THE HANDBOOK OF

THE MIDDLE EAST

REVISED EDITION

Michael G. Kort

TWENTY-FIRST CENTURY BOOKS · MINNEAPOLIS

For Carol, Eleza, and Tamara

The images in this book were used with the permission of: © Keyvan Behpour/Photonica/ Getty Images, all backgrounds pp. 1 (left), 3, 4, 6, 24, 62, 118, 156, 203, 260, 303, 305, 307, 310; © Corey Wise/Lonely Planet Images/Getty Images, background p. 1 (right); © Getty Images, pp. 260, 261 (top), 267, 268, 269 (both), 270, 274, 276 (bottom), 281 (bottom), 283, 284, 285, 286 (both), 289, 290, 293, 294, 295 (both), 296 (both), 297, 302; © Barry Iverson/Time Life Pictures/Getty Images, p. 261 (bottom); ELDAN DAVID/The State of Israel, p. 272; © Cynthia Johnson/Time Life Pictures/Getty Images, p. 276 (top); KORNE ZIV/The State of Israel, p. 281 (top); © Siavash Habibollahi/ZUMA Press, p. 282 (top); © Central Press/Hulton Archive/Getty Images, p. 282 (bottom). Maps on pp. 6, 8–9, 12–13, 27, 55, 65, 100, 108, 120, 131, 141, 158, 181, 207, 220, 226, 230, 233, 236, 240, by © XNR Productions.

Cover: © Keyvan Behpour/Photonica/Getty Images (main); © Corey Wise/Lonely Planet Images/Getty Images (background).

Text copyright © 2002, 2008 by Michael G. Kort

Twenty-First Century Books
A division of Lerner Publishing Group, Inc.
241 First Avenue North
Minneapolis, MN 55401 U.S.A.

Website address: www.lernerbooks.com

Library of Congress Cataloging-in-Publication Data

Kort, Michael, 1944–
    The handbook of the Middle East / by Michael G. Kort. — Rev. ed.
        p.   cm.
    Includes bibliographical references and index.
    ISBN: 978–0–8225–7143–8 (lib. bdg. : alk. paper)
    1. Middle East—Handbooks, manuals, etc.—Juvenile literature. I. Title.
DS44.K67 2008
956—dc22   2006034917

Manufactured in the United States of America
1 2 3 4 5 6 – JR – 13 12 11 10 09 08

C
O
N
T
E
N
T
S

Note: The names of capital cities and Middle Eastern
leaders appearing in the Encyclopedia are italicized in the
text at first usage.

On January 20, 1957, three maps appeared in the *New York Times*, a highly respected United States newspaper. All three supposedly showed the "Middle East." Yet these maps were quite different from each other. All three included Egypt, Israel, Lebanon, Syria, Iraq, Iran, Saudi Arabia, and Libya. Yet each map added a different list of countries to that core group. The map reflecting the British government's definition added Sudan in Africa, and Cyprus, a Mediterranean island nation that generally is considered part of Europe. The map based on the viewpoint of then U.S. secretary of state John Foster Dulles added Sudan and Ethiopia in Africa, and Afghanistan, Pakistan, and Turkey in Asia, but excluded Cyprus. The map consistent with a mid-1950s dictionary definition stretched 1,000 miles (1,600 kilometers) eastward in Asia to India and beyond, and westward in North Africa to Tunisia. Other definitions of the Middle East, some old and others new, eliminate everything east of Iran and south of Egypt but include Algeria, Tunisia, and Morocco in North Africa; include Afghanistan but eliminate Sudan; or include or eliminate other combinations of nations.

Obviously, the definition of what countries belong to the Middle East has changed over time; there is no consensus even today. The actual term *Middle East* dates from 1902. It was used that year by American military strategist Alfred Thayer Mahan to designate a region between Europe and the "Far East," the eastern part of Asia that includes countries such as China and Japan. This book uses two broad criteria to define the Middle East: geographic proximity to the Fertile Crescent and the Persian Gulf and a survey of current textbook definitions. According to these admittedly imprecise criteria, the Middle East includes sixteen countries: Bahrain, Egypt, Iran, Iraq, Israel, Jordan, Kuwait, Lebanon, Libya, Oman, Qatar, Saudi Arabia, Syria, Turkey, the United Arab Emirates, and Yemen, as well as territory controlled by the semi-independent Palestinian Authority (PA). Other books may include in the Middle East parts of North Africa or Central Asia not discussed here or exclude one or more of the countries included in this volume.

Whatever its precise boundaries, aside from its long history and contributions to civilization, the Middle East is important to Americans for several reasons. It contains the largest *oil* resources in the world, fully two-thirds of the world's total reserves. What happens in the Middle East therefore can affect whether Americans will have the fuel they need to drive their cars, run their electric power plants, and heat their homes. And a lot is happening. The Middle East is driven by serious and long-standing disputes that have led to numerous wars since the end of World War II, including the Gulf Wars of 1991 and 2003, in which American soldiers fought and died. The area poses a great threat because countries considered dangerous by the United States might acquire *nuclear weapons* or other weapons of mass destruction (WMD). The Middle Eastern countries that most worry the United States in this regard are Syria and especially Iran, both of which are listed by the U.S. State Department as powers that promote international *terrorism*. For these and other reasons, events in the Middle East are important enough to regularly make the front pages of newspapers, which is why each of us should be informed about that pivotal region of the world.

MIDDLE EAST

WHAT IS THE MIDDLE EAST?

No part of the world is more central to the story of human civilization than the Middle East. As a region, it is geographically unique, the only place on Earth where three continents—Europe, Asia, and Africa—meet and, in a historical and cultural sense, converge. It is appropriate that the shores of the world's geographic and historical "middle land" are washed by its "middle sea," the Mediterranean (from the Latin *medius* for "middle" and *terra* for "land"), which is encircled by Europe, Asia, and Africa and since prehistoric times has connected the inhabitants of those three continents. The Middle East's location has made it the oldest and most important crossroads in human history.

The Middle East was the original cradle of civilization. Between 10,000 and 11,000 years ago, people living near the present-day city of Jericho near the Dead Sea were some of the first human beings to practice agriculture. Jericho itself probably became the world's first city about 8000 B.C., complete with a wall that surrounded an area of about 10 acres (4 hectares). Signs of equally ancient town life have been found at a place called Catal Huyuk in Turkey. Catal Huyuk may also have been the place where people first practiced irrigation and domesticated animals. The first known civilization with a system of writing arose in the Middle East between the Tigris and Euphrates rivers around 3500 B.C. Since writing enabled people to keep records of what they did, it can be said that humanity's prehistory ended and its history began in the Middle East. The Sumerians, the ancient people who developed the world's first writing system, also are the first people known to have used the wheel. Their system of mathematics, based on multiples of sixty, gave us our system of measuring time with 60 seconds to a minute and 60 minutes to an hour, as well as our practice of dividing a circle into 360 degrees. Shortly after the beginning of Sumerian civilization, another civilization developed in the Nile River valley in Egypt. When Egypt was united, about 3100 B.C., the world had its first political unit large enough to be called a country. When King Sargon of Akkad conquered the surrounding city-states of Mesopotamia about seven hundred years later, the world had its first empire.

The Middle East, the birthplace of monotheism (the belief in only one God), is arguably the world's most influential religious epicenter. Judaism, the world's first genuinely monotheistic religion, was born in the Middle East among the ancient Israelites almost four thousand years ago. The world's other two great monotheistic religions, Christianity and Islam, also were founded in the Middle East, respectively about two thousand and fourteen hundred years ago. They are the two most widespread religions in the modern world. Monotheistic ideas also appeared at other times and places in the Middle East. They were part of a short-lived movement associated with the Egyptian pharaoh Akhenaton in the fourteenth century B.C.

Black Sea

BULGARIA

Bosporus

Kizil R.

Sea of Marmara

PLATEAU OF ANATOLIA

ITALY

ALBANIA

Dardanelles

GREECE

Aegean Sea

TURKEY

Lake Tuz

TAURUS MTNS.

TUNISIA

Crete

CYPRUS

Mediterranean Sea

LEBANON

ISRAEL

Dead Sea

Gulf of Sidra

Nile Delta

Negev Desert

Sinai Peninsula

JORDAN

Gulf of Suez

LIBYA

Libyan Desert

EGYPT

Gulf of Aqaba

Nile R.

Red Sea

S a h a r a

Lake Nasser

ALGERIA

NIGER

Nubian Desert

CHAD

SUDAN

MIDDLE EAST
PHYSICAL MAP

- ▲ Mountain
- — International border
- --- Unofficial border
- — River

The Zoroastrian faith of ancient Persia, which probably originated in the seventh century B.C. and was the dominant religion there until the Arab conquest fourteen centuries later, envisioned a good, ethical deity engaged in a constant struggle with the forces of evil. Another monotheistic religion, the Baha'i faith, began in Persia (present-day Iran) in the mid-nineteenth century. Severely persecuted in Iran today, the Baha'is have their world headquarters in Israel.

Two of the Middle East's sixteen countries, Egypt and Libya, are in North Africa. The rest are in Asia, although Turkey includes a small chunk of Europe. Some Middle Eastern countries, such as Saudi Arabia and Kuwait, are extremely wealthy because of enormous oil resources; others, such as Egypt and Yemen, are very poor. All of the region's countries except three—Turkey, Iran, and Israel—have a majority Arab population, and all except Israel are primarily Islamic in religion. Only Israel has a modern industrial economy. All of the countries in the Middle East, from the largest, Saudi Arabia, to the smallest, Bahrain, are going through rapid and often difficult changes that put enormous strain on their social structures.

The Middle East is a region of political turmoil. Only Israel is an established functioning democracy that guarantees its citizens political and civil rights. Turkey teeters precariously between democratic and military rule, while Lebanon, despite some democratic traditions, barely has a functioning government. The rest of the countries of the Middle East are either dictatorships, sometimes dressed up with powerless parliamentary institutions, or despotic monarchies. Three of them—Libya, Saudi Arabia, and Syria—were listed as being among the world's most repressive countries in the 2005 report by Freedom House, a highly respected independent organization dedicated to promoting civil liberties, political rights, and economic freedom throughout the world. Freedom House called that especially repressive group of nations "the worst of the worst." In 2006 Freedom House gave its lowest ranking—"not free"—to eight Middle Eastern states: Egypt, Iran, Iraq, Libya, Oman, Qatar, Saudi Arabia, and Syria. Six states—Bahrain, Jordan,

Kuwait, Lebanon, Turkey, and Yemen—were rated as "partially free," while only one Middle Eastern state, Israel, was rated as "free." In addition, of the states listed by the U.S. State Department as sponsors of terrorism as of mid-2006, two of them—Syria and Iran—are in the Middle East. Two other Middle Eastern states only recently were removed from that list: Iraq, after the overthrow of dictator *Saddam Hussein* by an American-led coalition of nations, and Libya, whose dictator *Muammar Qaddafi* changed his policies beginning in 2003.

THE GEOGRAPHIC SETTING: THE DRY WORLD

The Middle East has an area of about 3.4 million square miles (8.8 million square kilometers) and a population of approximately 300 million people. These figures are comparable to those of the United States, which has an area of 3.6 million square miles (9.3 million sq. km) and a population of 300 million people. The natural boundaries of the Middle East are the Black, Aegean, Mediterranean, Arabian, and Caspian seas, and the Caucasus Mountains. The Persian Gulf, sandwiched between the Arabian Peninsula and Iran and under whose shores and waters lie more than 60 percent of the world's oil resources, lies entirely within the region. The Gulf of Aden on the southern shore of the Arabian Peninsula and the Gulf of Oman to its northeast are extensions of the Arabian Sea.

The Middle East has several distinct regions, a large variety of topographical features, and environmental contrasts even within individual countries. There are extremes of cold and heat, flat plains and jagged mountain ranges, mighty life-giving rivers, and the salty and lifeless Dead Sea. At the same time, one overriding characteristic—an arid climate—unites the entire region. The Middle East has aptly been called "the dry world." For thousands of years, water has been the key to survival in the Middle East. Even today, despite the overwhelming importance of oil, nothing is of greater concern to its population than water.

Only about 3 percent of the region's land receives enough rain—more than 12 inches (30 centimeters) per year—to be agriculturally useful. Some of the Middle East's desert regions are among the driest places on Earth. Years can pass without rainfall in parts of Egypt, southeastern Saudi Arabia, and western Oman. Iran's Great Salt Desert reportedly is the largest area in the world with no vegetation at all.

A few areas along the fringes of the Middle East do get adequate rainfall—mainly parts of northern Iran and Iraq; the upland areas of northern Turkey; the Mediterranean coastal areas of Turkey, Syria, Lebanon, and Israel; and the mountainous areas of Yemen. Yet even in these areas, rainfall is a problem: it is concentrated in the winter months, while summers are hot and dry. Summer winds blowing in from the desert parch winter's well-watered landscapes. And there is always the danger in any given year (or period of years) that the rains will be too light and there will be drought.

The Middle East's largest and most reliable sources of water year-round are its two great river systems, the Nile and the Tigris-Euphrates. The Nile carries water into Egypt from the interior of Africa via two main branches, the Blue Nile and the White Nile, which join into a single river several hundred miles south of Egypt in Sudan. The Nile's waters make its river valley one of the most fertile and agriculturally productive places in the world. The Tigris and Euphrates both rise in Turkey and flow generally southeast until they meet just short of the Persian Gulf. The fertile land between them, where a series of ancient civilizations developed, is called Mesopotamia, which is Greek for "between the rivers." The third major river in the Middle East is the Jordan, the river that plays such a prominent role in the Bible. Compared to the Nile, Tigris, and Euphrates, the Jordan River is little more than a large stream, much of whose length forms the border between Israel and Jordan.

Another source of year-round water in the Middle East is groundwater, which in the form of springs has fed the region's oases for millennia. Recently discovered groundwater, buried in rock formations deep beneath baking desert sands, is being tapped in both Saudi Arabia and Libya. However, unlike the water from rivers or permanent springs, this groundwater is not a renewable resource. It has been there for thousands, and in some cases tens of thousands, of years. Some of it consists of deposits left over from the last ice age, when rainfall in the region was much greater, and is literally thirty thousand years old. The rest, about 6,000 years old, dates from more recent, but still prehistoric, periods of heavier rainfall. This so-called fossil water is not being replaced as it is used, which means its consumption must be managed carefully. Even then, this "new" source of ancient groundwater eventually will be used up.

Not surprisingly, deserts are the single most common land formation in the "dry world" of the Middle East. Most of Egypt and Libya is covered by North Africa's Sahara, the largest desert in the world. The vast Arabian Desert covers a huge plateau that dominates the Arabian Peninsula. Jordan, on the edge of that peninsula, is mainly desert, as is the southern part of Israel, which is known as the Negev. Yet another desert covers part of the plateau that makes up most of Iran.

The Middle East is divided into four major geographic regions. A huge mountainous plateau that runs from Iran through Turkey forms the region's northern tier. The western section of that region, which constitutes most of modern Turkey, is a peninsula known as Anatolia or Asia Minor, which separates the Mediterranean and Black seas. Anatolia, in turn, is separated from Europe by two narrow and strategic straits, the Bosporus in the northeast and the Dardanelles in the southwest, and by the Sea of Marmara, which lies between the two straits. South of that rocky highland is the Fertile Crescent. Its name comes both from its curved shape and, for the Middle East, its relative abundance of water. The Fertile Crescent runs from the Mediterranean coast of Israel and Lebanon northeastward into Syria and Iraq, where it turns southeastward, following the courses of the Tigris and Euphrates to the Persian Gulf. Its moisture comes from rainfall of approximately 24 inches (60 centimeters) per year in northern Israel, Lebanon, and southern Syria, and the waters of the Tigris and Euphrates. South of the Fertile Crescent is the barren

Arabian Peninsula, one of the hottest and driest places on Earth. Its most important features are underground: saucerlike rock formations, with their low point near the Persian Gulf. Eons ago these structures trapped the oil deposits that today are the largest in the world. The peninsula has mountainous areas in its southwestern and eastern corners. Finally, the North African section of the Middle East is part of the Sahara desert. Its parched landscape is broken only by the long and slender green strip of the Nile River valley and the huge triangular delta where the Nile flows into the Mediterranean Sea.

THE PEOPLES OF THE MIDDLE EAST

When we think of the Middle East, we usually think of Arabs, often in their traditional dress: men wearing a *kaffiyeh*, a headcloth held on by a cord, and women in modest, loose-fitting clothing, their hair covered by a scarf, their faces often hidden by a veil. This picture no longer fits many Arabs, who at least in urban areas have frequently adopted Western styles of dress. Nor are the Arabs the only people in the Middle East. They are the largest single group in the region and the vast majority in thirteen of its sixteen countries. But in the Middle East as a whole, Arabs constitute less than 60 percent of the total population.

Originally the term *Arab* referred to the inhabitants of the Arabian Peninsula, an ancient Middle Eastern people mentioned both in the Bible and in other contemporary records. Their conquests, beginning in the seventh century A.D., spread both Islam and the use of the Arabic language across the Middle East and North Africa. In the process, they assimilated non-Arab peoples such as the Egyptians into the Arab fold. The term *Arab* refers both to the original Arabs and the descendants of those conquered people who continue to speak Arabic as their native language. Arabic itself belongs to the Semitic family of languages. It is related to languages formerly spoken in the Middle East, such as Aramaic, as well as to Hebrew.

The Turks are the most populous non-Arabic-speaking people in the Middle East. By Middle Eastern standards, they are recent arrivals: the first Turkic groups settled in the region approximately one thousand years ago. The Ottoman Turks, founders of the empire that dominated much of the Middle East for five hundred years, arrived in Turkey only seven hundred years ago. They speak a language that originated in Central Asia and did not adopt Islam as their religion until after migrating to the Middle East.

The Iranians, the second-largest non-Arab group in the Middle East, are the direct descendants of the ancient Persians. They have lived in present-day Iran since ancient times, probably arriving in the region in the third millennium B.C. The Persians are mentioned as great conquerors in the Bible. In later centuries, they battled the ancient Greeks and Romans, as well as the Byzantines, for control of large parts of the Middle East. The Iranian language, Farsi, belongs to the Indo-European family of languages that includes English and most other European languages, as well as Sanskrit, the ancient language of India. Farsi is the third most widely spoken language in the Middle East, after Arabic and Turkish. Most Iranians follow the Muslim faith.

About twenty-five million Kurds live in the Middle East in a region called Kurdistan, which is divided between Turkey, Iran, and Iraq. They are, by far, the largest single Middle Eastern ethnic group without an independent country of their own. The Kurds, who trace their Middle Eastern roots to ancient times, are Muslims and speak a language related to Farsi.

Jews have lived in the Middle East for close to four thousand years. Over the course of their long history, they lived in virtually every part of the region. However, since 1948 Jews have fled persecution in Arab countries and settled in Israel. Sizable Jewish communities still survive in Iran, where all non-Muslims share a precarious existence, and in Turkey, where Jews are full-fledged citizens. Most Middle Eastern Jews live in Israel, where they constitute slightly less than half of the country's Jewish population.

All of the groups mentioned, with the exception of the Jews, are predominantly Muslim. The Muslims themselves are divided into two main sects, the Sunnis and the Shiites. The split between the two groups dates from the mid-seventh century. Between 85 and 90 percent of all Muslims are Sunni; most of the rest, who are concentrated in Iran and, to a lesser degree in Iraq, are Shiite. Sunnis and Shiites in turn are divided into many smaller sects.

Christians make up a small and declining proportion of the Middle East population. The largest Christian group in the Middle East is the Coptic community of Egypt, which accounts for about 6 percent of the country's population of seventy-eight million. About 39 percent of Lebanon's 3.8 million people belong to several different Christian churches. Approximately one million people in Lebanon, Syria, Israel, and Jordan follow the Druze faith, a secretive offshoot of Islam dating from the eleventh century. There are, of course, many small ethnic and religious groups scattered throughout the vast Middle East. Prominent among them are the Christian Armenian communities in Turkey, Syria, and Iran, and the Berbers in Libya.

A BRIEF HISTORICAL OVERVIEW

The long history of the Middle East can be divided into seven periods. The first, and by far the longest, dates from the origins of the ancient Sumerian and Egyptian civilizations shortly before 3000 B.C. to the conquests of the Greek king Alexander the Great between 334 and 323 B.C. That period saw the rise and fall of numerous great states and empires, beginning with Egypt and the empire of Sargon of Akkad in Mesopotamia, and followed by empires dominated by the Hittites, Babylonians, Assyrians, and Persians, among others. The development of monotheism by the Israelites began in the Fertile Crescent sometime after 1800 B.C., with the Israelite exodus from Egypt and settlement in present-day Israel probably occurring in the thirteenth century B.C. The first period of Middle Eastern history ended with the first conquest of the region by an outside power, Alexander the Great.

The second period, the era of Greek and subsequently Roman domination, lasted until the end of the fourth century A.D. Although Alexander's empire broke up after his death in 323 B.C., large parts of the Middle East from Anatolia southward along the Mediterranean coast into Egypt were absorbed into the Greek, or Hellenistic, world. Egypt especially became the center of a thriving Greek culture, although there and elsewhere in the Middle East that culture was limited to the ruling elite. During the second and first centuries B.C., Rome conquered the Hellenistic part of the Middle East. In the first century A.D., a time of extensive religious ferment, Jesus preached in Roman-dominated territory that lies mostly within present-day Israel, and Christianity was born. Christianity eventually became the official religion of the Roman Empire and thereby the dominant religion in much of the Middle East, a status it lost after the Arab conquests of the seventh century.

The Roman Empire was divided into western and eastern portions in A.D. 395 and ceased to exist in the west just fifteen years later. Rome's decline and fall marked the beginning of the Middle East's third historical period. During this period, which lasted until the seventh century, the Byzantine (or Eastern Roman) Empire, based in Turkey, and the Persian Empire, based in Iran, fought for dominance in the region. Having exhausted each other, neither could prevent the Arab armies that burst out of the Arabian Peninsula from overrunning much of the region. The Byzantine Empire lost much of its territory but still survived the storm, beating back several Arab assaults on its capital of Constantinople between 673 and 677. The Persian Empire was conquered between 637 and 650, after which the Persians gradually abandoned their native Zoroastrian faith for the religion of their conquerors.

The Arab conquest began the fourth period in the history of the Middle East. The Arabs brought a new religion, Islam, to the Middle East. Islam had originated on the Arabian Peninsula and was based on the teachings of Mohammad, who in about the year 610 began preaching what he claimed was the word of God as revealed to him. Mohammad's revelations were collected and written down in the Koran. By the time of his death in 632, most of the Arabian Peninsula had been won over to Islam, either as a result of Mohammad's preaching or by force. The Arabs then began a campaign of conquest to spread their new religion. The Arab armies had important advantages over their opponents. They were inspired by the idea of jihad, or holy war, which was to be waged, either militarily or by other means such as proselytism (active recruitment), until the entire world either converted to Islam or accepted Muslim rule. Arab warriors, fired by Islamic religious teaching that promised they would instantly be transported to paradise if they died fighting for their faith, often fought seemingly without fear, thereby terrorizing opposing soldiers. The Arabs were ruthless conquerors. They seized the land and property of those they defeated and also enslaved or deported large numbers of people. Once the conquered territories were firmly under Muslim control, large numbers of Arab colonists settled in these areas and became the new ruling class. However, as a rule the Arabs did not force Christians and Jews to convert to Islam, and Jews in particular often lived more securely and suffered less persecution under Muslim rule than under Christian rule. But the Arabs did compel Christians and Jews to live as inferiors to Muslims. As inferiors, or *dhimmi*, they had to pay an oppressive special tax and were subject to many humiliating restrictions, such as not being allowed to testify in Muslim courts or ride horses. In large part because of these restrictions and other persecution, Christianity declined in the Middle East, and Islam became the region's dominant religion, a status it retains to this day.

By the eleventh century, Arab military and political power had waned, and large parts of the Middle East passed to non-Arab control. Islam, however, remained the dominant religion. The main exception to Islamic rule was the existence of several Christian states established in the late eleventh century by the Crusaders from Europe along the eastern coast of the Mediterranean Sea. But the Crusader states lasted less than two hundred years. Muslim forces were able to regroup, and the last Christian stronghold fell to them in the late thirteenth century.

The rise of the Ottoman Turks in the fourteenth century marked the beginning of the fifth era, which lasted into the nineteenth century. The Ottomans, who were Sunni Muslims, succeeded an earlier group of Turkish conquerors known as the Seljuks. At its peak, the Ottoman Empire controlled most of the Middle East, with the exception of Persia and parts of the Arabian Peninsula. It also controlled the Balkan Peninsula in Europe and all of North Africa.

Although the Ottoman Empire survived until 1918, by the mid-nineteenth century it was in a state of decay. That decline opened the door for European powers to increase their influence in the region and began the sixth era of Middle Eastern history. It was during this period that the Suez Canal was built. Completed in 1869, the canal fulfilled an age-old dream of linking the Mediterranean and Red seas and opening a direct water route between Europe and eastern Asia. It immediately became one of the world's most strategically important waterways. European influence in the Middle East reached its peak after World War I, when the Ottoman Empire was dismantled. The empire's former territories that encompassed the Fertile Crescent were placed under the control of Great Britain and France by the newly founded League of Nations. These territories, however, were not held as colonies, but rather as what were called mandates, which meant that Britain and France were to prepare the local populations for eventual independence. France received the mandate for Syria (which included modern-day Syria and Lebanon), while Britain received the mandate for Iraq and the mandate for what was then called *Palestine* (the area that today includes Israel, Jordan, and the territories administered by the Palestinian Authority).

Meanwhile, in the 1920s, oil was discovered in the Middle East near the Persian Gulf. The discovery of the world's richest oil deposits made the Middle East a region of vital concern to the world's industrial powers. Control of the Middle East and its oil resources was critically important during World War II. In the battle of El Alamein in northern Egypt in 1942, one of the key battles of the war, the British stopped the Nazi German drive toward the Suez Canal and the invaluable oil wells of the Persian Gulf that lay beyond. The era of peak European influence lasted until after World War II, when the weakened European powers saw their empires in Asia and Africa dissolve.

The seventh and current era is one of independence from foreign control. The Middle East has sixteen independent states: thirteen Arab states and individual Turkish, Iranian, and Jewish states. The current era, however, has not been a peaceful one. Since World War II, Israel and Arab states that refuse to recognize Israel's right to exist have fought four wars. In addition there have been two wars against heavily armed militias controlled by non-state Arab organizations. These wars are part of what is known as the *Arab-Israeli conflict*. The Middle East has also been the scene of an eight-year war between Arab Iraq and non-Arab Iran, as well as wars and civil wars among Arabs themselves. Traditional monarchies have been overthrown in several Arab states and in Iran and have been replaced, depending on the case, by secular or religious dictatorships. Vast oil resources have made several states bordering the Persian Gulf wealthy, in some cases fabulously so. But riches from oil, and the economic development and social change that accompanied them, have also created problems. They have contributed to rivalries between countries and social unrest within countries where oil wealth is concentrated in very few hands.

In addition, from the end of World War II until the end of the 1980s, largely because of the region's oil resources, the Middle East was an important arena in the Cold War struggle between the United States and the Soviet Union. Both the Americans and the Soviets provided their allies and clients in the region with powerful ultramodern weapons that took their toll in lives during wartime and burdened countries with enormous military budgets in times of peace. When the Cold War finally ended in 1991, several of the region's most aggressive states, including Libya, Iraq, and Iran, continued their efforts to acquire nuclear, chemical, or biological weapons. These weapons are called weapons of mass destruction because they are capable of killing huge numbers of people in a single attack. While Libya and Iraq no longer seek these weapons, there is no doubt that Iran is attempting to develop nuclear weapons. As a whole, the countries of the Middle East devote a greater percentage of their gross national products to military spending than do countries anywhere else in the world. All this means that the Middle East, which since the dawn of civilization has been a region of great creativity and equally great conflict, faces an uncertain future.

TWO

NORTH AFRICA: EGYPT AND LIBYA

EGYPT

Egypt has the longest continuous history—more than five thousand years—of any country in the world. Modern Egyptians no longer speak the ancient language, worship the old gods, or live according to their original culture. But there remains a sense of continuity and national identity that runs back to when Egypt first was unified around 3100 B.C. The link goes beyond historical memory or sentiment: most experts agree that the modern Egyptians by and large are genetically similar to the people who lived there in ancient times. The name *Egypt* itself is a Greek adaptation of an ancient Egyptian word, *Kemet*, meaning "black land," a reference to the fertile black soil along the Nile River.

Egypt is no longer a world power or technological pacesetter, as it was in ancient times. It is, however, the political and cultural leader of the Arab world, a position it has held, with only one brief interruption, for generations. That role is the result of several factors. With about seventy-eight million people, Egypt has by far the largest population of any Arab nation. It is centrally located in the Arab world, midway between the North African states that stretch to the Atlantic Ocean in the west and the Fertile Crescent and Arabian Peninsula in the east. Egypt has a long tradition as a center of Islamic scholarship that dates from the founding of the Al-Azhar Mosque in *Cairo* during the tenth century. The nation has about 150 institutions of higher learning, including more than 20 universities.

Most important, however, Egypt's leadership in the modern Arab world evolved from its central role in the Arab revival after centuries of decline and foreign domination. That revival began in the early part of the nineteenth century and accelerated during the era of British control of Egypt that began in 1882 and lasted into the twentieth century. The era saw the birth of modern Egyptian nationalism. When Egyptian army officers overthrew the country's monarchy in 1952 and set up a military dictatorship, they firmly established Egypt as the leader of Arab nationalism throughout the Middle East and North Africa. The new regime, under President *Gamal Abdel Nasser*, also made Egypt the Arab world's leading military power, a position it holds to this day. Egypt also is the Arab world's center of literature, art, book publishing, music, theater, and film. The Arab world's most prominent fiction writer, Nobel Prize–winner Naguib Mahfouz, is a native and lifelong resident of Cairo. Egypt's broadcasting stations are the most powerful in the Middle East, and their transmissions are heard in many foreign languages as well as in Arabic. Egyptian Arabic is considered the common language of the Arab world. The country has played a central role in most major issues that have absorbed the Arab world, from the struggle against the Ottoman Empire and resistance to European colonialism to the Arab-Israeli conflict and the 1991 Gulf War against Iraq.

To be sure, Egypt remains terribly poor and is dependent on aid from the United States, Europe, and wealthy Arab oil powers such as Saudi Arabia. It is burdened by a huge and growing overpopulation problem that consistently overwhelms all development programs. Furthermore, as in several other Arab countries, Egypt's secular leadership faces serious and increasingly violent threats from Islamic fundamentalists. They want to overthrow the current regime and establish an Islamic state based on Muslim religious law, the Sharia. Yet so far no other Arab country has seriously challenged Egypt's place of primacy in Arab and Middle Eastern affairs.

GEOGRAPHY AND PEOPLE

GEOGRAPHY

Egypt is a large, almost square quadrilateral, slightly wider in the south than in the north, that occupies the northeastern corner of Africa and a small triangular chunk of western Asia called the Sinai Peninsula. Egypt is about 640 miles (1,030 km) from north to south, 600 miles (965 km) east to west in the north, and 770 miles (1,240 km) east to west in the south. Almost all of its total area of 385,229 square miles (999,739 square kilometers), about the size of Texas and New Mexico combined, is desert. The only exception, aside from a few scattered oases, is the region watered by the Nile River: a long, narrow valley, never more than 9 miles (14 km) wide, that extends southward into inner Africa, and a broad 11,000-square-mile (28,500-sq.-km) delta along the Mediterranean Sea. The Nile Valley and delta together account for about 4 percent of Egypt's land area but are home to 99 percent of its population. This region is one of the most densely populated places on Earth.

Egypt's northern boundary is the Mediterranean Sea. To the northeast, bordering on the Sinai Peninsula, is Israel. The rest of Egypt's eastern border is formed by the Red Sea. Egypt's western neighbor is Libya; its southern neighbor Sudan. Its largest city is Cairo (population 7.3 million). Several miles west of Cairo, in the desert, is the Giza plateau, home to Egypt's famous great pyramids, collectively the only remaining one of the ancient Seven Wonders of the World. A few hundred yards from the two largest

pyramids—the Great Pyramid of Khufu and the Pyramid of Khafre—is the Great Sphinx. Half man and half lion, 240 feet (73 meters) long and 66 feet (20 m) high, the Sphinx was carved at least forty-five hundred years ago from a single huge block of stone. It is known in Arabic as Abu al-Hol, the "Father of Terror." Along with the pyramids it seems to guard, the Great Sphinx is the most recognizable symbol of Egypt. Near these massive ancient monuments is Giza, officially Egypt's third-largest city (population 2.4 million) but really a part of greater Cairo. *Alexandria* (population 3.6 million), Egypt's second-largest city, is on the Mediterranean coast just west of the Nile delta.

With virtually all of Egypt desert, the country averages only 1 or 2 inches (2.5 to 5 cm) of rain per year. The main exception is a strip of Mediterranean coastline by the city of Alexandria, where winter rains average about 7 inches (18 cm) per year. Winters are warm and comfortable; summers are scorchingly hot, especially in the south. Whereas summer temperatures average around 85°F (30°C) along the Mediterranean coast, they soar to 122°F (50°C) at Aswan in the far south.

Two-thirds of Egypt consists of the Western—or Libyan—Desert, which covers all of Egypt from the Nile Valley to the Libyan border. The Western Desert, a part of the gigantic Sahara that covers North Africa, is a barren low plateau pockmarked by basins and depressions. They include the huge Qattara Depression, a 7,000-square-mile (18,130-sq.-km) expanse of salt marsh and quicksand lying below sea level that contains the lowest point (436 feet, or 133 meters, below sea level) in Africa. Along the Libyan border in the Western Desert is an expanse of dunes called the Sand Sea. The Western Desert was virtually impassable until invading Persians introduced camels to Egypt and North Africa in the sixth century B.C. But it often was more than a match even for camels. The Persians found this out to their sorrow in 525 B.C. when, according to the Greek historian Herodotus, one of their armies totaling fifty thousand men attempted to cross the desert but was lost and buried in a sandstorm.

The Western Desert is not entirely devoid of life. Jackals, hyenas, gazelles, and a variety of rodents and insects survive there. Humans also can live, and even thrive, in a few places. Deep beneath the desert's sands opposite the Nile Valley is an arch-shaped underground aquifer that supports five oases, pinpoints of green on the vast brown Western Desert canvas. The largest, Al-Dakahla, has 30,000 acres (12,150 hectares) of farmland and a population of 60,000. A sixth oasis, Siwah, is far to the west near the Libyan border. Siwah is unique in Egypt. Its isolation over the millennia has given it a distinct culture and language that persists to this day against the ever-growing inroads of the modern world. The Siwah oasis is crowded with 250,000 date palms that make it Egypt's main producer of highly prized dates. Just west of the Nile on the edge of the desert, about 60 miles (100 km) southwest of Cairo, is Al Fayyum, an oasis fed by an ancient canal leading from the Nile. Originally a swamp fed by the overflow from the Nile, this 1,620-square-mile (4,200-sq.-km) so-called "Garden of Egypt" was reclaimed by Pharaoh Amenemhet I almost 4,000 years ago. His efforts created a lake, Birket Quarun, and a productive agricultural area in the desert. Under pressure of increasing population and over-exploitation, the lake has shrunk to about 85 square miles (220 sq. km), half its former size, and has become as salty as the Mediterranean.

East of the Nile, the Eastern, or Arabian, Desert, extends to the Gulf of Suez and the Red Sea. East of the Gulf of Suez is Asia and the Sinai Peninsula, yet another desert. It contains Mount Sinai, where the Bible says Moses and the Israelites received the Ten Commandments from God after fleeing Egypt. (The actual Mount Sinai is unknown; the peak currently called Mount Sinai is only one of several candidates for the site where the Bible says this episode took place.) Another peak in the Sinai desert is Mount Catherine, at 8,652 feet (2,640 m) the highest point in Egypt.

More than two thousand years ago, the Greek historian Herodotus called Egypt the "gift of the Nile." It still is. Without the Nile River, the "long river between the deserts," Egypt simply would not exist. In fact, it seems fair to say that the Nile Valley and the Nile's delta are Egypt. The ancient Egyptians evidently thought so when they named their country Kemet after the "black land" along the river, in contrast to Deshret, the "red land" of the surrounding desert. For thousands of years, the main advantage of the deserts on either side of the Nile was to protect the inhabitants of the valley and delta from invasion. If nothing else, Egypt's Nile Valley—that slender 550-mile-long (885-km) green ribbon of life squeezed precariously between huge seemingly lifeless brown blocks of desert—is a lesson on the fragility of human existence. As if to emphasize that point, ancient Egyptians likened their country to a delicate lotus: the Nile and its valley were the stem, the Al Fayyum oasis its bud, and the Nile delta the flower.

Egypt traditionally was viewed as divided into Upper Egypt and Lower Egypt, names that reflect the course of the Nile rather than the directions north and south. Upper Egypt ran from Aswan in southern Egypt near the Sudanese border—that is, upstream along the Nile—to where Cairo stands, just south of the Nile delta. Lower Egypt began where the Nile fans out to form its delta—that is, downstream along the river—about 125 miles (200 km) from the Mediterranean. Traditionally, Aswan was the frontier where Egypt ended, the site of a natural barrier of rapids on the Nile called the First Cataract. (The Second Cataract was just north of the current Egyptian-Sudanese border. Both cataracts are gone, vanished hundreds of feet beneath the warm shimmering waters of Lake Nasser, the artificial lake that rises behind the huge Aswan High Dam, completed in 1971.)

The increasingly crowded Nile Valley is still a garden of water plants, including dozens of types of grasses, growing along the riverbank. It also remains a refuge for more than four hundred species of birds that feed on the river's fish. Some wild mongooses and ibis still roam the delta region. But these are the remnants of a biological past that was once rich and diverse. The elephant, Nile crocodile, lion, monkey, and baboon are gone. The lotus, the ancient symbol of Egypt, still grows in the delta. But papyrus, which at the dawn of history was made into a durable material on which to write, thereby playing a crucial role in the development of Egyptian literacy, has almost vanished.

All are victims of the unstoppable spread of agriculture and urbanization fueled by Egypt's growing population.

The Nile Valley is also a huge outdoor museum. In the northern part of the valley is Tel al-Amarna, the city built by the Pharaoh Akhenaton as the home for his short-lived monotheistic religion dedicated to the worship of the sun god Aton. In the center of the valley, where the Nile completes its semicircular detour eastward before returning to its southward course, stand the ruins of the ancient city of Thebes, Egypt's capital for almost five hundred years (1550–1070 B.C.). Here, less than 2 miles (3 km) apart, are two enormous temple complexes: Luxor and Karnak. At Luxor, successive pharaohs for several hundred years tried to outdo each other in their building projects. Pharaohs built at Karnak for more than 1,300 years. Both Luxor and Karnak are on the east bank of the Nile; across the river a few miles away in the desert is the Valley of the Kings. Here are buried some of Egypt's most famous rulers, including Ramses II, considered by some historians to be the pharaoh of the biblical Exodus; Hatshepsut, the only woman to rule as a pharaoh; and the boy-king Tutankhamen, whose small tomb, discovered in 1922, was the only one in the valley not looted by robbers and, therefore, still contained thousands of objects providing priceless information about life in ancient Egypt.

For eons the Nile flowed unobstructed from the interior of Africa to the Mediterranean Sea. The ancient Egyptians tried to dam the Nile about 2600 B.C., but that dam collapsed during construction. Although the British successfully built a dam on the Nile at Aswan in southern Egypt between 1898 and 1902, it was too small to control the mighty river. The great change for the Nile and the people living along its banks occurred between 1960 and 1971, when Egypt, with the help of the Soviet Union, built the Aswan High Dam. Located about 4 miles (6 km) south of the older and much smaller dam, the Aswan High Dam is a colossus, 364 feet (111 m) high and about 2 miles (3 km) long, dwarfing even the pyramids. Thirty thousand workers took eleven years to build it. Behind the dam, stretching for 500 miles (800 km), into Sudan, is Lake Nasser. The dam was a significant engineering accomplishment and has provided many benefits for Egypt. The country finally has a regular year-round water supply, allowing farmers to grow three crops annually. The dam increased Egypt's cultivable land by 2 million acres (810,000 hectares), or 30 percent, while its hydroelectric energy doubled Egypt's power supply. But these benefits came at a price, much of it unanticipated by the dam's builders. Because the Nile no longer floods annually downstream from Aswan, the farmland south of the dam no longer benefits from its yearly dose of soil-enriching silt. This means that farmers must resort to chemical fertilizers, which they often cannot afford. Meanwhile, the silt, now building up behind the dam, will someday fill the lake.

Nor is enough silt or water reaching the Nile delta, which contains more than half of Egypt's cultivable land. The delta, therefore, is increasingly threatened by the encroaching salt water of the Mediterranean and by erosion. It is, in fact, sinking, some parts by as much as a quarter of an inch (half a cm) a year. The cutback in fresh water downstream from Aswan is also harming local fishing, although Lake Nasser has become a major source of fish. Meanwhile, the slower flow of less water has allowed parasites that spread serious diseases to humans to flourish in the river.

Despite many problems, Egyptian agriculture—which consists mostly of small labor-intensive farms—is highly productive. The most important cash crop is cotton. Egypt is the world's sixth-largest producer of cotton and one of its leading exporters. Other crops include rice, wheat, millet, corn, citrus fruits, and dates. Egypt's main domestic animals are dairy cattle, goats, sheep, and water buffalo.

In recent decades, the percentage of Egyptians engaged in agriculture has fallen rapidly to about a third of the workforce. About a fifth of the workforce is engaged in manufacturing; the major industries are petroleum refining, chemicals, fertilizers, cement, and textiles. About 40 percent of the workforce is in services, much of that in the huge government bureaucracy. Egypt has a serious problem with child labor. Children under twelve make up a tenth of the workforce, and they are terribly exploited. For example, children who plant and harvest rice earn only eighty cents for working a twelve-hour day under the sweltering Egyptian sun.

Egypt's most important natural resource is oil, which is found in the Western Desert and the Sinai Peninsula. Although Egypt's oil deposits are tiny compared with the major Arab oil producers, it produces enough to supply its local needs and also be an exporter. Tourism, a major source of foreign currency, is very important to the Egyptian economy, one reason attacks on tourists by Islamic fundamentalists in the 1990s met with such a vigorous government response. Egypt's single-largest supply of foreign currency comes from tolls collected from ships passing through the Suez Canal. Another important source is money sent home by more than 3.5 million Egyptians living and working abroad, especially in the major oil-producing Arab countries.

PEOPLE

Egypt has a population of about seventy-eight million people, 99.8 percent of whom are Arabs. Approximately 94 percent of all Egyptians are Muslims, and Islam is the official state religion. Most non-Muslim Egyptians are Coptic Christians, the descendants of the Egyptians who did not abandon Christianity for Islam fourteen centuries ago. The Copts have been subject to discrimination in Islamic Egypt, and violence against them has increased dramatically in recent decades with the rise of Muslim fundamentalism. Other minorities—small ethnic European communities, Nubians in the south, and a few other groups—account for less than 0.2 percent of the population.

With so many citizens squeezed into a limited area, Egypt's most serious problem is overpopulation. Despite government efforts to encourage birth control, the population in the mid-1990s was growing at a rate of 2.3 percent per year, or one million every ten months. That has made it impossible to keep pace in terms of food, social services, jobs, and a host of other necessities. Egypt's rate of population growth, in the face of limited resources, is crippling. The country's population has risen from ten million in 1900 to thirty million in the 1960s to almost eighty million in 2006. In the mid-1800s, Egypt had 5 million acres (2 million hectares) to feed five million citizens; today it has 7 million acres (2.8 million hectares) to feed more than fifteen times that number. A country that was once the granary of the Roman Empire and that could feed itself until relatively recently, now imports half its food. Among the world's nations only Russia and Japan import more food.

EGYPTIAN HISTORY

FROM ANCIENT TIMES TO THE ISLAMIC CONQUEST

The ancient Egyptians were a Mediterranean ethnic group whose language belonged to the Hamito-Semitic language family spoken elsewhere in northern Africa and in southwestern Asia. They viewed themselves as ethnically and culturally distinct from their neighbors to the south in Africa and to the east in Asia. The Egyptians were ruled by pharaohs, their ancient god-kings, for almost three thousand years. This long epoch is divided into three main parts: the Old Kingdom (3100–2258 B.C.), the Middle Kingdom (2000–1786 B.C.), and the New Kingdom (1750–332 B.C.). The Old Kingdom, whose pharaohs built great pyramids and the Sphinx, was the era of Egypt's most significant cultural achievements. The Middle Kingdom was an age of empire, when Egypt's power extended southward into lands then called Nubia and Kush, westward into Libya, and eastward into Asia as far as the Euphrates River. It also was an age of monument building. The New Kingdom brought another age of empire. Its famous pharaohs included religious reformer Akhenaton and conquerors and builders like Ramses II. However, after 1000 B.C., Egypt was ruled intermittently by foreign powers, including the Assyrians and Persians.

The New Kingdom, and the era of the pharaohs, came to an end when the Greek king Alexander the Great conquered Egypt in 332 B.C. Alexander built a new city on the Mediterranean that he named Alexandria in his own honor. After his death, Egypt was ruled by a dynasty founded by the Greek general Ptolemy. The Greeks ruled as a tiny minority over a native Egyptian population. They made Alexandria the country's capital and the leading center of Greek learning in the Hellenistic world. The city was home to accomplished mathematicians, astronomers, historians, philosophers, and poets, and it contained the greatest library in the ancient world. The Ptolemaic dynasty ruled Egypt until it was overwhelmed by Rome in 30 B.C. During that troubled time, a fire swept through Alexandria's magnificent library, destroying almost 500,000 papyrus rolls and with them much irreplaceable knowledge of the ancient world. By the second century A.D., Christianity had taken hold in Egypt. In the mid-fifth century, disputes over religious doctrine gave birth to the country's Coptic Church. By then the western part of the Roman Empire had collapsed. Except for a twelve-year interlude of Persian control, Egypt would be ruled by the Byzantine Empire from its capital of Constantinople until the Arab conquest of the mid-seventh century.

FROM THE ISLAMIC CONQUEST TO 1952

The Arab conquest and the triumph of Islam was an important turning point in Egyptian history. At the time of the Arab conquest in the mid-seventh century, the Egyptians were speaking Coptic, a variant of their ancient native language. Over the next several centuries, most Egyptians converted to Islam, and Arabic replaced Coptic as the national language. This severed an important link with the past and gave Egypt a new identity, an Islamic one. The Arabs, however, could not bring political stability to Egypt. After being ruled by Arab dynasties based respectively in *Damascus* in Syria and *Baghdad* in Iraq, Egypt in the tenth century fell to the Fatamids, Arab invaders from the west. The Fatamids founded Cairo in 969 as Egypt's new capital. They also established the Mosque of Al-Azhar as a Muslim university, thereby making Egypt a center of Islamic learning. The Fatamids then weakened, in part under pressure from the European Crusaders. They were succeeded in the twelfth century by the short-lived Ayyubid dynasty founded by Saladin, best known for conquering *Jerusalem* from the Crusaders. From 1250 until

1517, Egypt was ruled by the Mamelukes, Turkish slave soldiers who had overthrown their Ayyubid masters. The Mamelukes were both great builders and warriors. In 1260 they defeated the Mongols in Syria, dealing the first serious defeat to invaders who conquered and terrorized much of Eurasia.

In 1517 Egypt fell to the Ottoman Empire. The country endured both economic and cultural decline under Ottoman rule. This was especially true beginning in the seventeenth century, when the Ottoman Empire began its own long decline that lasted into the twentieth century. The result in Egypt, as elsewhere in the empire, was misrule, corruption, and further decline. By the late eighteenth century, Ottoman control of Egypt was more official than real. A short period of French occupation (1798–1801) further weakened Ottoman control. The French occupation, however brief, was significant. In 1799 French soldiers found a basalt slab with identical texts written in three scripts: hieroglyphic (the ancient Egyptian script), demotic (a simplified form of ancient Egyptian writing), and Greek. The Rosetta Stone, as it was called, dated from the Ptolemaic era and enabled scholars, after years of effort, to decipher ancient Egyptian hieroglyphics. This enormously expanded our knowledge of ancient Egyptian history, culture, and life.

After the British drove the French from Egypt, the Turkish sultan appointed a new governor, or pasha, for Egypt named Mohammad Ali. Within a few years of taking office in 1805, he was operating as a virtually independent ruler. Mohammad Ali began the job of modernizing Egypt. He improved the government bureaucracy, expanded education, promoted new agricultural methods, and encouraged industrial development. Ali's successors continued his policies, promoting the cotton industry and, in the 1860s, the building of the Suez Canal by a French company. However, mismanagement and corruption left Egypt deeply in debt to the British and French, and in 1882 the British occupied Egypt, even though in theory it remained part of the decaying Ottoman Empire.

Official independence came in 1922, but it was less than what it seemed. Egypt had a king, Ahmed Fuad, and a parliament, but the parliament had little power and the British controlled the government from behind the scenes. When Ahmed Fuad died in 1936, he was succeeded by his son Farouk, but the British kept their influence in Egypt until after World War II.

In 1948 Egypt attacked the newly founded state of Israel, joining with four other Arab countries in an attempt to wipe the Jewish state from the map. The Egyptian army's poor performance and eventual defeat in the Arab-Israeli war of 1948–1949 infuriated many nationalists, and in 1952 a military group calling itself the Free Officers overthrew Farouk. They declared Egypt a republic, undertook a series of wide-ranging reforms, and began a new era in the country's history.

Under Nasser and Sadat: 1952 to 1981

Although General Mohammad Nagib was the apparent leader of the coup that overthrew the Egyptian monarchy, the strongman behind the scenes was Colonel Gamal Abdel Nasser. The new military government quickly arrested many prominent politicians, abolished all political parties, and declared Egypt a republic. In fact, it was a military dictatorship and a one-party state. By 1954 Nasser was Egypt's undisputed leader. He officially became president in 1956 in an election in which he ran unopposed. The voters also approved a new constitution that proclaimed Islam as Egypt's state religion but also granted women, for the first time in Egypt's history, the right to vote.

The Nasser regime had an ambitious agenda, one that matched its charismatic leader's grand vision of remaking not only Egypt but the entire Arab world. A primary goal was to modernize and industrialize Egypt's economy. Another objective was to reduce the great differences in wealth between a tiny minority who were very rich and the vast majority who were very poor. Nasser was equally intent on promoting Arab unity under his leadership. As part of that effort, Nasser was determined to avenge the Arab defeat of 1948–1949 and destroy the state of Israel. He also wanted Egypt to be a leader of the countries of Asia and Africa (called the Third World) that were neutral in the Cold War between the Soviet bloc and the West.

The new regime was not without opposition at home. Nasser's government was primarily secular in orientation. This soon brought it into conflict with Egypt's leading Islamic organization, the Muslim Brotherhood, which in 1954 tried to assassinate Nasser. The government responded by suppressing the Muslim Brotherhood, hanging several of its leaders and driving it underground. Meanwhile, the government promoted industrialization by expanding the role of the state in the economy, a policy Nasser called Arab socialism. The government seized foreign assets, including those of thousands of Jews who had been forced to flee Egypt in the years after 1948. It took over banks, newspapers, and most industrial and mining enterprises; by the 1960s it controlled 85 percent of all manufacturing and a third of the total economy. Arab socialism also meant breaking up large estates and turning farm land over to Egypt's millions of poor peasants, a program that won the government wide popular support. Laws establishing minimum wages and reducing working hours brought Nasser and the new regime further support from Egypt's poverty-stricken millions.

It was, however, in foreign affairs that Nasser made his reputation. By 1955 he was recognized as one of the Third World's most influential leaders. In 1956 Nasser seized control of the Suez Canal from its British owners. He intended to use its revenues to finance his dream project: the Aswan High Dam. Earlier, the United States had refused to finance the project because of Egypt's growing friendship with the Soviet Union. Great Britain and France responded to Nasser's bold step by attacking Egypt. They were joined by Israel, whose purpose was to end years of Egyptian-sponsored terrorist attacks on Israeli territory launched from the Sinai Peninsula and the Gaza Strip. The British-French-Israeli assault was successful militarily, but it failed politically. The attack won Nasser and Egypt international sympathy, including strong backing from the Soviet Union. Despite Egypt's military defeat, Nasser himself emerged as the Arab world's leading hero for standing up to the British and French colonial powers. International pressure forced the British and the French to withdraw from the Canal Zone and Israel

from the Sinai Peninsula. A United Nations (UN) force was
placed in the Sinai to prevent further military conflict between
Egypt and Israel. Egypt subsequently received large amounts of
aid from the Soviet Union, including funding for the Aswan
High Dam and Soviet experts to help build it.

But Nasser was not successful in promoting Arab unity
under Egyptian leadership. A union with Syria, called the United
Arab Republic, lasted only from 1958 to 1961 before Syria withdrew, leaving bitterness on both sides. A second union forged in
1958, this one with Yemen, also collapsed after three years.
Within a year Nasser was again involved in Yemen. In 1962 military officers who supported Nasser overthrew Yemen's conservative monarch and declared Yemen a republic. Royalists rallied
to oppose the new regime, and a civil war broke out. Nasser
intervened on the republican side, while Saudi Arabia backed the
royalists. Egypt ended up mired in a bloody and expensive struggle that involved fifty thousand of its troops. During the fighting, Egyptian troops committed numerous atrocities against
proroyalist villages, including, on Nasser's orders, attacking
them with chemical weapons. These actions embarrassed both
Egypt and Nasser in the Arab world before Nasser finally withdrew his troops from Yemen in 1967.

Still, Nasser overwhelmingly remained the most popular and
respected leader in the Arab world. One issue that served his
ambitions was the Arab-Israeli conflict. His rallying cry for unifying the Arab world centered on hatred of Israel and a determination to destroy the Jewish state. In 1967 Nasser's obsession with
Israel again led Egypt to war, and to a military disaster worse than
the debacle of 1948–1949. In the spring of 1967, he demanded
that UN peacekeeping forces leave Sinai. When the United
Nations complied, he massed thousands of troops along the
Israeli border and forged military alliances with Jordan and Syria.
Nasser also blockaded Israel's port of Elat by closing the Strait of
Tiran at the southern end of the Gulf of Aqaba.

Meanwhile, Nasser and other Egyptian officials proclaimed
that the time had come to crush Israel once and for all. After
weeks of waiting for international diplomatic action to restrain

the Egyptians, a response that never came, in early June the Israelis attacked Egypt and Syria. Jordan then joined the fighting on the Arab side. The Arab-Israeli war of 1967, which became known as the Six-Day War, ended with an overwhelming Israeli victory. Egypt's defeat, which again put Israel in control of the Sinai Peninsula, left Nasser a broken man. He remained Egypt's president but died in 1970 of a heart attack.

Nasser's successor was his little-known vice president, Anwar Sadat. Sadat turned out to be a man of many surprises. First, he was not pushed aside as expected but established himself firmly in power. Sadat relaxed Nasser's police-state measures, releasing some political prisoners and allowing political parties, banned since 1953, limited freedom to operate. To promote economic development, he reduced state interference in the economy in order to attract foreign investment. In foreign policy, he began to turn Egypt away from the Soviet Union and toward the United States, hoping to win U.S. support to force Israel to return the Sinai Peninsula to Egypt. In October 1973, frustrated by his lack of progress, Sadat got together with Syria and launched a surprise attack on Israel on the Jewish holy day of Yom Kippur. The initial battles of what is known as the Yom Kippur War gave the Arabs their first military victories over the Israelis. However, after bloody fighting and heavy losses on both sides, Israel again triumphed. Yet even in defeat Sadat won enormous prestige in the Arab world.

Sadat's last, and greatest, surprise was his role as peacemaker. In early November 1977 he stunned the world, and especially his fellow Arabs, by announcing in a speech to the Egyptian parliament his willingness to negotiate with the Israelis to establish peace; he thus became the first Arab leader to do so. Said Sadat:

> I am willing to go to the ends of the earth for peace. Israel will be astonished to hear me say now, before you, that I am prepared to go to their own house, to the Knesset [Israel's parliament] itself, to talk to them.

Sadat meant what he said. In mid-November, he went to Jerusalem and spoke to the Israeli parliament. Long and difficult negotiations followed. Finally, in September 1978, with American president Jimmy Carter playing a central role, Sadat and Israeli prime minister Menachem Begin signed a preliminary agreement, the Camp David Accords. Additional negotiations were needed to settle difficult issues. A conference of Arab nations met in November 1978 to plan measures against Egypt if it signed a peace treaty with Israel; the conference even offered Egypt five billion dollars in aid to scrap the peace process, an offer Sadat rejected. In March 1979, on the White House lawn, Sadat and Begin signed an Israeli-Egyptian peace treaty, ending more than three decades of war between the two nations.

While the peace treaty won enormous respect for Sadat in the United States and Europe, the Arab world reacted with fury. Sadat was accused of betraying his fellow Arabs. Almost every Arab country broke diplomatic relations with Egypt, and Egypt was suspended from the *Arab League*. The league moved its headquarters from Cairo to Tunis, the capital of Tunisia. The Arab states also imposed economic sanctions on Egypt, making it increasingly dependent on American aid. Syria, Iraq, and Libya even tried, but failed, to have Egypt expelled from several organizations related to the United Nations. The peace with Israel also was denounced in Egypt by critics who ranged from extreme Islamic fundamentalists to supporters of Nasser's policies.

These reactions did not deter Sadat, who continued to improve relations with Israel. In 1980 the two countries exchanged ambassadors. But Sadat's peace with Israel had made him too many enemies among the Arabs. On October 6, 1981, while watching a parade in Cairo commemorating Egypt's successful October 1973 attack on Israeli troops across the Suez Canal, he was assassinated. The killers belonged to a small Islamic fundamentalist group called al-Jihad ("Holy War"). While Anwar Sadat was deeply mourned in the West, and especially in Israel, there was little genuine mourning for him in Egypt. Three former American presidents—Richard Nixon,

Gerald Ford, and Jimmy Carter—attended his funeral, but there were no Arab heads of state there.

THE MUBARAK ERA: EGYPT SINCE 1981

Sadat was succeeded as Egypt's president by his vice president, *Hosni Mubarak.* In contrast to his two charismatic predecessors, Mubarak was a cautious and practical technocrat. His tendency was to seek a safe middle course whenever possible. The problems Mubarak faced fell into three broad categories. First, he had to promote economic development to relieve Egypt's massive poverty. Second, he had to cope with an increasingly violent Muslim fundamentalist challenge to secular rule. By the 1990s, this issue dominated Egypt's domestic agenda. Third, Mubarak wanted to restore Egypt to its leadership position in the Arab world while maintaining peace with Israel. Any one of these problems was daunting; having to deal with all three simultaneously was nothing less than overwhelming.

Mubarak made a little progress on the economic front. During the late 1990s, Egypt's economy grew at a strong rate of 5 percent per year. Furthermore, in appreciation, or perhaps more accurately, in payment, for Mubarak's central role in mobilizing Arab support for the 1991 Gulf War against Iraq, the United States and the wealthy Arab states of the Persian Gulf region each wrote off seven billion dollars (for a total of fourteen billion dollars) of Egypt's fifteen-billion-dollar foreign debt.

But these were little more than bright spots surrounded on all sides by darkness. Mubarak continued Sadat's attempt of slowly moving Egypt from a state-controlled to a market economy, while at the same time trying to curb the corruption that pervaded the country's economic life. Progress was painfully slow. By the late 1990s, after three five-year plans, most industrial plants were still owned by the government. Although the private sector's share of the economy increased, about half of Egypt's total gross domestic product (GDP) was still produced by the state. Loans secured in the early 1980s, when oil prices were high and foreigners were willing to lend, added their heavy weight to Egypt's crushing foreign debt. Egypt, an oil exporter, suffered badly when oil prices fell in the mid-1980s. There were serious food riots in 1984, as there had been under Sadat in 1977. By the 1990s, unemployment, fueled by unrelenting population growth, was growing at an alarming rate. Murderous attacks on foreign visitors by Islamic fundamentalists badly hurt the tourist industry, an important source of jobs and foreign earnings for Egypt. Egypt became increasingly dependent on foreign aid. American aid alone totaled thirty-five billion dollars in the twenty years after the Camp David Accords. In the mid-1990s, four million people staffed the government's bloated, inefficient, and expensive bureaucracy, yet another anchor on the economy. Another burden was Egypt's military forces, which were being equipped with modern high-tech weapons at the cost of billions of dollars. In fact, Egypt spent 70 percent of its American aid on armaments.

Mubarak also fought an uphill battle against *Islamic fundamentalism*. During 1980 and 1981, Sadat had used harsh measures against Islamic extremists, including a series of arrests in September 1981, just before his assassination. Sadat's murderers were tried and executed in 1984. Meanwhile, the number of fundamentalist groups was growing rapidly, as were the number of clashes between them and government security forces. Fundamentalists assassinated the speaker of parliament in 1990 and the head of Egypt's State Security Investigative Section in 1994. In 1995 they attempted to assassinate Mubarak himself while he was visiting Ethiopia.

In their battle to change Egyptian society, the Islamic fundamentalists targeted more than government officials. In 1992 the well-known writer and political figure Dr. Faraj Fuda was murdered because he had said that Egypt should be a secular society. Two years later, an Islamic extremist tried to kill Nobel Prize–winner Naguib Mahfouz, who was eighty-two at the time. Meanwhile, militant Muslims sued a highly respected professor of Arabic literature at Cairo University, Nasr Abou Zeid, to force him to divorce his wife. The militants argued that Zeid's writings showed that he had rejected Islam, which made him unfit to be married to a Muslim woman. Zeid had written that the

Koran should be viewed as a seventh-century document rather than as the basis for Egyptian society in the twentieth century. In 1995 Egypt's highest court accepted the argument of the Islamic militants and decreed that Zeid must indeed divorce his wife. Under threat of death from the militant Islamic group Holy War, Zeid and his wife left Egypt to live abroad.

Egypt's Coptic Christian minority, the largest Christian community in the Middle East, repeatedly fell victim to Islamic extremists. Hundreds of Copts were killed in numerous acts of violence that began with bloody assaults on villages in southern Egypt in 1991.

During the 1990s, Copts were victims of assaults and murders both in southern Egypt, where most of them live, and in other parts of the country as far north as the Nile delta region. The impact of these attacks was magnified by the government's failure to prosecute Muslims who committed them and by official anti-Christian discrimination, such as long-standing restrictions against building or repairing churches. The government made matters even worse by permitting Islamic clerics to denounce the Coptic faith in fiery sermons broadcast on government-run television. Probably the worst incident erupted in the southern village of al-Kosheh on December 31, 1999, the eve of the millennium, and culminated in riots by Muslim mobs on January 2, 2000, that left more than twenty Copts dead. Although the government arrested several people, the investigation and the trials that followed amounted largely to a cover-up, and all of the murder suspects were acquitted in February 2001.

Foreign tourists also became fundamentalist targets during the 1990s, and some were killed. An attack on a Cairo hotel in April 1996 left eighteen Greek visitors dead; the attackers claimed they were trying to kill Israelis. In September 1997, nine German tourists died in an attack on their bus. The worst incident was the gruesome murder of more than sixty people, among them fifty-eight foreigners, at Luxor in 1997. This act caused such public revulsion that the organization that carried it out announced it would no longer target tourists in its struggle with the government.

The Mubarak government cracked down hard. It arrested an estimated ten thousand Islamic fundamentalists in 1989 alone. In 1993 the government hanged convicted Islamic terrorists for the first time since the execution of Sadat's assassins. It also maintained the state of emergency that had been in effect since Sadat's assassination. That regulation, which gives the government sweeping military powers, has been renewed regularly, most recently in April 2006.

Of the many Islamic groups confronting the government, two stood out. The most active and dangerous organization was Gama'a al-Islamiya (Islamic Group), whose spiritual leader was Sheikh Omar Abdel Rahman. During the early 1990s, Islamic Group launched a terrorist campaign in an attempt to overthrow the Mubarak government and replace it with a strict Islamic regime. It attacked thousands of people and was responsible for the carnage in 1996 in Cairo and 1997 in Luxor. The insurgency lasted eight years and cost more than one thousand lives before the government finally crushed it. Meanwhile, Islamic Group's reach extended far beyond Egypt. In 1993 the Islamic Group tried to blow up the World Trade Center in New York City. Rahman, who was living in the United States at the time, was sentenced by an American court to life in prison without parole for his role in that bombing, in which six people died.

The Islamic organization with the broadest support in Egypt was and continues to be the Muslim Brotherhood, which was founded back in 1928. Like Gama'a al-Islamiya, the Brotherhood's goal is to establish an Islamic Egypt, but it opposes using violence to achieve that goal.

A small sign that the violence might decline came in March 1999 when Islamic Group announced that it would lay down its arms. The Egyptian government responded by freeing hundreds of its members but pointedly kept thousands more securely in jail. These actions, however, had little impact on Holy War, the assassins of Anwar Sadat. Holy War pledged to continue its fight. It condemned what it called Islamic Group's "cease-fire with the United States and Israel," saying it was "a step back in the face of a new Christian crusade which aims to uproot Islam and give Israel the upper hand."

Like Nasser and Sadat, Mubarak enjoyed his greatest successes in foreign affairs. One goal he achieved was to restore Egypt to its leadership position in the Arab world. This required a delicate balancing act, as Mubarak also was committed to Egypt's peace treaty with Israel. He maintained formal relations with Israel, but in such a distant and limited way that disappointed Israelis called their relationship with Egypt a "Cold Peace," as opposed to a normal peace in which countries interact on many levels. In fact, the only time Mubarak visited Israel was to attend the funeral of assassinated Israeli prime minister *Yitzhak Rabin*. At the same time, Mubarak was a diligent and effective peacemaker in intra-Arab disputes, such as that between Jordan and the *Palestine Liberation Organization* (PLO). He also encouraged other Arab states and the PLO to join Egypt in making peace with Israel.

Mubarak's efforts to restore Egypt's leadership position in the Arab world were helped by the fears of the oil-rich nations of the Persian Gulf. Those wealthy but militarily weak nations were increasingly concerned for their safety during the Iran-Iraq War of 1980 to 1988. The war was one reason the Persian Gulf states resumed financial aid to Egypt in 1987. By then Jordan had resumed diplomatic relations with Egypt. Most Arab states followed suit over the next five years. In 1989 Egypt was readmitted to the Arab League, and the organization returned its headquarters to Cairo.

In 1990, following the Iraqi invasion of Kuwait, Mubarak was instrumental in lining up Arab support for the international effort, led by the United States, to drive the Iraqis from their oil-rich neighbor. Egypt contributed thirty-five thousand troops to the multinational force that did the job in 1991.

At the same time, Mubarak worked hard to facilitate Israeli-Palestinian peace negotiations. Mubarak was anything but neutral in this process. Egyptian diplomats continuously worked behind the scenes to coordinate Arab strategy. Mubarak also tried to persuade the United States and Western Europe to increase their pressure on Israel to make concessions.

Beginning in 1995, Egypt faced problems on several fronts. The fundamentalist Islamic regime in Sudan, Egypt's neighbor to the south, was involved in a failed attempt to assassinate Mubarak. As a result, Egypt began openly supporting exiled opponents of that regime, which the United States had placed on its list of state sponsors of terrorism back in 1993. Relations with Israel worsened after 1996 when Israel, under its new prime minister Benjamin Netanyahu, took a harder line in negotiations with the Palestinians. In 1998 it took an American threat to discontinue aid to get Egypt to sign the renewal of the Nuclear Non-Proliferation Treaty (NPT).

Still, when in September 2001 nineteen members of the Muslim fundamentalist al-Qaeda terrorist organization killed more than three thousand people in attacks against the World Trade Center in New York City and the Pentagon in Washington, D.C., Mubarak immediately condemned the attacks. Although al-Qaeda was led by a Saudi Arabian exile named Osama bin Laden and most of the nineteen terrorists who carried out the attacks were Saudis, there was also a strong Egyptian connection to the events. Bin Laden's second-in-command was Ayman al-Zawahiri, an Egyptian doctor who had been imprisoned for three years after the Sadat assassination and later formed his own terrorist organization, Egyptian Islamic Jihad. Another Egyptian, Mohammad Atef, was Bin Laden's chief military planner until U.S. forces killed him in Afghanistan. At home, Mubarak responded to the 9/11 attacks with arrests of more than 250 Muslim fundamentalists, a crackdown that continued into 2002. In 2004, the government launched its largest crackdown in years against the Muslim Brotherhood, arresting dozens of its members and closing several publishing houses. Egypt also endorsed the American war on terrorism after 9/11. However, Egypt did not support the 2003 U.S.-led invasion of Iraq that overthrew Saddam Hussein. In several public statements, Mubarak said he was concerned that the war in Iraq would encourage the spread of Islamic fanaticism throughout the Arab world.

Mubarak meanwhile remained active in efforts to promote negotiations between Israel and the Palestinians. In early 2000, he met with newly elected Israeli prime minister *Ehud Barak*. Over the next several years, Egypt sponsored several meetings between various Palestinian factions, partly in an effort to stop attacks by certain Palestinian groups against Israeli civilians inside Israel. Egypt also supported the so-called "roadmap," a plan for peace negotiations devised by the United States, the European Union (EU), Russia, and the United Nations. In 2004 Mubarak met with Barak's successor, *Ariel Sharon*, to help implement Israeli plans to withdraw from the Gaza Strip.

In early 2005, responding to criticism both at home and abroad that his government was too authoritarian, Mubarak announced his support for a constitutional amendment that would allow more than one candidate to run for president. The amendment was approved by Egypt's voters in May, and Egypt's first multicandidate election took place that September. Two fairly well-known opposition leaders challenged Mubarak: Ayman Nour, a forty-year-old former journalist and lawyer who had just been released from prison, and Noman Gomaa, a longtime politician who promised to abolish the country's emergency laws. They were joined by seven minor candidates. Although the election was something new for Egypt, it aroused little voter interest, probably because everyone assumed Mubarak would win. They were right. Mubarak was reelected overwhelmingly, amid complaints from his defeated opponents that the election was rigged.

A more significant election followed a few months later, as Egypt's voters went to the polls to elect a new People's Assembly. This was not a free election as practiced in democratic countries. There was violence around polling places, opposition campaign workers were jailed, and an independent monitoring group reported a systematic and planned campaign to keep opposition voters from going to the polls. Nevertheless, observers agreed that despite extensive government restrictions, it was the freest election in Egypt in more than fifty years. Everyone expected the ruling National Democratic Party (NDP) to win, and it did, taking almost three-quarters of the seats. The best any of the opposition could do was to win six seats, an achievement by a group called the New Wafd Party.

Two other parties managed to win three seats between them.

It was the independent candidates who made news. More than one hundred of them were elected, including almost ninety who were openly loyal to the banned Muslim Brotherhood.

The Muslim Brotherhood ran on the slogan "Islam is the Solution," which meant turning Egypt into a country run according to Islamic law and eventually re-creating the Islamic caliphate that existed more than one thousand years ago. As one successful candidate put it, "This is an Islamic state; we can't say otherwise." The group's candidates also expressed views that were strongly anti-American. This was not surprising, as the Muslim Brotherhood had a long history of hostility toward the United States.

Perhaps the main losers in the elections were the younger leaders of the NDP, some of whom actually lost their seats. In addition, expert observers worried that the election showed a dangerous and growing division in Egyptian society. As one political scientist at Cairo University said, "We have a religious current on the one hand and a party that has lost its legitimacy and credibility and is desperately clinging onto power on the other." Other experts, especially within the NDP, were more optimistic, but even they admitted they recognized the growing power in Egypt of the Muslim Brotherhood.

EGYPTIAN POLITICS, THE PRESS, AND THE LAW

Egypt has an authoritarian form of government. It is, however, not nearly as brutal as the dictatorships of Iran or Syria or as absolutist and oppressive as the monarchies of Saudi Arabia and the Persian Gulf states. Prior to 1952, Egyptian political life was freer and more open than it is today, but that interlude ended with the Free Officers Revolution. Egypt became a one-party state, whose leader ruled with dictatorial power. In 1962 Nasser named the Arab Socialist Union (ASU) as Egypt's ruling party. Anwar Sadat loosened Nasser's system a little. Amendments to the constitution in 1980 permitted a limited multiparty system. But Egypt's political system still operated under tight controls. The country's leading party, which inevitably won every election, was Sadat's NDP. In presidential elections, the candidate was nominated by the parliament and ran in an election where he was the only candidate. Thus in 1994 Mubarak won his third six-year term as president in a typical election in which he took 94.9 percent of the vote. In 1999 Mubarak was nominated to a fourth term and reelected with just under 94 percent of the popular vote. The constitutional amendment of 2005 that permitted more than one candidate to run in presidential elections did not change much. In the election that followed that year, Mubarak was victorious, with more than 88 percent of the vote. That election meant that Mubarak, who already had been president for twenty-four years, would remain Egypt's leader for at least six more, assuming the seventy-seven-year-old president remained healthy. It therefore was not surprising that some Egyptians quietly referred to their president as the last Pharaoh.

Egypt's parliament, called the People's Assembly, is only slightly less of a monopoly than the presidency. Under both Sadat and Mubarak, opposition parties have been allowed to win a few seats. The People's Assembly has 454 members: 444 are elected for five-year terms and ten are appointed by the president. The president also appoints the country's prime minister and council of ministers, who are in charge of day-to-day governing. There is, in addition, an advisory body called the Shura Council, which generally is considered the upper house of parliament. Established in 1980, the Shura Council has 264 members; 176 are elected, and 88 are appointed. Its members serve six-year terms. As a result of elections held late in 2005, Mubarak's ruling NDP held 324 seats in the People's Assembly and 255 seats in the Shura Council.

Egypt's leading opposition party is the New Wafd Party (*wafd* means "delegation" in Arabic). It is a descendant of the most popular party that existed before 1952 and represents Egypt's middle class and business interests. The New Wafd Party has chafed under the restrictions of Egyptian political life. In 1995 it called the parliamentary elections the "worst in history," and it boycotted the 1997 elections. Several other parties also exist, although they are basically insignificant. Far more important than the legal opposition parties are the illegal Islamic groups. They include the Muslim Brotherhood, which has elected representatives to parliament as independents, and Islamic Group and Holy War.

Egypt's press reflects the country's form of government. As with political parties, the press was freer before the 1952 revolution than after it. The government owns 51 percent of all major newspapers and is careful to control much of what they print. After a period of relative freedom in the 1980s, the government imposed harsher censorship. A new law in 1995 provided for long prison sentences and harsh fines for various crimes, including insulting public officials. The law was modified and made less severe in 1996, after international criticism.

Egyptian law for the most part does little to support individual rights. Before 1980 the constitution identified the Islamic legal code (Sharia) drawn from the Koran as a source of Egyptian law. In 1980 Sharia became *the* source of Egyptian law. Egypt also continues to have strict censorship laws. In May 1999, the parliament passed a law severely restricting human rights groups. Another 1999 law put all nongovernmental organizations more firmly under state control. Still, Egyptian law, even while imposing limitations unacceptable by Western standards, allows citizens considerably more freedom than in most Arab countries. For example, in January 2000 parliament changed the country's divorce laws to make it easier for women to get a divorce. Previously it was almost impossible for a woman to get a divorce without her husband's consent, while a husband could divorce his wife simply by saying "I divorce thee" three times or by filing a paper with the government stating that he was divorcing his wife. The new law, while still leaving wives at some disadvantage relative to their husbands, allows a woman to demand a divorce if she and her husband cannot get along with each other and requires that he help support her if he is able to do so. Only Tunisia among the world's Arab nations grants women similar rights when it comes to divorce.

Egyptian cultural life is a colorful and cosmopolitan mixture of traditional and modern that reflects the impact of outside influences. The movie industry is a prime example. The first Egyptian movie was made in 1927, the same year Hollywood produced the world's first talkie. More than three hundred films were produced in the 1960s, the heyday of Egyptian filmmaking. Egyptian directors borrowed many of the plots they used from Hollywood. Today it is not easy to make a good film in Egypt. Egyptian filmmakers must walk a thin line in dealing with political and sexual themes to avoid getting into trouble with religious authorities and government censors.

Egypt's greatest film star of the twentieth century was Umm Kalthoum, the "Star of the East," who also was Egypt's most popular singer and a superstar throughout the Arab world. In 1956 the director Salah Abou Seif won the critics' prize at the Cannes Film Festival, one of the international film industry's most prestigious awards. The Egyptian actor who probably achieved the most international recognition is Omar Sharif. His most notable role was as the Russian physician Dr. Zhivago in the British-made classic of that name. The country's most distinguished director is Youssef Chahine, who has excelled at his trade for half a century. He won a lifetime achievement award at the 1997 Cannes Film Festival.

Theater also remains popular in Egypt. Adel Imam, currently the most popular local movie actor, is a leading actor in the theater as well. The belly dancer Fifi Abdou is one of Egypt's leading theater actresses. Belly dancing, whose roots run deep into Egyptian history, remains popular, although since the 1990s it has been under attack by Islamic extremists.

One of the more interesting aspects of twentieth-century Egyptian culture has been the development of painting and sculpture. These art forms flourished in ancient Egypt, as tombs and monuments amply demonstrate. However, Islam, which forbids painting or sculpting living creatures, severely limited these traditions for centuries. Stimulated by Egypt's growing contact with Europe, art and sculpture revived in the twentieth century, growing along with Egyptian nationalism. Influenced by nationalist thinking, Egyptian artists tried to create a distinctly Egyptian style. Their influence can be seen today in the work of artists such as Adel al-Siwi and Chant Avedissian.

No discussion of Egyptian cultural life would be complete without a reference to the coffeehouse. Coffeehouses are popular gathering places throughout the Middle East, where along with conversation, patrons enjoy drinking strong coffee and smoking tobacco. Sipping and puffing—the latter often through a *sheesha*, or water pipe—are interspersed with games of dominoes, dice, and cards. Interestingly, both coffee and tobacco are foreign imports into the Middle East. Coffee probably was introduced in Egypt, Turkey, and Syria from Ethiopia via the Arabian Peninsula in the sixteenth century. English merchants probably brought tobacco to the region a century later. There are about thirty thousand coffeehouses in Cairo alone, many catering to specialized groups of customers of every conceivable variety, from physicians, musicians, and retired generals to political radicals, Muslim extremists, and homosexuals. Many coffeehouses also serve a variety of concoctions that are supposed to cure ailments from stomach problems to coughs.

Coffeehouses remain, as they have been for centuries, largely a male bastion. A common complaint today in Egypt, as elsewhere in the world, is that the home-based entertainment available from television and other electronic media has had a negative impact on local traditions and culture, such as coffeehouse life.

LIBYA

If Egypt is the country with the world's oldest continuous history, Libya, its North African neighbor directly to the west, is at the opposite end of the spectrum. Libya had no history as a nation prior to becoming independent in 1951. The term *Libya* is an ancient one that traditionally referred to most of North Africa. The name was revived in 1934 when Italy cobbled together three areas it controlled in North Africa—Tripolitania,

Cyrenaica, and Fezzan—and called its new creation Libya. After gaining independence, whatever its troubles, Libya functioned more or less normally as a country for eighteen years. That ended in 1969 when military officers led by Muammar Qaddafi overthrew the monarchy of King Idris I. Since then, rather than functioning as a country in the normal sense of the word, Libya has been dominated and even defined by one man: Qaddafi. The only comparable situation in the second half of the twentieth century is in Cuba, where Fidel Castro has been in power since 1959, ten years longer than Qaddafi. But not even Castro, it seems fair to say, has cast a personal shadow over his country as completely as Qaddafi. And if Castro has his detractors and bitter enemies, there are few who would go so far as to call him insane, something that cannot be said for Qaddafi.

Libya's official name, changed several times by Qaddafi, currently is the Great People's Socialist Libyan Arab Jamahiriya. *Jamahiriya* means "state of the masses." Islam is Libya's official religion, and Arabic is its official language.

GEOGRAPHY AND PEOPLE

Libya is a huge country of 679,358 square miles (1,759,540 sq. km), slightly larger than Alaska. It is the fourth-largest country in Africa, and the second largest, after Saudi Arabia, in the Middle East. Libya's northern border is the Mediterranean Sea. To the east are Egypt and Sudan, to the west Tunisia and Algeria, and to the south Chad and Niger. Almost all of the country is desert and barren rock; it has no rivers that flow year-round. More than 90 percent of Libya's people live within 10 miles (16 km) of its 1,100-mile-long (1,770-km) Mediterranean coastline. The climate is cooler along the coast than in the searing desert, where temperatures as high as 135°F (57°C) have been recorded. Western coastal areas receive enough rainfall to make agriculture possible. Libya's main crops are wheat, citrus fruits, and olives. A few oases dot the bone-dry southern part of the country, deep in the Sahara desert.

Crete
(GREECE)

M e d i t e r r a n e a n   S e a

LIBYA

TUNISIA

Tripoli ☆
Al-Aziziyah ○   Al-Khums ○
                 Misratah ○

Tripolitania

Ghadamis

Gulf of Sidra

Al-Bayda ○
          Benghazi ○   Tobruk ○

Surt ○

Mersa
Brega ○

C y r e n a i c a

EGYPT

■ Houn

S   *A*   *H*   *A*   *R*   *A*

■ Sabha

■ Germa

■ Murzuq

F e z z a n

○ Ghat

*Libyan
Desert*

■ Al-Kufrah

ALGERIA

Tropic of Cancer

▲ *Bette Peak*

NIGER

CHAD

SUDAN

LIBYA
- ✪ **Capital city**
- ○ **City**
- ▲ **Mountain**
- ■ **Oasis**
- — **International border**

N
W ✦ E
S

0   100   200 mi
0   100   200 km

Libya consists of three regions that have few historic ties. Tripolitania, the western coastal area, makes up about 16 percent of the country. *Tripoli* (population 1,150,000), Libya's largest city and capital, is in that region. Tripolitania is most closely linked to the western part of North Africa called the Maghreb, which consists of Algeria, Tunisia, and Morocco. South of Tripolitania is the desert region of Fezzan. Libya's eastern half is called Cyrenaica. Historically linked most closely to Egypt and the east, Cyrenaica is where most of Libya's oil and gas deposits are located. Part of Cyrenaica's coastline cradles the Gulf of Sidra, the scene in 1981 of an air battle between American and Libyan jets. Benghazi (population 637,000), Libya's second-largest city, lies on the northeastern coast of the Gulf of Sidra.

Libya has a population of about 5.8 million people, a number that is increasing rapidly at the rate of more than 2 percent per year, in part because of government encouragement. Almost half the population is less than fifteen years old. Virtually all Libyans are Sunni Muslims, and most are Arabs. There is a significant community of Berbers, the indigenous people of North Africa. The Berbers probably migrated to North Africa from southwestern Asia at least five thousand years ago. They have been partially, but not entirely, assimilated into Arab culture, and many still speak the ancient Berber languages, which are related to ancient Egyptian.

Libya has natural resources such as iron, potash, and gypsum. Oil, however, discovered in the late 1950s, is by far Libya's most important resource. While the oil industry employs less than 2 percent of Libya's workforce, it accounts for a third of the country's domestic product and virtually all (along with natural gas) of its export earnings. Libya is the world's thirteenth-largest oil producer, but it consumes less than 10 percent of what it pumps from the ground. The rest is exported, mainly to Europe. Libyan oil is in demand because it contains very little sulfur and therefore burns cleanly. Oil wealth has enabled the regime to provide a vast range of social services, including free education until age fifteen and medical care, that has helped it keep the population economically satisfied and under control.

Since ancient times, a variety of groups, including Phoenicians, Greeks, Romans, Byzantines, Arabs, Spaniards, and Ottomans, have ruled Libya. Between 1711 and 1835, when Ottoman control weakened, the city of Tripoli and its environs was ruled by a local dynasty. Tripoli earned its income, as did the other so-called Barbary states of North Africa, from piracy or from collecting tribute from countries in return for not attacking their ships. In effect, what was going on was state-sponsored terrorism. To protect its ships and citizens after enduring more than a decade of attacks, a young and vulnerable United States under President Thomas Jefferson sent a naval squadron to attack Tripoli. The successful capture of the city in 1805 by a small force of U.S. Marines secured the safety of American ships. The achievement was memorialized in the U.S. Marine Corps hymn by the line "To the shores of Tripoli."

After 1835 Tripoli returned to Ottoman control until 1911, when Italy seized what became is Libya. Libya remained an Italian colony until British and French forces occupied it during World War II. In 1951, in accordance with a 1949 United Nations resolution, Libya became independent under King Idris I. A period of conservative rule and stability followed. Libya under Idris had good relations with the conservative Arab monarchies of the region and with Britain, the United States, and other Western powers. Both the United States and Britain were permitted to have military bases in Libya, and Western oil companies developed the country's newly discovered oil deposits.

LIBYA UNDER QADDAFI

After military officers led by twenty-eight-year-old Muammar Qaddafi seized power in 1969, Libya was transformed from one of the most conservative states in the Arab world to arguably the most radical. Qaddafi's idol was Nasser, but the Libyan leader quickly went far beyond Nasser in his radicalism. Qaddafi rejected Western capitalism and democracy as well as Soviet communism. His ideology is a unique and volatile mixture of Islamic

THE HANDBOOK OF THE MIDDLE EAST

theology, revolutionary socialism (but not Marxism), Arab nationalism, populism, anti-Semitism, and an absolute faith in his fate as a man of destiny. Qaddafi's revolutionary vision for the Arab world, or "Third Universal Theory," was outlined in his Green Book. Part one was published in 1976, followed by parts two and three respectively in 1978 and 1979.

The Qaddafi regime moved swiftly. It closed down British and American military bases (the day the last U.S. forces left became a national holiday), nationalized all banks, took over all heavy industry and mining, and negotiated far more favorable terms for Libya with foreign oil companies. It also seized the property of Italians and Jews and forced them to leave the country. Eventually the regime seized all foreign oil assets. A new organization, the Arab Socialist Union (ASU), became the country's only political party. In 1973, declaring that the Libyan people were not sufficiently revolutionary, Qaddafi announced a cultural revolution that rejected all non-Islamic thinking. In the mid-1970s, after spending most of 1974 in seclusion, Qaddafi introduced what he called direct people's power. Libya's government was now called the General People's Committee. Private economic activity was severely restricted, and traditional Koranic law—including punishing thieves by cutting off their hands—became the country's basic legal code.

By the late 1970s, Libya supposedly was being run by people's or revolutionary committees. In fact, even though Qaddafi resigned his position as head of the government in 1979—announcing he was leaving his post to devote himself full time to "preserving the revolution"—Libya remained a strict military regime under his personal dictatorship. There were at least five serious attempts to overthrow Qaddafi, but none of his opponents were able to topple him.

Life for ordinary Libyans has ranged from unpredictable to dangerous. Among the things most feared are the purification committees of army officers and students the government often uses to enforce its laws and decrees. For example, in October 1998 Qaddafi decided the prices in private shops were too high. He warned shopkeepers that "prices must be cut by whatever means, and if they are not, there will be violence." Shopkeepers took Qaddafi seriously, terrified that purification committees would find them in violation of the new decree. While Qaddafi's enforced price slashing was popular with the poor—salaries in Libya have been frozen since 1981—many shopkeepers simply shut their businesses, unable to make a living under the new rules. The wife of one spoke for many when she complained, "This is not fair, but what is fair in this country anyway?"

Libya from the start was much too small a stage for the historical role Qaddafi envisioned for himself. Only the international arena, including not only the Arab world but well beyond it, could provide a venue large enough to match his grandiose ambitions. Libyan foreign policy under Qaddafi therefore was militant, unconventional, and aggressive. Qaddafi is bitterly anti-Western in general and anti-American in particular. He supported extremist Islamic movements and what he considers "liberation movements" worldwide, from the Middle East to Latin America, Western Europe, and East Asia. Many of the movements receiving Libyan money, training, and arms were terrorist groups. The Libyan government also was directly involved in terrorist acts. All this made it one of the world's leading sponsors of international terrorism.

In the Middle East, Qaddafi has uncompromisingly opposed all attempts to peacefully solve the Arab-Israeli conflict. Instead, he supports the most extreme Palestinian groups that share his vision of seeing Israel completely destroyed. This position at times has brought Libya into conflict with Egypt. Libyan attempts to undermine the Sadat regime in the 1970s led to armed clashes along their mutual border. Libya also played a leading role in ostracizing Egypt from the rest of the Arab world after Sadat made peace with Israel.

Qaddafi's confrontations with the United States also have led to clashes. In 1981 American and Libyan jets fought in the Gulf of Sidra when Qaddafi claimed the gulf lay within Libyan territorial waters, an assertion belied by the geography of the region. In 1986 American aircraft bombed Libya after Libyan agents were linked to the bombing of a nightclub in Germany in which several American soldiers were killed. The United States also imposed a trade embargo on Libya.

In addition, two Libyan intelligence agents were linked to the bomb explosion that destroyed an American passenger airplane (Pan American Flight 103) in midair over Lockerbie, Scotland, in 1988. This terrorist act cost 270 lives (259 on board, 11 on the ground). When Qaddafi refused to turn the agents over for trial, undoubtedly fearing the trial would point the finger of guilt directly at him, the United Nations Security Council imposed economic sanctions on Libya. Those sanctions—which, significantly, did not include a boycott of Libyan oil exports—remained in place until Libya, fearing the sanctions were about to be tightened, finally turned the agents over to international authorities in May 1999. In July of that year, Libya in effect admitted involvement in a 1986 bombing of a French airliner over Africa when it paid the families of 170 victims in that incident thirty-one million dollars. A year and a half later, in February 2001, a Scottish court convicted one of the two Libyan agents tied to the Pan American bombing of murder. The second agent was acquitted.

Libya's international influences also extended into Africa. For fifteen years, Libya intervened in Chad, Libya's poor African neighbor to the south. Qaddafi's goal was to annex Chad's northern region, called the Aouzou strip, which reportedly has rich uranium deposits. Supported by French and American aid, Chad finally expelled Libya from the Aouzou strip in 1987. Qaddafi's ambitions in Africa ranged farther than Chad. As one American analyst commented in 1999, "there has been a consistent effort in the past to destabilize West Africa."

In 2003 Libya finally began to modify some of its aggressive policies. A key reason was the U.S.-led invasion of Iraq and the overthrow of Saddam Hussein, a campaign that apparently convinced Qaddafi that he might be next on America's list. During 2003 and 2004, Libya agreed to pay $2.7 billion to the families of persons killed on Pan American Flight 103 ($10 million per family), $170 million to the families of the victims of the French airliner shot down over Africa, and $35 million to the non-American victims of a nightclub bombing in Germany. Meanwhile, in December 2003 Libya announced its willingness to give up its program to develop nuclear weapons and other weapons of mass destruction. This occurred a few months after U.S. intelligence agents intercepted a shipment of centrifuges—devices used to enrich uranium so it can be used for weapons—being shipped to Libya. During 2004 Libya, under international supervision, destroyed its chemical weapons. Its equipment for making nuclear weapons was shipped to the United States. That year Libya once again began exporting oil to the United States.

In May 2006, the United States restored formal diplomatic relations with Libya after a break of twenty-eight years and, equally important, removed Libya from its State Department list of countries that sponsor terrorism. Libya had been on that list since 1979. While these events significantly changed Libya's international standing, and the country enjoyed an economic boost from higher world oil prices, life under Qaddafi's dictatorship in Libya itself remained as repressive as ever. In its 2006 report, Freedom House gave Libya its lowest possible rating for both political rights and civil rights. The key question for Libya is what will happen when the post-Qaddafi era finally arrives. One thing is certain, with or without him, life in Libya is likely to be unpredictable and unstable.

ISRAEL, THE PALESTINIAN AUTHORITY, AND JORDAN

ISRAEL

During their long history, the Jewish people have settled on every hospitable continent and in some of the most remote areas in the world. Their roots, however, are in a tiny part of the Middle East, where in the twentieth century, after a lapse of nineteen hundred years, they re-created the state of Israel. The goal of the founders of the modern state of Israel was to build a country in their ancient homeland where Jews could live securely and freely. An independent Israel would enable Jews to escape the insecurity and persecution they had known as a scattered minority and become a nation able to defend itself and develop its national culture.

The ancient Israelites, the ancestors of modern Jews, emerged as an identifiable people almost four thousand years ago along the eastern shore of the Mediterranean Sea, approximately where modern Israel is. Unlike other ancient peoples that appear in history books, the

Israelites' main distinguishing feature was not cultural sophistication or military conquests or impressive monuments or expertise in science and technology. Rather, they were remarkable for their unusual religion, one that assumed the existence of a single God who demanded that his followers live according to a strict moral code. That religion—Judaism—was the world's first monotheistic faith. It later provided inspiration for two other monotheistic religions, Christianity and Islam, which are the two most widely followed religions in the modern world.

After several centuries of being organized into twelve separate tribes, the Israelites established a unified but short-lived kingdom in the eleventh and tenth centuries B.C. After that kingdom split in two in the late ninth century B.C., the Israelites were ruled by a succession of powerful empires. Still, for the next one thousand years, they were able to develop their religious life and moral principles while occasionally reasserting their political independence.

In the first and second centuries A.D., two unsuccessful revolts against the mighty Roman Empire brought catastrophe. The Romans drove most of the Jews, as they were called by then, from the land known as Judea at the time. The Romans then changed its name to Syria Palestina, or Palestine, which means "Land of the Philistines" (the Philistines had lived in the region centuries earlier), in order to sever its ties with the Jewish people. That name, although it referred to a people long since vanished, would remain in use until 1948.

For about eighteen hundred years, the Jews lived in the region as a minority of the overall population. But beginning in the late nineteenth century, Jews from distant countries returned in growing numbers to what they called Eretz Yisrael, the "land of Israel," to reestablish their national life. Unlike the Egyptians, who never left the Nile Valley but who have lost direct touch with their ancient religion and language, modern Israelis follow the religion and speak the language—an updated Hebrew—of their ancient ancestors. They also share with their ancestors the burden of living in a region that remains, as it was long ago, one of the most tumultuous and dangerous in the world.

Geography, Economy, and People

Geography

Israel is a narrow sliver of land with great topographical variety along the eastern coast of the Mediterranean Sea. Its boundaries and area still are not permanently settled. In many places, they remain jagged armistice lines left over from a series of wars between Israel and its Arab neighbors. According to the armistice lines that existed between 1949 and 1967, Israel has an area of 7,992 square miles (20,700 sq. km). If one includes the eastern part of the city of Jerusalem, which Israel annexed in 1967, and the Golan Heights, which Israel took over in 1981, Israel's area is 8,473 square miles (21,946 sq. km). In either case, Israel is about the size of New Jersey.

Israel also exercises external military control (but not direct day-to-day administrative control) over part of an area known as the West Bank, a region east of Jerusalem that lies between the 1949 armistice lines and the Jordanian border. Many Israelis refer to that territory by its biblical names: Judea (the southern part) and Samaria (the northern part). Israel also exercises full control over additional parts of that region, especially along the Jordan River and the Dead Sea.

Israel's 170-mile-long (273-km) Mediterranean coastline is its western border. Egypt lies to the southwest. Due south from its southernmost point is the Gulf of Aqaba, which Israelis call the Gulf of Elat. Jordan borders Israel to the east, Syria sits to the northeast. Due north of Israel is Lebanon.

Despite its small size, Israel has four distinct geographic zones. The heart of the country is the fertile and densely populated coastal plain. At its center on the Mediterranean coast is *Tel Aviv*, Israel's second-largest city (population 375,000). Approximately two million people, almost one in three Israelis, live in the Tel Aviv metropolitan area, which has the country's largest concentration of population. Farther north on the coastal plain is Haifa, Israel's third-largest city (population 272,000), its most important port, and its high-tech industrial center.

Haifa begins at the seashore and then climbs the steep, wooded slopes of 1,792-foot-high (546-m) Mount Carmel, a dramatic and scenic 13-mile-long (20-km) mountain ridge that towers over the coastal plain.

Not far inland is Israel's second geographic zone, a region of hills bisected by the fertile Jezreel Valley (Valley of Israel), the largest valley in Israel. The area north of the Jezreel Valley is Galilee. Its shimmering liquid jewel is the 64-square-mile (165-sq.-km) Sea of Galilee (Lake Tiberias), Israel's only freshwater lake and its most important water resource. Its Hebrew name, the Kinneret, probably comes from the Hebrew word for "harp" (*kinor*), referring to the lake's shape. Looming above the lake and the Galilee is a dark block of gray volcanic rock called the Golan Heights, a 444-square-mile (1,150-sq.-km) plateau. The Golan's highest point, and the loftiest in Israel, is Mount Hermon, at 7,300 feet (2,224 m). South of the Jezreel Valley are the Judean Hills. Perched on a peak in those hills is Jerusalem, Israel's capital and largest city (population 705,000) and possibly the most fought-over piece of real estate in human history.

Israel's third zone is the Jordan Valley, where the Jordan River flows from the Sea of Galilee to the Dead Sea. The Jordan Valley is a small section of the Great Rift Valley, a huge gash in the earth, the largest of its kind, that runs 3,000 miles (4,830 km) from northern Syria in southwest Asia to Mozambique in East Africa. The Jordan, Israel's longest and most important river, also marks a large part of its border with the Kingdom of Jordan to the east. The Dead Sea, eight times as salty as the ocean, is actually a salt lake with no outlet. At 1,292 feet (394 m) below sea level, it is the lowest point on the surface of the earth. Summer temperatures in the hot and arid Dead Sea basin reach 122°F (50°C). The main relief from the baking heat is the oasis of En Gedi, a series of springs and cliffs covered with lush vegetation that also is a nature reserve. Gazelles, ibex, oryx, foxes, jackals, leopards, and many other animals and birds flourish there.

Israel's fourth geographic zone, and by far its largest, is the Negev Desert. The Negev—its name comes from a Hebrew word meaning "to dry"—is a large, arid triangle that occupies about 60 percent of the country. Its main city is Beersheba, a sprawling, vibrant town of about 150,000 people on its northern fringe. At the Negev's southern tip stands Elat, a port and resort city that is Israel's main outlet to the Far East. The Negev is not all desert. Its northern and western sections around Beersheba comprise a dusty plain that really is a transition zone that supports agriculture. Winter rains here often produce flash floods. Farther south is the rocky and desolate, but also dramatic, landscape of the real desert. The eastern fringe of the Negev is the Arava Valley, another section of the Great Rift Valley and a stretch of desert between the Dead and Red seas.

Israel lies at the southeastern edge of the Fertile Crescent. This is reflected in the country's rainfall statistics, which vary considerably despite its small size. Northern Israel has a Mediterranean climate, with warm, reasonably wet winters and hot, dry summers. Rainfall reaches about 28 inches (71 cm) in the far north and 19 to 21 inches (48 to 53 cm) in the central part of the country. Farther south, the Fertile Crescent ends and the desert begins. The northern fringe of the Negev, the transition zone, gets about 12 inches (30 cm) of rain per year, enough to support agriculture with the aid of highly efficient Israeli irrigation techniques. Rainfall declines to virtually zero near the city of Elat. The Arava gets less than an inch (2.5 cm) of rain per year.

Israel's rainfall, although marginal, enables its farmers to feed the country and produce many crops for export. Israel is the world leader in making maximum use of limited quantities of water in agriculture. In the 1960s, it built the National Water Carrier, a huge network of pipelines, pumping stations, tunnels, aqueducts, canals, artificial reservoirs, and dams. It carries water from the Sea of Galilee, the upper Jordan River and its tributaries, and other water sources in the north to the drier parts of the country. Israeli farmers make extensive use of a technique invented in the country called drip irrigation, in which water is delivered on a timed basis directly to individual plants through pipes or hoses with tiny holes in them, rather than being sprayed wastefully over an entire field. Recent improvements in drip irrigation include computer controls and the addition of fertilizer to the irrigation water. Effective irrigation has enabled Israel to increase its farmland by 250 percent since 1948. Local farmers also make extensive use of greenhouses and plastic sheeting to cover plants, which allows them to grow crops out of season for the export market.

THE ECONOMY

Although Israel must import certain items, such as cereals and feed grains, on balance it is self-sufficient in food. Major export crops include citrus fruits, a variety of noncitrus fruits and vegetables (eggplants, tomatoes, avocados, melons, bananas, and peaches), and flowers; most of them find customers in Western Europe. Other important crops include cotton, olives, and grapes. Israeli agriculture has a feature that is unique in the world: the majority of its farmers live and work on democratically run cooperatives. There are two main types of cooperatives: the kibbutz and the moshav.

The kibbutz is essentially based on communist principles. All property is collectively owned, work is done cooperatively, and earnings are distributed equally among the members. Earnings are not distributed in the form of wages but as necessities and services such as housing, medical care, education, and vacations. Many kibbutzim also engage in manufacturing, so that along with a third of the country's agricultural products, they produce more than 6 percent of its manufactured goods. A moshav is a village in which each family farms an individual plot and profits accordingly, but the village buys its supplies and sells its product cooperatively. About 125,000 people live on 267 kibbutzim, while about 160,000 people live in 411 moshavim. All Israel's cooperatives lease the land they farm from an agency called the Jewish National Fund. A few Israelis operate private farms.

Israel focused on developing agriculture during its early years. Agriculture produces just 2.6 percent of the country's total output, employs only about 2.5 percent of its population, and accounts for about 2 percent of its exports. This is because Israel has become a modern industrial society. The country has a highly competitive and rapidly growing high-tech sector. That sector has been boosted by investment from American and European companies seeking to make use of the country's highly skilled workforce. Israeli-made software, computer chips, and other electronic equipment—including sophisticated medical and printing equipment—have excellent international reputations. So does the high-tech military equipment that Israel produces. The U.S. military is a leading buyer of Israeli equipment. Israel's leading exporter, Israel Aircraft Industries, manufactures both military equipment such as unmanned reconnaissance aircraft and, increasingly, civilian products such as executive jets. Israeli industries also produce modern plastics, petrochemicals, and metal products. In addition, the country is a leader in the production of polished diamonds and other precious stones.

Israel has almost no natural resources. *Golda Meier*, Israel's third prime minister, used to joke that Moses led the ancient Israelites through the wilderness for forty years and then took them to the only place in the Middle East where there is no oil. (Actually, Israel has a tiny amount of oil and is exploring for more.) Its only valuable mineral resources are bromides, potash, magnesium, and other materials extracted from the Dead Sea. Israel is the world's largest exporter of bromides, which are used to make photographic chemicals, antiknock mixtures for gasoline, and a number of other products. About a third of Israeli exports go to the European Union, about 36 percent to the United States, and 20 percent to the Far East. Israel also benefits from traffic flowing the other way in the form of tourists, most of whom come to see its many sites connected with the Bible.

Like every industrial country, Israel suffers from pollution and environmental problems. Industrial pollution and urban sprawl threaten both Israel's limited farmland and its precious natural open space. At the same time, Israelis have dramatically improved the environment of their country. Since 1948 they have planted hundreds of millions of trees in what was once an almost totally deforested countryside. These ongoing efforts have expanded the tree cover from almost nothing to 770 square miles (2,000 sq. km), about 10 percent of Israel's total area. The trees have helped regenerate Israel's soil and enabled the land to absorb rainwater, thereby restoring dried-up wells to productivity. The Israeli government also has established more than 250 nature reserves; they cover a fifth of the country's total land area and provide a refuge for wildflowers and animals. Some native animal species such as the white oryx and Mesopotamian fallow deer that had disappeared from the region have been reintroduced, while others, among them the magnificent golden eagles, have returned on their own.

PEOPLE

In 2006 Israel's population topped seven million. Just over 76 percent of the population are Jews. Muslim Arabs account for about 16 percent of the population; Christians—most, but not all, of whom are Arab—about 2 percent, and Druze about 1.6 percent.

Statistics do not convey the complexity of Israel's population profile. Israel is a very young country that since its founding has attracted Jewish immigrants from all over the world. Although they shared a common religion, they came from radically different cultural backgrounds. Some came from modern industrial countries, others from traditional agricultural societies. Blending them together into a single nation has been an ongoing and sometimes difficult task that remains unfinished after more than fifty years.

What virtually all the immigrants had in common was that they were escaping from persecution or, as in the case of more than 270,000 Holocaust survivors in the years immediately after World War II, far worse. The Holocaust survivors were joined by hundreds of thousands of Jews fleeing persecution in Arab countries, from Morocco in the west to Iraq in the east to Yemen in the south. Some of those communities were twenty-five hundred years old. The 700,000 refuges who reached Israel by 1951 helped swell its Jewish population of 650,000 in 1948 to 1.4 million. In the 1970s, a new wave of immigrants escaping persecution came from the Soviet Union. That wave swelled after the Soviet Union collapsed in 1991, and by 1999, the wave totaled over one million people. Tens of thousands of immigrants came in the 1980s and 1990s from the African country of Ethiopia. Smaller numbers of immigrants who were not fleeing persecution but who wanted to live in the Jewish state also arrived from the United States and Western Europe.

Israel's Jewish population is divided into two main groups: Ashkenazic and Sephardic Jews. Ashkenazic Jews, who make up slightly more than half the Jewish population, trace their roots to the medieval Jewish centers of Central and Eastern Europe. Sephardic Jews are the descendants of Jewish communities from the Iberian Peninsula, Greece, Turkey, North Africa, and the Middle East. The two communities have somewhat different religious rituals, but the most important differences between them are economic and social. Israel was founded by Ashkenazic Jews, who have comprised most of the country's political and economic elite ever since. Sephardic Jews, by contrast, began arriving in Israel in large numbers after the founding of the state. The great majority came from Arab countries and were poorly educated, with few skills suitable for a modern economy. In addition, they arrived virtually penniless, most of their property having been confiscated by Arab governments when they departed for Israel. Most of these Sephardic Jews therefore found themselves near the bottom of Israeli society in economic terms.

Over time this situation began to change as Sephardic Jews gradually improved their social, economic, and political positions. In the government formed after the 1996 elections, three of the most senior positions—defense minister, foreign minister, and deputy prime minister—were held by men born respectively in Iraq, Morocco, and Iran. In 2000, for the first time, a Sephardic Jew, *Moshe Katsav*, became Israel's president. Intermarriage between Ashkenazic and Sephardic Jews also is common. Still, significant economic, educational, and social gaps remain; most poor Israeli Jews are Sephardic. This continues to create intergroup tensions. At the same time, because of the high rates of immigration throughout Israel's history, about one third of its Jewish citizens—whether Ashkenazic or Sephardic—were born abroad.

A third, smaller group, numbering about fifty thousand, are black Jews from Ethiopia. Their origins are uncertain; they probably are an amalgam of Jews who arrived in Ethiopia in ancient times and native converts. In any event, Ethiopian Jews were cut off from the rest of world Jewry for two thousand years. They lacked any knowledge of Jewish learning and traditions that had developed since ancient times. Yet in exceedingly difficult circumstances they preserved their Jewish identity. Israeli authorities brought them to Israel from the turmoil and starvation in Ethiopia, initially by sea in 1981 and then in two airlifts: Operation Moses in 1984–1985 and Operation Solomon in 1991. In a young country, they are a young community. Half of all Ethiopian Jews are under eighteen years of age.

Jews in Israel are divided in another way that transcends ethnic origins: the division between secular and religious (often called Orthodox). It is difficult to say precisely where this dividing line is. Orthodox and ultra-Orthodox Jews, who strictly observe traditional Jewish religious law, are themselves divided into many groups. Ultra-Orthodox Jews wear distinctive traditional clothing and live in their own neighborhoods, such as the famous Mea Shearim section of Jerusalem. The state of Israel is a secular state. However, from the beginning the Orthodox community was given control over certain areas of life that seemed to be most closely connected to religion, such as marriage and burial. Other accommodations were made as well. For example, automobile traffic was banned in Orthodox neighborhoods during the Jewish Sabbath. Orthodox and ultra-Orthodox Jews, who account for perhaps 20 percent of Israeli Jews, also traditionally have voted for their own political parties. They usually have held the balance of power in the Knesset (Israel's parliament) and used that position to win concessions for causes they support. The result has been a degree of tension between secular and Orthodox, especially ultra-Orthodox, communities.

That tension, however, should not be seen simply as a secular-Orthodox divide. There are significant differences between Orthodox groups, who usually get along well with the secular majority, and the ultra-Orthodox sects, who themselves have major areas of disagreement. There are, to be sure, also divisions in the secular community, which means that the shifting tides of political life cause bewildering alignments and realignments that defy a simple secular-Orthodox distinction.

Most of Israel's non-Jews are Muslim Arabs. Israel's one million Muslim Arabs occupy an awkward and difficult position in Israeli society. They live on a tightrope, suspended between their relatively new identity as Israeli citizens and their much older identity as Arabs in a world where Arab states (and Muslim Iran) remain the greatest threat to Israel's security. Israel's Arab citizens enjoy full legal rights. But they usually live apart from the country's Jewish majority, mainly in all-Arab villages or in Arab sections of towns and cities. Most Israeli Arab parents send their children to Arabic-language schools, which also teach them Hebrew. The main legal difference between Arabs and Jews in Israel—and it is a big one—is that Arabs are not subject to being drafted into the army. (They may, however, volunteer.) Because army service is so important for social acceptance in Israel, not serving creates a stigma. Israel's main enemies are Arab states, and the Israeli army inevitably must fight and kill Arabs when it goes to war. Israeli Arabs ordered to defend Israel would have to choose between loyalty to their country and to their fellow Arabs in opposing armies.

Israeli Arabs maintain that the government has taken land that legally belongs to them and that their communities do not receive services equal to those given to Jews. While they have legitimate complaints, the fact remains that they have done well in Israel. The Arab literacy rate has climbed since 1948 from 5 to 95 percent. (It is 57 percent in Arab nations.) Arabs have prospered economically and have the same access as Jewish citizens to the best medical treatment in the Middle East. Israeli Arabs enjoy a free press and the political rights of a democratic society, neither of which exist in the Arab states. Arab women, who make up most of the illiterate population in the Arab world, in particular benefit from living in a modern democratic society. In Israel they enjoy legal equality with men and legal protection unmatched by women in Arab countries. In the last three elections to the

120-person Israeli parliament (the Knesset), 13 Arabs were elected in 1999, 9 in 2003, and 11 (and 1 Druze) in 2006. These representatives may address the Knesset in Arabic, which along with Hebrew has the status of an official language in Israel. Arabs have served on important Knesset committees, such as the foreign affairs committee. An Arab was the deputy foreign minister in the government formed in 1999, and an Arab is one of eight Knesset deputy speakers. Since 2004 a Christian Arab, Salim Jubran, has been a permanent member of Israel's nine-person supreme court. In January 2007, Raleb Majadele became the first Muslim Arab to hold an Israeli cabinet position when he was appointed minister of science and technology Yet while Israeli Arabs have increased their participation in Israeli political life, there also is a disturbing trend in the opposite direction. In recent years, many Israeli Arabs, including college students, increasingly have been identifying less with Israel and more with Arabs living under the Palestinian Authority. This trend worries both Jewish and Arab Israelis who are working to encourage Jewish-Arab coexistence in Israel.

The Druze religion is an eleventh-century offshoot of Islam. About 100,000 Druze live in Israel. Since 1957 they have been recognized as a separate religious community. Still, the Druze speak Arabic and most of them seem to view themselves as Arabs. Nonetheless, in 1948, many Druze sided with Israel against the invading Arab armies, and since 1957, by their own request, they have been subject to conscription in the Israeli army. Their long tradition of self-defense makes the Druze excellent soldiers, and many serve in elite Israeli army units such as the paratroopers.

The great majority of Israeli Christians are Arabs. Most belong to three Christian groups: Greek Orthodox, Greek Catholic, and Roman Catholic. Although they are not Muslims, the Arab Christians of Israel usually side with the Muslim Arab community in its disputes with the Jewish community and Israeli government. But not always. In 1998 a dispute broke out in the city of Nazareth, the largest Arab city in Israel, whose population of about sixty thousand is about two-thirds Muslim and one-third Christian. The trouble began with Christian plans to build a plaza on a half acre of land in front of the city's church in preparation for the millennium. The church itself stands on the site where tradition says the angel Gabriel told Mary she was pregnant with Jesus. Muslims protested and responded with plans for their own project, a huge mosque financed by Persian Gulf nations, on that same half acre, which they claim is a Muslim holy site.

Nazareth's Muslims were in a position to carry out their project because in the most recent elections, they had taken over the city council for the first time in decades. Among those who tried unsuccessfully to dissuade local Muslims from going ahead with their project was *Yasser Arafat*, who feared the dispute would hurt tourism in Bethlehem, which the Palestinian Authority governs. Tension built until it boiled over into fights and rock throwing between Muslim and Christian youths on Easter Sunday of 1999. In the end, the Israeli government, which actually owns the land in question and found itself caught in the middle of the dispute, imposed a compromise. The Muslims could build their mosque, but it would have to be smaller than planned so as to leave some room for the Christian plaza. Not surprisingly, the compromise satisfied neither side.

At the same time, the Christian presence in Israel is not limited to Arabs. Christian groups of all sizes from all over the world maintain a presence in Israel, where their faith was born two thousand years ago. One of their major concerns is with the many Christian holy sites in Israel, a shared interest that not infrequently leads to competing claims and disputes.

POLITICAL SYSTEM

Israel is a democracy, the only one in the Middle East. Its parliament, the Knesset, has 120 members, who are elected by proportional representation. Every political party that receives more than 1.5 percent of the vote receives seats according to its percentage of the vote. Proportional representation, while very democratic in theory, can be divisive. It allows small political parties to proliferate and makes it very difficult for one party to win a majority of the vote. In fact, no single party has ever won a majority in an Israeli election; every government, including the current one, has been a coalition of several parties. In recent years, the number of parties has increased, complicating the task of governing the country. The person ultimately responsible for that job is the prime minister, who heads the cabinet. From 1948 until 1996, the prime minister was the leader of the largest party in parliament. However, in 1996 the system was changed so that the country's voters as a whole chose the prime minister in an election similar to the presidential election in the United States. The hope was to increase the authority of the prime minister and overcome some of the division and weakness in parliament caused by the proportional representation system. That hope was disappointed. In the elections of 1996 and 1999, voters split their ballots. In the election for prime minister, they voted for a candidate from one party, while in the parliamentary election they voted for another party. The result was a weakening of Israel's two largest parties, increased division in parliament, and two unstable governments in a row, neither of which lasted very long. By 2001 most Israelis understood that the reform had failed. After the prime ministerial election in February 2001, parliament restored the old system by which it chooses the person for that office.

THE HISTORY OF MODERN ISRAEL

THE ZIONIST MOVEMENT AND THE ESTABLISHMENT OF ISRAEL

The history of modern Israel begins in the late nineteenth century with the founding of the Zionist movement. Zionism is the belief that Jews should return from the countries where they live as a minority and build their own nation in Israel, the land of their ancestors. Zionism is properly considered the modern Jewish nationalist movement, basically similar to many other nationalist movements that also began in the nineteenth century. At the same time, it is more than twenty-five hundred years old, dating back to the time when the ancient Israelites first were exiled from their homeland by the Babylonians in the sixth century B.C. Psalm 137, written during that exile, contains the famous admonition:

> If I forget thee, O Jerusalem, let my right
> hand forget her cunning.
> If I do not remember thee, let my tongue
> cleave to the roof of my mouth.

The founder of the modern Zionist movement was Theodor Herzl, a Jewish journalist born in Austria. He organized the first Zionist Congress in 1897. Between his death in 1904 and 1914, about thirty thousand Jews from Eastern Europe settled in the ancient homeland of their people, which was at the time called Palestine and was part of the Ottoman Empire. In November 1917, during World War I (1914–1918), the British government responded to Zionist appeals and issued the Balfour Declaration, which called for the "establishment in Palestine of a national home for the Jewish people." After World War I, the British took control of Palestine under the League of Nations mandate when the Ottoman Empire was dismantled. The League mandate repeated the Balfour Declaration's endorsement of a Jewish national home in Palestine. However, as early as 1920, the same year they officially received the League mandate, the British imposed restrictions on Jewish immigration into Palestine. Those restrictions were tightened in the 1930s, just when Jews in Europe were attempting to escape Nazi persecution.

The British imposed these restrictions because the Arabs of Palestine, at the time the overwhelming majority of the population, strongly objected to Jewish immigration. During the 1920s and 1930s, their anger erupted into protests and acts of violence directed at the Jews, whose population nonetheless rose from 50,000 in 1917 to 350,000 in 1939. Yet Jews were far from the only immigrants entering Palestine. In fact, during the years the British restricted Jewish immigration, they did nothing to restrict extensive Arab immigration from neighboring countries, which had been going on for decades. By the 1930s, most of the Jewish immigrants were refugees from Nazi persecution in Germany. They had help in adjusting to their new situation from the well-organized Jewish community in Palestine. Among its most effective leaders was *David Ben-Gurion*, later Israel's first prime minister.

During World War II (1939–1945), more Jewish refugees entered Palestine. This occurred despite strict restrictions put in place by the British, who during the war were worried about growing Arab support for Nazi Germany and did not want to antagonize the Arabs by allowing too many Jews into Palestine. After the war with Germany, the British found it increasingly difficult to keep peace in Palestine in the face of intensifying Arab-Jewish conflict. At the same time, there was widespread international sympathy for the Jewish people because of the murder of six million Jews by Nazi Germany during the Holocaust. There also were hundreds of thousands of Jewish refugees—the survivors of the Holocaust—in European displaced persons camps with no place to go. The Jews of Palestine tried to smuggle refugees into the country, usually on old ships that were barely seaworthy, but the British navy caught most of those ships and interned the Jews in detention camps in Cyprus.

In 1947 the British, burdened by their own domestic problems, announced they would withdraw from Palestine. The United Nations General Assembly then voted in November of 1947 to partition the country into two states, one Arab and one Jewish. The proposed borders were based largely on population patterns, that is, where each group was the majority. The Jewish community of Palestine accepted the partition, but the Arabs rejected it, demanding complete control of the country. They warned they would fight any attempt to establish an independent Jewish state. On May 14, 1948, the British withdrew from Palestine, and the Jews, led by Ben-Gurion, declared the independence of the state they called Israel. Five Arab armies from neighboring countries immediately invaded the new country. The head of the Arab League was very clear about what his side intended to do: "This will be a war of extermination and a momentous massacre which will be spoken of like the Mongol massacres and the Crusades."

FROM WAR TO WAR: ISRAEL, 1948–1982

The fighting lasted from May of 1948 to the spring of 1949. Israel defeated the armies of Egypt, Syria, Iraq, Jordan, and Lebanon—which were supported by units from Saudi Arabia, a volunteer group called the Arab Liberation Army, and other forces—in what Israelis call their War of Independence. But victory came at a very high price in terms of lives, destroyed property, and money. And the end of the fighting did not bring peace. The Arab states refused to sign peace treaties with Israel and agreed only to an armistice. The armistice also left Egypt in control of a small but strategic coastal area called the Gaza Strip. The Kingdom of Jordan got control of a large kidney-shaped area called the West Bank, which it soon officially annexed. Jerusalem ended up divided. Jordan controlled the eastern part of the city, which included the Old City and its Jewish Quarter— from which the Jordanians expelled all the Jewish inhabitants— and the Western Wall, Judaism's holiest site. Israel controlled the new, western part of Jerusalem.

The war also produced about five hundred thousand Arab refugees. The Arab flight began in late 1947 immediately after the United Nations voted to partition the country, when thousands of wealthy business leaders moved their families and assets to the safety of Egypt and Lebanon. By spring 1948, before the British left but after fighting had begun between local Arab and Jewish forces, many Arab political and community leaders joined a second wave leaving the country. By the time Israel declared its independence in May of 1948, about 175,000 Arabs had left to escape the fighting. Then, as the tide of battle turned in favor of the Israelis, large numbers of ordinary Arab town dwellers and peasants, having seen their leaders flee, left their homes to seek safety behind Arab lines. Often these refugees had been frightened by rumors and by false claims of atrocities. In a few cases, Israeli troops expelled Arab civilians from villages they felt had strategic military importance, including along the highway connecting Tel Aviv and Jerusalem. In any event, the Arab refugees were unable to return to homes that ended up on the Jewish side of the 1949 armistice lines. No Jews were allowed to remain in Arab-controlled territory; all were expelled, most of them from areas seized by the Jordanians. The jagged armistice lines of 1949 gave Israel about 21 percent more territory than provided by the original UN partition plan.

Even if the Arabs had won the war of 1948–1949, there would still not have been an independent Arab state in Palestine. The Arab countries that launched that war wanted to destroy Israel and add to their own territories, not to found a new Arab country. Jordan expected to annex all of Palestine. Egypt wanted as much as it could seize in the southern part of the country. Syria and Lebanon each hoped to obtain territory in the north, while Iraq hoped to further its expansionist aims in the region as a whole. The fact that their ambitions conflicted with each other probably helped the Israelis win the war and establish their state.

Meanwhile, in the decade after 1949, Israel took in hundreds of thousands of Jewish refugees, mainly from Arab countries where growing hostility had made life for Jews impossible. The newcomers changed the face of Israel. In 1948 it had been largely European and Ashkenazic, but by the 1960s it was about 50 percent Middle Eastern and Sephardic. Under the Law of Return, passed in 1950, Jews from anywhere in the world were given the right to come to Israel and immediately become citizens.

In 1956 Israel again went to war, this time with Egypt. Israel attacked Egypt, hoping to end Egyptian-sponsored terrorist raids from the Sinai desert and Gaza Strip that had claimed hundreds of civilian lives. These raids had increased dramatically during 1955. A second goal, shared by Britain and France, countries that also attacked Egypt in 1956, was to bring down the Nasser regime. Israel defeated the Egyptian army in the Sinai Peninsula and occupied the region, but it bowed to international pressure and withdrew in 1957.

Israel's prime minister from 1948 until 1963, with the

exception of 1953 to 1955, was David Ben-Gurion. His political party, a socialist group called Mapai (now the Labor
Party), controlled the government in coalition with smaller
partners even longer, until 1977. The 1950s and 1960s were
tense for Israel. All its Arab neighbors officially maintained a
state of war with the Jewish state. Furthermore, the Arab
League enforced an economic boycott against Israel. Arab
states not only refused to trade with Israel, but they pressured
European, American, and Asian companies not to do business
with Israel on pain of losing Arab business. Still, Israel
enjoyed a period of rapid development and growth. Hundreds
of thousands of refugees, most of them penniless and unedu-
cated when they arrived in Israel, became productive citizens.
Israel built a powerful army and air force. It constructed its
National Water Carrier, drained swamps, planted forests on
barren hillsides, and established new industries in the cities.
These included armaments factories that made Israel less
dependent on foreign weapons suppliers.

In 1967 Israel faced its most serious crisis since its War of
Independence in 1948–1949. It began when Egypt's President
Nasser demanded that the UN withdrew peacekeeping troops in
the Sinai Peninsula. Nasser then quickly moved tens of thousands of Egyptian troops up to the Israeli border. He signed military alliances with Syria and Jordan, and blockaded Israel's port
of Elat by closing the Strait of Tiran at the southern end of the
Red Sea to Israeli shipping. On May 27, he announced, "Our
basic objective will be the destruction of Israel." Three days
later, Cairo radio proclaimed that Israel either "will be strangled
by the Arab boycott, or it will perish by the fire of Arab forces."
By early June, the Egyptian force along Israel's southern border
included nearly 120,000 well-trained troops and almost 2,000
tanks.

The Israelis were convinced that they could not afford to
let the Arabs strike first. On June 5, 1967, they launched a pre-
emptive attack against Egypt, the enemy they feared most. Six
days later, Israel had won a total victory and controlled the
Gaza Strip and West Bank, the Sinai Peninsula, and the Golan

Heights. It also controlled all of Jerusalem, including the holy sites in the eastern half of the city from which all Jews had been barred since 1948. Upon entering Jerusalem's Old City, Defense Minister Moshe Dayan spoke for the country when he said, "We have returned to all that is holy in our land. We have returned never to be parted from it again."

Israel's victory in what is known as the Six-Day War was a great boost to morale and left the country, at least temporarily, much more militarily secure than ever before. But it also left many urgent problems unsolved. The Arab world remained united in its opposition to Israel's right to exist. Israel now ruled over more than one million Arabs living on the West Bank and in the Gaza Strip who were not Israeli citizens and who were bitterly hostile to Israeli control. In addition, Israeli Arabs were increasingly restive. Until 1966 they had lived under special military rules that limited their freedom of movement. After 1967 they were influenced by their increased contacts with the West Bank and Gaza Arabs. This heightened their sense of Arab identity at the expense of whatever ties they felt with the state of Israel.

There also was a new and destabilizing element in the already volatile Middle Eastern political mix. In 1964, at a time when Israel did not yet control the West Bank, Gaza Strip, or eastern Jerusalem and the Old City, the Arab League decided to set up the Palestine Liberation Organization (PLO). The PLO's goal was the destruction of the Jewish state and its replacement by an Arab-dominated state from which most Jews living in Israel would be expelled. After the defeat of Arab armies in 1967, the PLO's importance grew. It received effective leadership for the first time in 1969 when Yasser Arafat became its chairman. In the years that followed, Israel increasingly found itself under attack by terrorists sent by the PLO or other Palestinian terrorist organizations.

Israel's prime minister at the time of the Six-Day War had been Levi Eshkol. When he died in 1969, he was succeeded by Golda Meier, the first woman head of state in the Middle East. In 1973 it became Meier's fate, like that of her predecessors, to lead Israel as it fought another costly war. The war began with a coordinated Egyptian-Syrian attack against Israeli forces in both the Sinai Peninsula and Golan Heights that caught the Israelis unprepared. The attack came on October 6, the night of Yom Kippur, the Day of Atonement, the holiest day of the Jewish year (hence the name the Yom Kippur War). Outnumbered twelve to one at the front, initially the Israelis were thrown back, but they then regrouped. With the help of a massive airlift of supplies from the United States, they defeated the Egyptian and Syrian forces, but at a price in lives that stunned the nation. Israel lost nearly twenty-six hundred soldiers in the war. Only the War of Independence had cost more lives. For Israel, whose population was about 3 million at the time, 2,600 dead was the equivalent of 250,000 dead in a country the size of the United States. Almost 9,000 soldiers were wounded. Three weeks of intense warfare had cost nine billion dollars, more than Israel's gross national product for an entire year.

The Yom Kippur War was a catalyst for political change. In April 1974, Golda Meier resigned following criticism that her government had not been prepared for the 1973 attack. Her replacement as prime minister was Yitzhak Rabin, the general who had led Israel's forces during the Six-Day War. Rabin, who after retiring from the army had served as ambassador to the United States, was the first native-born Israeli to lead his country. During his term in office, almost one hundred people—most of them Israelis but also some non-Israeli Jews—were taken hostage by Palestinian and German terrorists. The terrorists had hijacked a passenger airliner in Europe and diverted it to Entebbe, Uganda, 2,600 miles (4,100 km) from Tel Aviv. On July 3, 1976, Israeli soldiers, having secretly flown seven hours from Israel and landed at Entebbe in the dead of the night, freed the hostages. A financial scandal—Rabin's wife had illegally kept a foreign bank account—forced Rabin's resignation in 1977. His successor was *Shimon Peres*, a former close aide to Ben-Gurion and a long-time rival of Rabin in the Labor Party. Peres had played a key role in building Israel's defense industries and its nuclear program. His problem, as his party faced parliamentary elections in May, was that after almost thirty years in power, the Labor Party had lost touch with many Israelis, especially the Sephardic community. The 1977 election ended Labor's long era in power. The winner was the Likud Party, led by Polish-born Menachem Begin.

Begin's Likud Party differed from Labor in two main policy areas. During Labor's years in power, Israel had a mixed economy—most of it was in private hands, but there also was a large government-run sector. Likud strongly favored free-market reforms to reduce the role of government in the economy. The more important difference concerned the territories Israel had won in the Six-Day War. From the start, Labor had favored territorial compromise in exchange for peace. Labor did not even want to retain areas with a large Palestinian Arab population, fearing that such control would undermine Israeli democracy. Labor did insist on keeping Jerusalem as the united capital of Israel, a position that had almost universal support among Israelis. When it came to other territories—the Sinai Peninsula, the thinly populated Golan Heights and Jordan Valley, and selected parts of the West Bank and the Gaza Strip—the decisive issue was security. Areas deemed not essential to security could be given up in return for peace; those deemed vital would remain under Israeli control.

Begin and Likud had a different view from Labor. They were prepared to yield territory that was not part of biblical ancient Israel, such as the Sinai Peninsula, but not land that was part of what they considered Israel's biblical heritage. For that reason, while Labor restricted Jewish settlements to thinly populated and strategically critical areas, Likud promoted Jewish settlement throughout the West Bank and the Gaza Strip, even in areas with large Arab populations.

In the end, however, it was Begin, the hard-liner, who made Israel's first peace with an Arab country. In 1977 he reacted positively to Egyptian president Anwar Sadat's offer to come to Jerusalem. Begin then negotiated the Camp David Accords, a framework for peace, with Sadat and U.S. president Jimmy Carter in September 1978 and a peace treaty in March 1979. In that treaty, in exchange for peace Israel returned the Sinai Peninsula to Egypt. The treaty also called for further negotiations to establish autonomy for the Arabs of the West Bank and Gaza Strip. Begin then moved to shore up Israel's legal position over areas he considered crucial. In 1980 the Knesset passed a law declaring Jerusalem Israel's permanent and undivided capital, and in 1981 Israeli law was extended to the Golan Heights, in effect annexing that territory. However, neither act received international recognition. That same year, Begin sent Israeli warplanes to bomb a nuclear reactor being built in Iraq. Begin feared that Iraq, a country still officially at war with Israel, was planning to build nuclear weapons. (The Israeli raid, criticized at the time in Europe and America, likely spared the United States and its allies from facing a nuclear-armed Iraq in the Gulf War ten years later.)

In June 1982, Begin sent the Israeli army into civil-war-torn Lebanon to destroy bases the PLO had been using to attack Israel. The war in Lebanon, despite achieving its military goal, turned into a long and bloody occupation that deeply divided Israeli society. The first major crisis of the war occurred in September when Christian Lebanese forces, who were allied with Israel, murdered hundreds of Palestinian refugees in two refugee camps near *Beirut.* Although it was Lebanese and not Israeli forces who committed that crime, many Israelis began to turn against the war. The second crisis developed over time as Israel kept its troops in southern Lebanon and ended up fighting Lebanese and Palestinian guerrillas there.

In 1983 Begin resigned as prime minister, in part because of his despair over the growing Israeli casualties in Lebanon. His successor was Yitzhak Shamir, a veteran Likud politician. When the 1984 elections produced a virtual Labor-Likud standoff, the two parties formed a national unity government. They agreed that Shimon Peres would be prime minister from 1984 to 1986 and that Shamir would take over from 1986 to 1988. In 1985, the midpoint of Peres's short term, Israel finally left most of southern Lebanon. It withdrew to a narrow security zone just north of the Israeli border, which its army patrolled along with local Lebanese Christian allies.

Meanwhile, there was trouble closer to home. In December 1987, a Palestinian uprising, known as the intifada (the term means "shaking off" in Arabic), began in the Gaza Strip and spread to the West Bank. The intifada reflected the deep frustrations of Palestinian Arabs, especially the youth, with the ongoing Israeli occupation. While the intifada began spontaneously, within a month the PLO controlled many of its activities. Two radical Islamic fundamentalist groups, *Hamas* and *Islamic Jihad*, also were deeply involved in the intifada. When Israel tried to crack down on the demonstrators, who often were teenagers, its public image abroad suffered. At home, Israelis understood when their soldiers had to go to war against Arab armies, but many were troubled watching their soldiers use tear gas and clubs against rioting Palestinians, even rioters armed with guns and explosives.. But the continued political stalemate—there was another indecisive election in 1988—prevented new initiatives that might lead to useful negotiations between Israel and the Palestinians.

In 1991 Israel became involved in the Gulf War, but not as a direct participant. The war was fought between Iraq, which had invaded Kuwait in 1990, and a U.S.-led coalition formed to force the Iraqis to withdraw. During the war, Iraq attacked Israel with dozens of guided missiles. The United States urgently requested Israel not to retaliate, fearing an Israeli response would cause the Arab states allied with the U.S. to quit the coalition. The Israelis honored the request. The next year, Israel finally held an election that produced relatively decisive results. The Labor Party, led by Yitzhak Rabin, won a solid plurality and formed a new government with Rabin as prime minister. For the first time in almost a decade, Israel had a government capable of taking decisive action on urgent issues facing the country.

When Yitzhak Rabin took office in July 1992, he told his fellow Israelis, "We are going to change the national order of priorities." His main goal would be to "promote the making of peace and take vigorous steps that will lead to the end of the Arab-Israeli conflict." He also directed some of his remarks to the Palestinians, urging them, "Don't lose this opportunity that may never return. Take our proposals seriously." During 1993, while public talks that had begun back in 1991 were getting nowhere, Israeli and PLO officials met secretly for months in Oslo, Norway. In August they surprised the world by announcing an agreement, or Declaration of Principles, popularly known as the Oslo Accords. The agreement provided for a transition to Palestinian self-rule in the Gaza Strip and West Bank over a five-year period. Israel would turn over territory to a newly created Palestine Authority in stages, beginning with most of the Gaza Strip and the West Bank city of Jericho. Exactly how much territory Israel eventually would retain and how close autonomy would come to actual independence were two of the many difficult issues left unsettled. A third critical issue left unsettled was the final status of Jerusalem.

On September 9, Israel and the PLO exchanged letters in which Israel recognized the PLO as the representative of the Palestinian people and the PLO recognized Israel's right to exist and promised to abandon the use of terror against the Jewish state. The two sides formally signed the Oslo agreement in Washington, D.C., on September 13, 1993. Additional essential details took further negotiations that were worked out in an agreement signed in Cairo on May 4, 1994. The peace process and establishment of Palestinian self-rule was supposed to be completed in five years.

The Oslo Accords, despite deeply felt skepticism and mistrust of the PLO and Arafat, initially won widespread support in Israel. Rabin admitted to his people that it was not easy to make peace with people he called murderers, but he added that Israel had to consider what he called the comprehensive picture. Significantly, the former general, known for his careful and meticulous planning, bluntly and simply said, "We have to take risks." The benefits of the peace process for Israel became more evident to many when Israel and Jordan signed a peace treaty in October 1994, finally ending a forty-six-year state of war between the two nations. Low-level diplomatic relations and economic ties also were established with several other Arab states.

But Israeli faith in the process was shaken by a series of terrorist attacks by Islamic fundamentalist groups that killed a total of seventy-seven people in the sixteen months following the accords. Nevertheless, in September 1995 Israel and the PLO reached an agreement often called Oslo II. It provided for Israel's withdrawal from six more West Bank towns, a legislature called the Palestinian Council, and the election of a president of that council. Oslo II also divided the West Bank and Gaza Strip into three unequal areas: territory under full Palestinian control (the smallest at 3 percent, but including the major urban areas), territory under Palestinian administration and Israeli military control (24 percent), and territory under full Israeli control (73 percent).

Oslo II was controversial in Israel and barely won Knesset approval in October. Then the peace process and virtually everything else in Israel was disrupted on November 4, 1995, when an extremist Jewish law student assassinated Rabin just after his appearance at a peace rally in downtown Tel Aviv. The assassination united Israelis of virtually all political camps in shock and mourning. Although the assassin belonged to a tiny fringe group opposed to territorial concessions to the Palestinians, his deed grimly highlighted the deep and bitter divisions in Israel over the peace process and how to guarantee the country's security.

Shimon Peres succeeded Rabin as prime minister and prepared for elections in May 1996. For the first time, voters would not only cast ballots in a parliamentary election but also would vote directly for Israel's prime minister. Although Labor and Peres were favored, a new series of deadly terrorist attacks by Palestinian groups opposed to the peace process cost Peres and his party support. The voters narrowly chose Likud leader Benjamin Netanyahu as prime minister. Netanyahu was a critic of what he said were excessive Labor concessions to the Palestinians under the Oslo agreement; his campaign stressed that Israel must negotiate a secure peace. Once elected, Netanyahu had to cobble together a coalition of eight parties to form a majority in the Knesset. This was further testimony to the growing fractionalization of Israeli political life.

Netanyahu's domestic program called for reducing the government's role in the economy, cutting the budget deficit, and encouraging foreign investment in Israel. In foreign affairs, Netanyahu focused on the peace process, but with a tougher and more cautious stance toward the PLO than that of Labor. Netanyahu and Likud, also in contrast to the former government, encouraged additional Israeli settlement on the West Bank. In addition, the new Israeli government demanded stricter Palestinian compliance with agreements already signed. Its demands included carrying out Arafat's long-standing but unfulfilled pledge to eliminate numerous articles in the PLO Covenant that called for Israel's destruction and for real efforts to combat terrorism.

Notwithstanding Netanyahu's skepticism about the Oslo agreement, in January 1997 his government and the Palestinian Authority negotiated the Hebron Protocol, under which Israeli troops withdrew from most of the West Bank city of Hebron. After the Hebron agreement, the peace process again ground to a halt. In October 1998, Netanyahu and Arafat began a summit meeting with American president Bill Clinton at the Wye River Conference Center in Maryland. Later they were joined by King Hussein of Jordan, already seriously ill with cancer. It took nine days of intense negotiations to reach an agreement, the Wye River Memorandum. Israel agreed to withdraw its troops from an additional 13 percent of the West Bank in three stages. In return the Palestinians again agreed to step up antiterrorist efforts and eliminate the clauses from the PLO Covenant calling for Israel's destruction. This pledge, made five times since 1993, finally was carried out by a vote of the PLO's governing body, the Palestinian National Council (PNC), in December 1998. The PNC voted to approve a January 1998 letter from President Arafat to President Clinton that stated fifteen articles (out of thirty-three) had been "nullified" and parts of nine others "modified."

In May 1999, Israel once again held elections. Labor's candidate, former general Ehud Barak, the most highly decorated soldier in Israel's history, decisively defeated Netanyahu in the prime minister's race. Barak was considered tough and security minded but also more flexible than Netanyahu in terms of negotiating with the Palestinians. His reputation as being strong on security was important. Between the signing of the Oslo Accords in 1993 and the end of 1998, 279 Israelis were killed in terrorist attacks, more than in any comparable period in recent years. Most died in suicide attacks by bombers who blew themselves up along with their victims. Barak appeared to many as the man who could wear the mantle of Yitzhak Rabin and negotiate a secure peace for Israel.

When he took office, Barak told Israelis his main priority would be a "true lasting peace." He directed remarks to Israeli mothers "who don't sleep at night," but also told Palestinians he recognized their "suffering." Less than two months later, on September 3, after tough negotiations in which the United States again played an important role, Barak and PA president Arafat signed an agreement in Sharm al-Sheikh, Egypt. Its significance was that it restarted the peace process. Israel agreed to complete the withdrawals agreed to at Wye in three stages, which would leave the Palestinian Authority in full or partial control of 40 percent of the West Bank. The Palestinians agreed to carry out security measures that included arresting terrorists wanted by Israel, collecting weapons from Palestinian civilians, and reducing the size of its police force to the limits specified by the Oslo Accords. The two sides also agreed to reach a final settlement by September 10, 2000. The first Israeli withdrawal, fixed for September 10, 1999, took place a day earlier than scheduled.

ISRAEL SINCE THE MILLENNIUM

The hopes for peace raised by the election of Ehud Barak and the Sharm al-Sheikh agreement did not survive the year 2000. The year began well enough when Israel completed the withdrawals agreed to in the Wye River Memorandum in March. Late in May, Israel withdrew its soldiers from its security zone in southern Lebanon, where they had been for fifteen years. The occupation, while bringing some security to Israel's northern villages and towns, had been extremely costly. Hundreds of Israeli soldiers had been killed in battles with various Lebanese and Palestinian guerrilla groups, in particular the Lebanese Shiite group *Hezbollah*, which drew much of its inspiration and financing from Iran. It was against this background that U.S. president Bill Clinton called for a summit between Prime Minister Barak and President Arafat at Camp David, Maryland, the same presidential retreat where more than two decades earlier President Jimmy Carter had negotiated the agreement with Israeli and Egyptian leaders that had led to the peace treaty between the two countries. Clinton set an ambitious goal: to resolve the most difficult issues remaining in the Israeli-Palestinian peace effort dating from the 1993 Oslo Accords.

The negotiations at Camp David lasted two weeks, from July 11 to July 25. Barak offered the Palestinians unprecedented concessions. He was prepared to turn over about 95 percent of the West Bank and Gaza to an independent Palestinian state. That state would have sovereignty over part of eastern Jerusalem and over the surface of the Temple Mount, where two Muslim mosques stand. Barak offered to allow one hundred thousand Palestinian refugees to return to Israel under a one-time family reunification program. He offered to uproot more than forty thousand Israeli settlers living on territory that would become part of the Palestinian state and to cede some land inside Israel's 1949 borders adjoining the Gaza Strip. In return Israel would annex about 5 percent of the West Bank where three major blocs of Jewish settlements housing about 130,000 settlers stood.

These concessions went far beyond anything Israel had offered before and shocked and dismayed many Israelis, who believed he was doing irreparable harm to Israel's security. President Clinton, both in private during the negotiations and in public comments to the press later on, made it clear that he believed that these were terms that Arafat and the Palestinians should accept. But Arafat wanted more, and the negotiations dragged on. Finally, with time running out, Clinton gave Arafat a series of yes-or-no options that could have led to an agreement and an independent Palestinian state. Arafat said no. The Camp David negotiations were over, the best opportunity for the Palestinians to have a state of their own since 1947 had been lost, and the Israeli-Palestinian peace process had broken down.

Although the Camp David negotiations officially collapsed over the specific issue of Jerusalem, the Israeli public was perhaps even more disturbed and deeply shaken by another Palestinian demand, one that directly challenged the assumption that the Palestinians finally were prepared to accept Israel's existence. The Palestinians insisted on the right of all refugees from the 1948–1949 war and their descendants— about three million people—to return and live in Israel. Israel rejected the demand, which would have ended Israel's existence as a Jewish state.

It was not long before large-scale violence resumed in the form of an explosion of Palestinian demonstrations and attacks against Israelis throughout the West Bank and Gaza Strip. Initial reports depicted the violence by Palestinians as a spontaneous reaction to a visit by Israeli hard-line politician Ariel Sharon to the Temple Mount—a visit approved by the PA. In fact, it soon became clear that the campaign of violence, soon known as the second intifada, had been planned by PA authorities well in advance, after Yasser Arafat's return from the failed Camp David negotiations.

The second intifada escalated the violence that had taken place during the original intifada of the late 1980s and early 1990s. It involved the direct participation of militias controlled and armed by *al-Fatah* ("conquest" in Arabic), the group headed by Arafat since the 1950s. They used an arsenal of weapons that included automatic rifles, machine guns, mortars, hand grenades, explosives, and antitank missiles to attack Israeli soldiers. Israeli civilians living in settlements on the West Bank also came under attack, often by rifle fire. In October, a Palestinian mob destroyed a Jewish shrine, Joseph's Tomb, in the West Bank city of Nablus. A week later, another mob in the city of Ramallah killed two Israeli soldiers. The Palestinian Authority, meanwhile, released hundreds of jailed Hamas and Islamic Jihad terrorists, a practice it had followed on and off since 1994 in violation of the Oslo Accords and subsequent agreements. In a report issued in 2001, the U.S. State Department said that the members of the PA security services and groups associated with al-Fatah had "instigated and participated in anti-Israeli violence."

In only six months, events seemingly had come full turn, and for the worse. Far from sensing that peace was at hand, as many had hoped in mid-2000, Israelis once again worried about the danger of a full-fledged war. Many Israelis who had considered themselves part of the peace camp were deeply disillusioned. With Israel facing the worst violence in years, the government of Ehud Barak fell apart, and in February 2001 Israelis again went to the polls, for the third time in less than five years, to elect a new prime minister. This time, more than 62 percent of the voters turned to Ariel Sharon, leader of the Likud Party.

Sharon was one of Israel's most charismatic and controversial politicians. He was a war hero from the 1973 Yom Kippur War. He had led Israeli troops across the Suez Canal to trap the Egyptian army on the other side. He also had been defense minister during the 1982 invasion of Lebanon, which many

Israelis believed had been a costly mistake. He was known for his daring and toughness and for his hard-line views when it came to dealing with the Palestinians. Within Israel, he had both fervent admirers and bitter enemies. By 2001 he also was the man most Israelis believed could at least provide them with some measure of security.

Sharon's new government, which included the first member of the Druze community ever to hold a cabinet post in Israel, was immediately confronted by a series of terrorist attacks. In one incident, a Palestinian drove a bus into a crowd at a bus stop near Tel Aviv, killing eight people; in another, a suicide bomber killed two teenagers. Israel responded by temporarily reoccupying a town in the Gaza Strip. On June 1, a Hamas suicide bomber blew himself up inside a Tel Aviv discotheque, an event that shocked the world because this time the target was not only civilians, but young people. Most of the twenty-one Israelis killed in the attack were between fourteen and eighteen years of age. That was followed in August by a suicide bombing in a Jerusalem pizzeria that killed 15 people and wounded more than 130. Israel's response included an intensified effort to kill Palestinian terrorist leaders involved in planning and carrying out these attacks.

The next month, Israelis reacted with grief and sympathy when the United States became the victim of Islamic terrorists. In response to the September 11 attacks by al-Qaeda airplane hijackers that killed more than three thousand people in New York City and Washington, D.C., the Israeli government declared September 12 to be a national day of mourning. There was a nationwide emergency blood drive to help the injured, and in Jerusalem the city's main street, Jaffa Road, was renamed New York Avenue for one month in sympathy with victims of the 9/11 attacks.

Meanwhile, Palestinian terrorist attacks against Israel continued, including the assassination of Israel's tourism minister, Rehavam Ze'evi, in October 2001. At that point, Israel suspended all contact with the Palestinian Authority. In January

2002, a nurse and al-Fatah activist became the first woman suicide bomber when she blew herself up on a main street in
Jerusalem. The PA media praised her action, and she immediately became a heroine to thousands of Palestinian children.
That same month, Israeli naval forces intercepted a ship, the
Karine-A, headed for the Gaza Strip and loaded with fifty tons
of heavy weapons supplied by Iran. In the wake of further terrorist attacks, including a suicide bombing that killed 28 people and injured 134 at a Passover meal at a hotel in the seaside
town of Netanya, Israel took two major steps. During March
and April, it sent military forces into several West Bank cities to
destroy Palestinian weapons factories and other means of carrying out terrorism. In June Israel began building a security
fence along its border with the West Bank to prevent terrorists
from entering Israel from that territory. Original plans called
for completing the 440-mile-long (708-km) structure by the
end of 2005, but delays and disputes over its exact route
pushed the completion date back by several years. While the
fence, in the areas where it was completed, significantly cut
down terrorist activity, it could not stop it entirely. Dozens of
attacks followed, which pushed the total of Israeli casualties
from terrorism between late 2000 and mid-2006 to almost one
thousand dead and about seven thousand injured, many of
them severely.

Early in 2003, Sharon and the Likud Party scored a solid
victory in parliamentary elections. Shortly thereafter the United
States, the European Union, Russia, and the United Nations—
collectively referred to as the quartet—announced a new peace
plan they called the roadmap. The Israeli cabinet endorsed the
plan, but it did not produce any more results than previous plans
did. With the roadmap stalled, in December 2003 Sharon
announced what he called his disengagement plan. It called for
Israel to unilaterally withdraw from the Gaza Strip, evacuating
all Jewish settlements in the region, and to also dismantle several settlements in the northern West Bank. The plan, which left
open the question of final borders between Israel and a future
Palestinian state, was supported by the United States. In Israel,

public opinion was divided. However, Israel's parliament approved the plan in early 2005, and it was carried out in August. The government removed by force Israelis who did not voluntarily leave their homes in the dismantled settlements.

Although Sharon had won the support of parliament for his disengagement plan, he faced strong opposition to it within his own Likud Party. Therefore, in November 2005, Sharon resigned from Likud and formed a new political party, which he called Kadima ("forward" in Hebrew). His strategy was to build support among Israelis for his program by leading the party to victory in the upcoming March 2006 parliamentary elections. However, in January 2006 Sharon suffered a massive stroke that left him disabled and permanently removed him from public life. *Ehud Olmert*, a longtime Sharon supporter and former mayor of Jerusalem, became acting prime minister and replaced Sharon as leader of Kadima. In March Kadima placed first in the parliamentary elections. Olmert then formed a governing coalition that included the Labor Party, the second-place finisher in the elections.

Olmert and his country faced enormous challenges. According to what he called his convergence plan, Israel by 2010 would set permanent national borders by withdrawing from most of the West Bank. While Olmert was not specific about the details of those borders, he indicated his plan would leave Israel in control of three major settlement blocs where almost two hundred thousand Jews live, the Old City of Jerusalem, and a security border in Jordan Valley. Olmert said Israel was prepared to negotiate borders with the Palestinian Authority but would take matters into its own hands if the Palestinian Authority did not respond to his proposals. As he put it, "We will give the Palestinian Authority the opportunity to show that it is aware of its responsibilities and willing to change, but we won't wait forever."

By 2006 the Palestinian Authority was, if anything, more hostile to Israel than ever. Yasser Arafat had died in November 2004 and was succeeded as PA president by his longtime associate *Mahmoud Abbas*, who won a special election in January 2005 with

62 percent of the vote. However, in January 2006 Hamas won the elections for a new Palestinian parliament. Hamas, an Islamic fundamentalist organization, was totally opposed to Israel's right to exist, and its leaders reemphasized this after the elections. After its election victory, Hamas and other terrorist organizations launched hundreds of rockets from the Gaza Strip against Israeli towns near the border. More than six hundred rockets struck Israel between September 2005 and June 2006.

A greater immediate threat to Israeli security lay in the north. From its bases in southern Lebanon, Hezbollah periodically attacked northern Israeli communities with artillery, mortar fire, rockets, or other weapons, killing and wounding both civilians and soldiers on the Israeli side of the border. There were almost twenty such attacks between Israel's withdrawal from Lebanon in 2000 and July 2006 despite the fact that in September 2004 UN Security Council Resolution 1559 had called for the disarming of all militias on Lebanese territory. By 2006 Hezbollah had more than twelve thousand rockets, some with a range of up to 120 miles (193 km). Many of these rockets, especially the advanced ones, were supplied by Iran, which both financed Hezbollah with about one hundred million dollars per year and trained its military forces. Iran itself was committed to developing nuclear weapons and was led by Islamic fundamentalists who continually threatened to destroy Israel.

In July 2006, Hezbollah launched its most severe attack yet on Israeli territory. It bombarded Israeli towns and military positions along the border with rockets and mortars while simultaneously sending a raiding party across the border that killed three Israeli soldiers and kidnapped two others. Israel responded with a military campaign designed to end the Hezbollah threat once and for all. That effort, which Israelis called the Second Lebanon War, met with only partial success. While the Israelis knew about Hezbollah's rockets, they were unaware that Iran had supplied Hezbollah with a full range of antitank and other weapons. Nor did they know that, with Iranian help, Hezbollah had built heavily fortified bunkers throughout southern Lebanon. The short-range rockets

Hezbollah relied on most could be set up and fired quickly. Frequently they were launched from civilian areas inside Lebanon, leaving the Israeli military no choice but to attack those areas in order to protect Israeli civilians. In just under five weeks of fighting, almost four thousand Hezbollah rockets landed in Israel. Meanwhile, Israeli ground forces in south Lebanon faced a determined foe that was well equipped and well dug in.

The fighting finally ended on August 14, on the basis of UN Security Council resolution 1701, which called for the dis- armament of Hezbollah and Israel's withdrawal from southern Lebanon and for a UN force and the Lebanese army to take con- trol of the region. The hope was that these conditions would provide the basis for a stable peace that would allow Israel and Lebanon, both of which suffered greatly in the war, to recover. However, it quickly became an open question whether the inter- national community would stand behind the UN resolution and guarantee its enforcement. Israel withdrew from southern Lebanon, but neither the Lebanese army nor the new UN force in Lebanon took effective action to disarm Hezbollah or to stop the arms smuggling across the Syrian-Lebanese border. By early 2007, Hezbollah effectively had rearmed. In April 2007, UN secretary-general Ban Ki-moon warned that UN resolution 1701 was not being enforced. Continued arms smuggling from Syria threatened the cease-fire in Lebanon.

This was the situation Israel faced as of early 2007. The country has achieved a great deal in its nearly sixty years of exis- tence and has become a modern and prosperous society. It inte- grated Jewish immigrants from all over the world and built a modern industrial economy. Israeli schools train world-class sci- entists and engineers. Its high-tech products make up 60 percent of its exports (excluding diamonds). The Israeli military is among the world's most respected. It is working with the U.S. military to produce the Arrow antimissile system, the world's first, and a powerful laser to destroy short-range rockets often used by guer- rillas. The country has a vibrant cultural life. Writers like Amos Oz and A. B. Yehoshua are known internationally, and Israeli-

trained classical musicians like Itzhak Perlman and Pinchas
Zuckerman are among the world's most renowned in their fields.
Its problems, from secular-religious tensions to the environment,
are serious and daunting, but all have taken second place to the
search for a secure peace. Nothing can change the reality that
Israel faces great dangers in the future.

PALESTINIAN AUTHORITY

The Palestinian Authority (PA) is an autonomous political entity located on parts of the West Bank and Gaza Strip, areas that
were under Israeli control from 1967 to 1994. The PA controls
all of the Gaza Strip, a small and densely populated stretch of
land along the Mediterranean coast 28 miles (45 km) long and
only 5 miles (8 km) wide, squeezed between Israel and Egypt. It
also fully or partially controls 40 percent of the West Bank, the
hilly eastern region of the former Palestine mandate. Both areas
were occupied by invading Arab powers in the 1948–1949
Arab-Israeli war, the Gaza Strip by Egypt and the West Bank by
Jordan. They were taken by Israeli forces in the 1967 war. The
West Bank and Gaza Strip make up most of the area that would
have formed an Arab state had the Arabs accepted the 1947 UN
partition of Palestine.

About 1.75 million Muslim Arabs live on the West Bank.
Christians make up about 2 percent of the region's Arab population. However, life for Christians is insecure under PA rule,
and their numbers are declining rapidly because of emigration.
About 160,000 Israelis live in scattered settlements in the region
established in the years after the 1967 Six-Day War. The population of the Gaza Strip is about 1.1 million, virtually all of
whom are Sunni Muslim Arabs. A quarter of the population lives
in *Gaza City*, the region's largest urban area. One-third of the
population consists of refugees from the 1948–1949 war and
their descendants. They live in eight large camps that over the
years have taken on the look of permanent towns. About six
thousand Israelis once lived in several small settlements in the

WEST BANK AND GAZA

- ○ City
- ─── 1949 armistice line
- ─── International border
- ─── River

Mediterranean Sea

ISRAEL

"Green Line"

Qalqilya ○

Tulkarm ○

Jenin ○

Nablus ○

West Bank

Jordan R.

JORDAN

Ramallah ○

Jericho ○

Jerusalem ○

Bethlehem ○

Dead Sea

Hebron ○

Gaza City ○

Dayr al Balah ○

Khan Yunis ○

Rafah ○

Gaza Strip

EGYPT

0   10   20 mi

0   10   20 km

WEST BANK AND GAZA

Gaza Strip, but the Israeli government dismantled those towns and villages in 2005.

The autonomy of the PA refers to its uneasy and unresolved relationship with Israel. In 1994 Israel yielded some of its control to the PA in a series of agreements. Israel, however, maintains that the ultimate fate of the region must take into account its security concerns. The West Bank in particular is a wedge that practically divides Israel in two. It also contains high ground overlooking Israel's coastal plain that provides a strategic advantage in any military conflict. The West Bank could become, as it was in 1948 and 1967, a staging ground for an

Arab attack on the Jewish state. Israelis therefore are deeply
concerned about exactly what territory the PA controls and the
degree of its control.

The Palestinians argue for complete independence of the West Bank and the Gaza Strip. They want all Israeli settlements established since 1967 in the West Bank to be dismantled. In addition, they want control of all of eastern Jerusalem, which Israel annexed in 1967 and considers part of its united capital city.

The PA came into being as a result of the Declaration of Principles signed by Israel and the PLO in September 1993. In May 1994, after further negotiations, the PA took control of the city of Jericho on the West Bank near the Jordan River and the majority of the Gaza Strip. At the end of 1995, after the Oslo II agreement, Israel withdrew from six of the remaining seven major West Bank cities: Nablus, Ramallah, Jenin, Tulkarm, Qalqilya, and Bethlehem. Hebron, important to both Muslims and Jews because they consider it the burial place of the patriarch Abraham, was not included in the 1995 agreement. However, 450 Palestinian villages and towns were turned over to PA administration, with Israel maintaining control over security. Outside those densely populated areas, large chunks of West Bank territory remained under complete Israeli control.

In 1997 Israel withdrew from 80 percent of Hebron but kept control over the rest of the city to protect the small group of Jewish settlers there. The agreements of 1993, 1995, and 1997 left the PA with full control of 3 percent of the land on the West Bank and civilian administrative control of an additional 24 percent, as well as full control of 60 percent of the Gaza Strip. The Wye River Memorandum of 1998 and the Sharm al-Sheikh agreement that superseded it expanded the PA's total or partial control to 40 percent of the West Bank. These agreements also left well over 90 percent of all Palestinians living in the West Bank and Gaza at least under PA civilian rule. Just under a quarter of the territory transferred to PA control under the Wye and Sharm al-Sheikh agreements was set aside as a nature reserve where building is prohibited.

In January 1996, Palestinian voters elected a parliament

called the Palestinian Council. Yasser Arafat's al-Fatah organization, the core of the PLO, won 49 out of the 88 seats. The voters also elected a president of the council. In that election, Arafat won more than 87 percent of the votes over a rival who opposed the Oslo peace agreements. In May of that year, Arafat appointed what in effect was a cabinet.

The PA has had a rocky history. Almost entirely dependent on foreign contributions for funding, the PA has been undermined because its officials consistently have mismanaged and stolen those funds. For example, a 1997 audit revealed officials had misappropriated $326 million. In 1998 investigators discovered that $70 million in customs duties had not been deposited in the PA treasury. When the International Monetary Fund audited the PA's finances in 2003, it concluded that between 1995 and 2000 about $900 million had been transferred into accounts controlled personally by Yasser Arafat. Documents captured by Israelis in 2001 revealed that funds provided by the European Union had been used by the terrorist militia associated with Arafat's al-Fatah organization. For these and other reasons, the PA was widely viewed as being corrupt, even by local Palestinians. It also was criticized for operating undemocratically and committing many human rights abuses.

The PA also has had serious economic problems. It remains heavily dependent on Israel—for imported goods, as a market for its exports, and as a place where many Palestinians find jobs. The economy therefore was hurt each time Israel closed its borders with the PA, which happened on several occasions after terrorist suicide bombing attacks killed Jews in Israel. During the late 1990s, notwithstanding billions of dollars in international aid, almost every relevant statistic indicated economic decline. The intifada that began in 2000 further hurt the PA economy. During 2004 two billion dollars in international aid prevented a complete collapse of the economy. Unemployment stood at staggering levels, about 23 percent in the West Bank and 29 percent in the Gaza Strip as of 2005.

Along with its internal problems, the PA consistently locked horns with Israel. PA leaders were angered and disappointed by the pace and the extent of Israeli withdrawals from West Bank territory. What emerged in the course of those withdrawals was a fundamental difference in what each side expected. The Palestinians expected Israel to withdraw from virtually all of the West Bank, including all of eastern Jerusalem, which the Palestinians wanted as their capital. Israel intended to withdraw from perhaps 50 percent of the region and to retain complete control of Jerusalem.

Israel had its own list of complaints about the PA. It accused the PA of violating written commitments not to foment hatred against Israel. These violations included speeches by PA president Arafat, who when speaking to Arab audiences repeatedly called for jihad, or holy war, against Israel. Arafat and other PA officials also compared agreements signed with the Jewish state to a temporary truce the Prophet Mohammad had made with a Jewish tribe in the seventh century. Mohammad later broke the truce and destroyed the Jewish tribe.

Israel also was disturbed about what the PA was teaching the next generation of Palestinians. Palestinian schoolchildren, rather than being prepared to accept Israel's existence and live alongside it in peace, were being taught to hate both Israel and Jews and to believe that Israel would be destroyed someday. PA textbooks compared Zionism to Nazism and contained many anti-Semitic slurs, and PA-distributed maps of the region, including more than one hundred in various textbooks, failed to show Israel. In dozens of textbooks published by the PA ministry of education since 2000, including thirty published in 2004 for grades 5 and 10, Israel still was not recognized as a sovereign state and did not appear on any of the maps. Nor was peace with Israel mentioned.

One particularly disturbing incident that graphically illustrated Israel's complaints was a 1998 Palestinian television program that showed footage of Palestinian children at summer camp training with automatic weapons and chanting, "I foresee my death and I rush toward it!" and "A hero's death, the death of a suicide warrior!" This was not an exception; there were many programs with similar messages. In one, a Muslim cleric preached the following message:

> Have no mercy on the Jews no matter where they are, in any country. Fight them, wherever you are. Wherever you meet them, kill them. Wherever you are, kill those Jews and those Americans who are like them.

In another program, aired in April 2006, a young girl recited a poem in which she compared Jews to monkeys and proclaimed that she would never accept the existence of Israel. Sitting in the audience in the front row with other PA officials and applauding was Mahmoud Abbas, Yasser Arafat's successor as PA president.

Late in 1998, the Palestinians took two contradictory steps. The PA passed a law mandating the death penalty for both seller and buyer when any Palestinian sold land to an Israeli. At the same time, in December the PLO at last amended its covenant to eliminate clauses calling for the destruction of Israel. That decision was denounced by Islamic fundamentalist organizations bitterly opposed to the peace process. The most important of these were Hamas and Islamic Jihad, the groups responsible for most of the suicide bombings since the 1993 Oslo Accords. Yet PA efforts to restrain Hamas and Islamic Jihad from terrorist acts were interspersed with cooperation with those organizations. This pattern typified a revolving-door policy regarding jailed terrorists, who often were released shortly after their arrests or convictions. Meanwhile, the PA had little leverage of its own in dealing with Israel, whose power far exceeded its own. Any headway Arafat made toward his goal of an independent Palestinian state depended on outside help. The most important outsider was the United States, whose close relationship with Israel at times enabled it to persuade the Israelis to make concessions and to apply pressure when persuasion did not work.

By 2000 the series of agreements reached with Israel since 1993 had created optimism among Palestinians that their goal of an independent state was within reach. However, that picture changed with the failure of the Camp David peace talks in July and the new Palestinian intifada. The fighting brought death and economic hardship to both Palestinians and Israelis. Aside from the loss of life, the first half year of the intifada left the Palestinian economy in ruins. Unemployment, which had dropped to 11 percent by 2000, soared to 45 percent. Per capita income dropped from two thousand dollars to fourteen hundred dollars, leaving half the population living in poverty. Loss of income—including lost wages because Palestinian workers could no longer go to their jobs in Israel and trade with Israel—approached one billion dollars. The United Nations increased its aid programs to try to fill the gap, and European nations sent sixty million dollars to pay PA salaries. But the Arab nations, despite large promises, sent almost nothing to help the PA.

Along with the United Nations, the United States was a key source of aid to the PA. Nonetheless, many Palestinians deeply resented the United States because of what they considered American support for Israel at their expense. That resentment became a serious problem for the PA leadership when it burst into view immediately after the al-Qaeda attacks on the United States that killed more than three thousand people on September 11, 2001. While Arafat himself denounced the attacks, spontaneous celebrations broke out in several Palestinian cities in the West Bank and Gaza. The PA tried to stop foreign journalists from videotaping the celebrations, efforts that included threatening journalists and the organizations they worked for. According to the *Washington Post*, Palestinian police stopped photographers from filming a rally where "drivers honked their horns, gunmen fired into the air, and revelers handed out sweets." In response to these attempts to control the news, the Associated Press filed an official complaint with the PA, while the Foreign Press Association condemned what it called "direct threats" and "harassment" of journalists.

During the next several years, little changed for the positive in areas under PA control. Then, in November 2004 Yasser Arafat died. He had headed the PA since its inception and, even more, had been the most significant Palestinian leader since the 1960s. In an election held in January 2005, the man chosen to replace Arafat as PA president was Mahmoud Abbas, a founding member of al-Fatah and Arafat's longtime associate. Abbas also served under Arafat as the first PA prime minister when that post was created in 2003. Among the many challenges Abbas faced as president was to clean up the corruption that had so discredited the PA and to reestablish some kind of working relationship with the Israelis.

He soon found himself facing another challenge as well. Actually, it was a dual challenge, both to his status as the leader of the Palestinian people and to the status of al-Fatah as the dominant group in the PA. The challenge emerged dramatically in January 2006 when the PA held parliamentary elections and Hamas swept to victory, taking 76 of the 132 seats. Al-Fatah trailed badly, with 43 seats. Hamas is a radical Islamic fundamentalist organization that is bitterly and unalterably opposed to Israel's right to exist. Since its founding in the 1980s, Hamas has carried out some of the deadliest terrorist attacks against Israel. Hamas leaders, including Ismail Haniyeh, who took over as the PA prime minister a month after the elections, made it clear in many public statements that Hamas's views remain unchanged. A typical comment came from Mahmoud al-Zahar, the new PA foreign minister "Palestine means Palestine in its entirety. . . . Why should we recognize . . . Israel's right to exist?"

The election results shocked not only the Israelis but much of the international community. Officials in Europe and the United States were dismayed that the Palestinians had turned to a terrorist organization whose core beliefs made it totally opposed to the peace process. Although Mahmoud Abbas still was PA president, the elections had shifted real power to Hamas, and that threatened to throw the entire region into turmoil. To try to weaken Hamas, or to at least force it to accept Israel's right to exist, Israel and the United States both cut all ties with the PA. The United States and the European Union, which between them provided the PA with about one billion dollars a year in aid, half its income, cut off that aid. Humanitarian aid from various international organizations continued to reach the PA, and the European Union began providing some aid later in the year. Meanwhile, Israel kept open a key crossing point into Gaza to allow that aid through. Still, as of mid-2006, the Palestinians have painted themselves and the PA into a corner, one that promises to become increasingly uncomfortable in the foreseeable future.

JORDAN

Modern Jordan occupies an area where the ancient kingdoms of Edom and Moab stood in ancient times. Mentioned often in the Bible as enemies of the Israelites, the Edomites and Moabites nonetheless were closely related to them. Both peoples disappeared from history when the Arab conquest of the seventh century permanently made the region part of the Arab world. Other conquerors—the Crusaders, Mamelukes, Ottomans, and British—took their turns ruling the country into the twentieth century. Jordan finally became fully independent in 1946.

GEOGRAPHY AND PEOPLE

GEOGRAPHY

Jordan is a jagged-shaped country. Mostly desert, its only outlet to the sea is 15.5 miles (26 km) of coastline on the Gulf of Aqaba. Its only lake is its section of the salty and lifeless Dead Sea. Jordan has an area of 34,442 square miles (89,206 sq. km), about the size of Indiana. Its eastern border, formed in part by the Jordan River and Dead Sea, faces Israel and the West Bank. Syria lies to the north, Iraq toward the northeast, and Saudi Arabia to the east and southeast. *Amman* (population 1,292,000) is Jordan's capital and largest city. Other major urban centers are Irbid (population 257,000), in its northwestern corner, and Zarqa, also in the

Mediterranean
Sea

LEBANON

N
W E
S

JORDAN

SYRIA

SYRIAN

DESERT

IRAQ

Golan
Heights

ISRAEL

Yarmuk
R.
Irbid

Jordan
Valley   Jerash

Zerqa R.

Zarqa
Ruseifa

Amman

Azraq

West
Bank

Jordan R.

Madaba

Dead
Sea

SAUDI
ARABIA

Karak

al-Hasa

Wadi al-Abyad

ARABIAN

Maan

DESERT

Aqaba
Gulf of Aqaba

0   25   50 mi

0   25   50 km

JORDAN

✪ Capital city
○ City
── International border
--- Unofficial border
── River

northwest. Jordan's only port, Aqaba, in the far south, has a population of about 104,000. Its main rivers, aside from the Jordan, are two of the Jordan's tributaries, the Yarmuk in the north and the Zarqa in the south. The Yarmuk forms part of Jordan's border with Syria and supplies water to a major irrigation project before reaching the Jordan just south of the Sea of Galilee.

Jordan has three distinct topographical areas. Its western edge is the Jordan Valley. The valley's mild winters and hot summers, combined with fertile soil and adequate water supply, make it a rich agricultural region. People have lived in the Jordan Valley for millennia. Stone tools have been found there dating back almost one million years. Evidence of farming and raising livestock is ten thousand years old. The center of the country is an upland area above and east of the Jordan Valley. Its northern section near the Syrian border contains a small forest region that makes up 1 percent of Jordan's territory. Jordan's eastern section is a parched, barren plateau that belongs partly to the North Arabian desert in the south and the Syrian Desert in the north.

The 10 percent of Jordan's land that is arable produces wheat, barley, lentils, tomatoes, eggplants, citrus fruits, and grapes. Sheep and goats are raised for their milk and meat. Jordan's industries produce or process phosphates, potash, fertilizers, cement, and a tiny amount of oil. Most oil, consumer goods, and more than half of Jordan's food must be imported. Jordan prospered during the oil boom of the 1970s and 1980s when about 350,000 of its citizens, including many educated and skilled professionals, took jobs in the wealthy oil-producing Persian Gulf states. The money they sent home to their families stimulated the local economy. The collapse of the oil boom at the end of the 1980s cost Jordanians their jobs and ended the flow of money. At the same time, aid from the wealthy Gulf states dried up. Jordan was hurt again in the wake of the 1991 Gulf War when Kuwait expelled 300,000 Palestinian workers. Many ended up in Jordan, where they added to the ranks of the unemployed. Overall, as the new century began, Jordan was burdened by poverty, large foreign debts, and unemployment.

PEOPLE

Jordan's population is 5.9 million, about 98 percent of whom are Arabs. Approximately 96 percent of the population are Sunni Muslims, while 4 percent are Christians. Jordanians are well educated. The literacy rate is more than 93 percent for men and almost 80 percent for women. Jordan has the highest number of university graduates of any Arab country. Its official language and religion are respectively Arabic and Islam.

The homogeneity of Jordan's population suggested by the percentage of Arabs and Sunni Muslims is deceiving because there are different groups of Arabs. Jordan's ruling dynasty, the Hashemites, is a relatively recent arrival from the Arabian Peninsula. Its base of support is the Bedouin Arab community, which until recently lived the traditional nomadic life. The Bedouin continue to make up a large part of the Jordanian army and the core of the officer corps on which the Hashemites have always depended. Yet they constitute at most 10 percent of Jordan's population.

The single largest group in Jordan's population is the Palestinians. Many of them arrived in Jordan in the last fifty years. Some simply moved from the West Bank, but hundreds of thousands came as refugees after the 1948–1949 and 1967 wars with Israel. All were granted Jordanian citizenship. This movement of people is not surprising, as it is nothing new. The personal and business ties between towns on opposite sides of the Jordan River have long been very close. Many prominent Jordanian families that have been in the country for centuries, including that of a recent prime minister, trace their roots to West Bank towns. In fact, it often is impossible to distinguish who is a Palestinian and who is a Jordanian. Yet it is clear that Palestinians dominate much of Jordan's economic life, from banking to retailing to the import-export trade. At the other end of the economic spectrum, hundreds of thousands of Palestinians live in poverty in refugee camps. Whatever their status, Palestinians often are neutral or hostile toward the Hashemite dynasty. They also have opposed various Jordanian efforts since 1949 to reach a peaceful solution to the Arab conflict with Israel, since those attempts would leave the Palestinians without a state of their own.

HISTORY OF MODERN JORDAN

The Hashemite Kingdom of Jordan takes its name from the dynasty that has ruled the country throughout its brief history. The Hashemites ended up the rulers of Jordan in the wake of World War I and the partition of the Ottoman Empire because they were willing to cooperate with Great Britain, the new dominant power in the Middle East. In 1920 the area that is Jordan was included in Britain's Palestine mandate that was supposed to be set aside for a Jewish national home. In 1922, however, the British detached the territory west of the Jordan River, about three-quarters of Palestine's total area, from the mandate. They installed Abdullah ibn Hussein as emir (Arabic for "prince") in what from 1923 was the semi-independent Emirate of Transjordan. When the British granted full independence in 1946, Abdullah became king of the Kingdom of Transjordan.

Abdullah, uniquely among Arab leaders, did not oppose Zionism or the creation of a Jewish state in Palestine. He met with Zionist leaders, including Golda Meier, who later became Israel's foreign minister and prime minister. In 1948 Arab pressure forced Abdullah to send his British-led and British-equipped Arab Legion across the Jordan River to join the campaign to destroy the newly born state of Israel. However, he was satisfied with taking over the part of Palestine set aside for an Arab state and controlling eastern Jerusalem. Abdullah's army performed better than any of the other Arab forces, and he added valuable territory to his realm. At war's end in 1949, he controlled the West Bank and eastern Jerusalem, including the Old City and its holy sites.

Abdullah officially annexed the West Bank and eastern Jerusalem in 1950, granted the local inhabitants Jordanian citizenship (having expelled all the Jews from the territories he had seized in 1948), and changed his country's name to the

Hashemite Kingdom of Jordan. The international community did not accept that annexation, which was recognized only by Britain and Pakistan. Abdullah was assassinated in 1951 while preparing to pray in the Old City's al-Aqsa Mosque. His assassin was an Islamic fanatic who considered Abdullah a traitor to the Arab cause. When Abdullah's son and successor was found to be mentally ill, the crown passed to his young grandson, *Hussein ibn Talal*. Hussein officially became king of Jordan on his eighteenth birthday, in 1953. The new teenage king surprised almost everyone by surviving the crisis that put him on the throne and many other challenges thereafter. The worst of them, his participation in the 1967 Six-Day War, cost his country the West Bank and eastern Jerusalem. Yet Hussein was destined to rule Jordan until his death in 1999 and eventually earn a reputation as one of the Middle East's outstanding statesmen.

THE REIGN OF KING HUSSEIN

King Hussein sat on a shaky throne from the very start. In the sharply divided world of Arab politics, he sided with the region's other conservative monarchies such as Saudi Arabia. One of the earliest threats to his reign came from Jordanian groups favoring closer cooperation with radical Arab states such as Syria and Egypt. In 1957 Hussein thwarted a military coup. The young king declared martial law and dissolved all political parties to deal with the unrest that followed. The next year, Hussein survived a Syrian assassination attempt and in 1959 another military coup. That same year, Jordan's prime minister, a close ally of the king, was assassinated. Hussein responded by further tightening political restrictions.

The founding of the PLO in 1964 was yet another threat to Hussein. The PLO competed with Jordan for the loyalty of its Palestinian population and constantly tried to provoke a conflict with Israel, something Hussein wanted to avoid. In 1967, however, like his grandfather in 1948, Hussein found himself unable to resist widespread Arab pressure to join the war effort against Israel. The swift Israeli victory left Jordan as the war's biggest loser, shorn of both the West Bank and eastern Jerusalem, the

Hussein's showdown with the PLO came in 1970. By then various guerrilla and terrorist groups that made up the PLO had created a state within a state in Jordan. They controlled large parts of the border area and used them as staging grounds for raids against Israel. In September 1970, Hussein concluded that the Palestinians had become a threat to his throne and sent his army against them. When Syria prepared to intervene on the PLO's behalf, Israel mobilized troops along the border, forcing the Syrians to back down. The king's army decisively defeated the Palestinians, killing thousands, in what the latter have since called Black September. The fighting lasted until mid-1971. Some PLO fighters so feared Hussein's forces that they swam across the Jordan River and surrendered to the Israelis. The defeated PLO, along with several hundred thousand refugees, retreated into Lebanon.

The 1970s and 1980s were good times for Jordan. In 1973 Hussein kept Jordan out of the Yom Kippur War until its late stages, when he sent soldiers to help Syrian troops on the Golan Heights. Meanwhile, Jordan's economy grew, fueled by money sent home by its citizens working in the oil-rich Persian Gulf region. Hussein's own popularity at home also grew, and his widening base of support helped stabilize his regime.

Jordan's complicated relationship with the Palestinians gradually began to sort itself out, although not always with Hussein's approval. That process, in turn, helped to define Jordanian identity. In 1974 the Arab League, with reluctant Jordanian support, recognized the PLO as the sole representative of the Palestinian people. Hussein held back from Egyptian president Anwar Sadat's initiative that in 1979 produced the Egyptian-Israeli peace treaty, bowing to Arab pressure to sever ties with Egypt. Meanwhile, the king continued to retreat from Jordan's claims to the West Bank. In 1984 he changed the constitution to allow Jordan to hold elections without West Bank participation, and in 1988 he renounced all Jordanian claims to the West Bank.

In 1989 Hussein felt confident enough to ease his tight grip

on Jordanian political life. He permitted the country's first parliamentary elections since the 1950s. Jordanian women, to
whom the king had granted the vote in 1974, voted for the first
time. However, the election results were disappointing and even
dangerous. Islamic fundamentalist parties, whose goal was to
subject Jordan to Islamic law, won about 40 percent of the seats.
They became the largest bloc in the parliament. This did not
stop Hussein from legalizing political parties, banned since
1957, in a new law that took effect in 1992. In 1993, having
changed the electoral law to minimize Islamic strength, Hussein
suddenly dissolved parliament and ordered new elections. This
time the largest bloc elected to parliament consisted of moderate politicians loyal to Hussein and the Hashemite regime.

Meanwhile, Hussein and Jordan endured the agony of the
Gulf War. The crisis that led to the war began in August 1990
when Iraq invaded Kuwait. King Hussein was a moderate man,
strongly pro-Western and pro-American and interested in making
peace with Israel. Yet many Jordanians, especially Palestinians, fer-
vently supported Iraq in its invasion of Kuwait, largely because of
Iraqi dictator Saddam Hussein's militant anti-Israel stance. (The
two men were not related; Hussein is a common Arabic name.)
King Hussein therefore kept Jordan neutral in the crisis, a stance
that provoked Western, and especially American, anger. The war
and blockade of Iraq, an important Jordanian trading partner, also
hurt Jordan economically, as did its losses in foreign aid from the
United States and the Persian Gulf countries.

Still, by 1992 Jordan was back in good graces with its traditional allies. In the summer of that year Hussein went to the
United States for cancer treatment. He returned home, apparently cured, to huge and enthusiastic welcoming crowds. By 1994,
with Israel and the PLO finally engaged in the peace process,
Hussein moved quickly toward his long-standing goal of making
peace with Israel. He and Israeli prime minister Yitzhak Rabin
signed the treaty at an Israeli-Jordanian border village in October
1994. After the ceremony, the king said, "This is my proudest
accomplishment: leaving my people a legacy of peace." However,
not all Jordanians agreed with Hussein. The opposition to the

treaty was vocal and more extensive than expected, and the king
responded with a political crackdown. Parliamentary elections in
November 1997 led to new confrontations between the Hussein
regime and its Islamic fundamentalist opponents. They boycotted the elections in protest of Hussein's stripping parliament
of many of its powers. Not surprisingly, the election produced a
progovernment majority.

In 1998 King Hussein again fell ill with cancer. This time
treatment in the United States was unsuccessful. As his health
declined, Hussein changed the line of succession. He removed
his brother Prince Hassan as heir, a position Hassan had held
since 1965. The new heir was Hussein's eldest son, thirty-seven-
year-old Abdullah. King Hussein ibn Talal, who had survived so
much and led his country for forty-seven years out of its fifty-
three years of independence, died on February 7, 1999. The
long list of foreign dignitaries who attended his funeral was testimony to his international standing as a statesmen. His son,
Abdullah II, speaking to the nation as king for the first time,
pledged to continue his father's policies.

JORDAN AFTER HUSSEIN

King Abdullah had enormous shoes to fill and moved quickly to
solidify his hold on power. Within a month of becoming king,
he removed several cabinet ministers closely associated with his
uncle and former heir, Prince Hassan. The new king also
released more than five hundred political prisoners from prison.
In foreign affairs, he took steps to improve relations with Syria,
Lebanon, and Kuwait, while also stressing he was strongly committed to peace with Israel. During 1999 Abdullah also closed
the Jordanian offices of Hamas and expelled several of its leaders from the country.

Still, Abdullah sat uneasily on his throne. While supporters
of the monarchy did well in municipal elections held in mid-
1999, Islamists also showed strength. Their growing influence
was one reason that Abdullah postponed parliamentary elections originally scheduled for 2001. He then issued a decree
strengthening Jordan's antiterrorism efforts. Parliamentary

elections finally took place in mid-2003, shortly after coalition forces led by the United States overthrew Saddam Hussein's brutal regime in Iraq. Once again, progovernment forces won, but Islamic fundamentalists and other conservative groups also did well. They then blocked or seriously weakened reforms designed to improve women's rights.

One reform that failed to be enacted was a law that would have imposed harsher penalties on so-called honor killings, murders of women who supposedly dishonored their families, which usually are carried out by their fathers or brothers. Acts that have resulted in honor killings include having an extramarital affair, refusing to accept an arranged marriage, or simply flirting or even talking with a man. Jordan is one of many Muslim countries where such killings were common. Parliament rejected the proposed new law in September 2003. A few days later, a particularly brutal crime took place in which three brothers killed their two sisters.

Meanwhile, a trial began of Islamic militants involved in the assassination of an American diplomat the year before. One of the defendants convicted and sentenced to death for the crime when the trial concluded in 2004 was Abu Musab al-Zarqawi. However, the sentence on Zarqawi could not be carried out because he had never been captured. By 2004, in fact, he was leading al-Qaeda forces in Iraq in their campaign of terror against Iraqi civilians and American soldiers. But the Jordanians did not forget about Zarqawi. In 2006 they provided intelligence that played a key role in enabling American forces in Iraq to find and kill Zarqawi.

In late 2004, Abdullah followed the example his father had set in 1999 by removing his half brother as heir and making his ten-year-old son heir to the throne. That step probably strengthened the monarchy's stability. Meanwhile, although the 2003 Iraq war hurt Jordan economically, by 2004 the country's economy was doing better than it had in years. This was in part because, with the fall of Saddam Hussein, UN sanctions against Iraq ended, and Jordan once again had access to one of its most important trading markets. The future, however, is uncertain.

Abdullah, like his father, is pro-American and supports peace with Israel. However, many Jordanians, in particular those of Palestinian decent and Islamic fundamentalists, bitterly oppose him on both issues. By 2006 local Islamists were encouraged by the growing strength of the Muslim Brotherhood in Egypt and the success of Hamas in PA elections. These deep divisions in Jordanian society plagued King Hussein for decades and induced him to keep most power in his hands rather than allowing democratic reform. Whatever his early successes, King Abdullah faces the same dilemma as his father.

LEBANON, SYRIA, AND IRAQ

LEBANON

No Middle Eastern country has been more divided and torn by ethnic and religious strife than Lebanon. Between 1975 and 1989, a country that once was considered the financial capital and playground of the Middle East was ripped apart by civil war. Further complicating the picture were 350,000 Palestinian refugees who came to Lebanon in several waves after 1948. Order finally was restored in 1990 but only at the price of leaving Lebanon a satellite of Syria, which occupied key parts of its small neighbor with thirty-five thousand troops. Over time the size of that force was reduced, but the occupation continued until 2005, when international pressure finally forced the Syrian government to withdraw its last fifteen thousand troops. Then, in the summer of 2006, the terrorist organization Hezbollah, which controlled southern Lebanon with its well-armed militia, dragged Lebanon into a five-week-long war with Israel that caused a great deal of new damage to a country with many old problems to solve.

Lebanon's most fundamental problem is Syria. Most Syrian leaders consider Lebanon to be a part of their country. Syria has never formally recognized Lebanon's independence; Syrian educational materials and official maps refer to Lebanon as a Syrian province. To this day, Syria does not have an embassy in Lebanon. Syria currently does not seem interested in annexing Lebanon as its many internal ethnic problems might destabilize Syria itself. Instead, the Syrian government is content to manipulate events from Damascus, using the political figures and parties it controls or influences.

GEOGRAPHY, ECONOMY, AND PEOPLE

GEOGRAPHY

Lebanon is a small wedge-shaped country of 3,950 square miles (10,230 sq. km), wider in the north than in the south, about three-quarters the size of Connecticut. Its western border is its 135-mile (220-km) Mediterranean coastline. To the north and west is Syria; Israel is Lebanon's neighbor to the south. Coastal Lebanon has a Mediterranean climate of mild, wet winters and hot, dry summers. Its short winter lasts about three months. Altogether, about three hundred days of each year are sunny. Farther east in the mountains, heavy snow falls in winter and summers are cooler. It is perhaps symbolic of Lebanon's political divisions that its two main rivers, which rise near each other in the country's Bekaa Valley, flow in opposite directions. The Litani, the country's longest river, flows generally southwestward before turning due west and emptying into the Mediterranean Sea. The Orontes River rises just north of the Litani but flows northward into Syria. The Jordan River also rises in Lebanon and flows due south into Israel.

Lebanon has four distinct geographic regions that run parallel to each other along a north-south axis. In the extreme

west, a narrow coastal plain that broadens out in the north runs the length of the country. Approximately midway on the plain stands Beirut, Lebanon's capital and largest city (population 1.8 million). South of Beirut are the port cities of Sidon and Tyre. Tripoli, another port and Lebanon's second-largest city (population 213,000), is in the far north. The coastal plain is broken at several points by protrusions from a amountain range called the Lebanon Mountains, the country's second geographic region. It contains Lebanon's highest point, Qurnet as Sauda (10,131 feet, 3,088 m). Gorges and rivers cut through the mountains, whose slopes are home to the small remaining stands of the famous cedars of Lebanon, trees that were highly valued in ancient times and are mentioned in the Bible. Most of Lebanon's remaining trees are oak, cypress, fir, juniper, and carob. About 60 miles (96 km) northeast of Beirut, Lebanon's last cedar forest clings to mountain slopes 6,500 feet (2,000 m) above sea level. The Lebanese call these magnificent trees *ars-ar-rab*, "God's cedars." Bears and small mammals, as well as a few large predators including wildcats, still roam the forests of the Lebanon Mountains.

Immediately to the east of the Lebanon Mountains is the fertile but narrow Bekaa Valley, only 5 to 8 miles (8 to 12 km) in width. Perched at an altitude averaging about 3,280 feet (1,000 m), the valley produces crops year-round. East of the Bekaa Valley is another range of mountains, the Anti-Lebanon range. It forms Lebanon's border with Syria. At the southern end of this range is Mount Hermon, which straddles Lebanon, Syria, and Israel. Because it is the highest point (9,232 feet, or 2,814 m) in a region contested by Israel and Syria, Mount Hermon is of considerable strategic importance.

ECONOMY

Lebanon was once called the "Switzerland of the Middle East" because it was the region's commercial and banking center. The country's long and destructive civil war (1975–1989) has deprived Lebanon of that status, at least for the immediate future. The fighting left in ruins Beirut's business section, where most of the country's banks, hotels, and international businesses were located. The country's once-thriving tourist industry is a shadow of its former self. The civil war badly damaged Lebanon's economic infrastructure and cut its overall output in half.

Still, the basis for a recovery has remained. Two oil pipelines—one beginning in Iraq and ending in Tripoli and the other originating in Saudi Arabia and ending in Sidon—cross Lebanon and are potential revenue sources if they can be restored to operation. The country's main crops, grown either on the coastal plain or in the Bekaa Valley, include citrus fruits, apples, pears, grapes, olives, potatoes, tomatoes, and tobacco. Another important and profitable crop from the Bekaa Valley, grown and exported illegally, is hashish. Small- and medium-scale manufacturing industries produce processed foods, textiles, and tobacco products. The relative stability of the 1990s has attracted foreign investment and international businesses, and large parts of Beirut's business district are being rebuilt. However, the recovery has not been across the board. The gap between rich and poor widened in the 1990s, sowing the seeds for economic discontent that adds to Lebanon's formidable ethnic and religious problems.

PEOPLE

Although more than 90 percent of Lebanon's estimated 3.8 million people (including Palestinian refugees) are Arabs, its population actually is a volatile mixture of religious groups that has turned it into a country of quarreling, and often warring, minorities. There are no completely reliable statistics on Lebanon's population. Early in the twentieth century, the country had a Christian majority, but that has changed because of Christian emigration and higher birthrates among Muslims. The best guess is that Christians account for perhaps a third of the population. The largest single group is the Maronite Catholic community, whose presence in Lebanon dates from the fifth century A.D., when the Byzantine Empire ruled the region. The Maronites number about 20 percent of Lebanon's total population and are concentrated in the Lebanon Mountain region as well as in

Beirut. Greek Orthodox, Greek Catholics, and Armenian Christians make up the rest of the Christian community.

On the Muslim side, the Shiites (about 35 percent of the total population) are the most numerous. Many Shiites, traditionally the poorest Lebanese, live in southern Lebanon, the Lebanon Mountain region, the Bekaa Valley, and Beirut. Sunni Muslims, about 21 percent of the population, live in the major coastal cities, including Beirut, and in the Bekaa Valley. Lebanon's Druze, who make up about 7 percent of the population, have settled in the Lebanon Mountain region, in the coastal towns, especially Beirut, and in the Bekaa Valley. Large numbers of Palestinians, who are Sunni Muslims, are found in refugee camps in the Beirut area and in the south.

The fundamental division in Lebanese political life, and in the struggle over control of the country, has been Christian—mainly Maronite—versus Muslim. Usually the Druze have sided with the Muslims. However, alliances often have shifted, sometimes in bewildering ways, especially with Palestinians factored into Lebanon's ethnic-religious equation. The Syrians and the Israelis have made the situation even more complicated.

LEBANESE HISTORY TO 1946

Ancient Lebanon was home to the Phoenicians, the greatest sailors of the Mediterranean world for seven hundred years, from about 1250 B.C. to 550 B.C. More important, by about 1200 B.C. they had developed the world's first standardized phonetic alphabet. The Phoenicians and their civilization disappeared during the Roman era. Lebanon subsequently became Christianized and, significantly, remained predominantly Christian after the Arab conquest when most of the Middle East adopted Islam. Lebanese Christians aided the Crusaders from Europe before the country fell under Muslim rule. Ottoman rule began in the early sixteenth century.

Druze massacres of Lebanese Christians in 1860 led to French intervention on their behalf in 1861. The French forced the

Turkish sultan to create a Lebanon Mountain district with a Christian governor. Its population was 80 percent Christian and more than 60 percent Maronite. After the dissolution of the Ottoman Empire after World War I, France received the League of Nations mandate for Syria and Lebanon. The French then expanded Lebanon at Syrian expense, adding territory that included Beirut and land to its south, Tripoli and surrounding territory in the north, and the Bekaa Valley. The new "Greater Lebanon" was only about 57 percent Christian and less than half Maronite. In effect, the seeds of future ethnic conflict had been sown.

Lebanon became independent officially but not in fact in 1941. Genuine independence came when French troops withdrew a year later. Lebanon was admitted to the United Nations in 1945. In 1943 a census was taken that became the basis of the Lebanese system of government. The 1943 National Covenant provided that Christians would predominate over Muslims in parliament by a ratio of six to five. The presidency would be Lebanon's most powerful executive post and the president, elected by parliament, would be a Maronite Christian. The prime minister would be a Sunni Muslim and the speaker of parliament a Shiite Muslim. This system would remain in place until 1989.

MODERN LEBANON

Independent Lebanon's history is divided into three periods: three decades of relative order and prosperity from 1946 to 1975, the civil war of 1975 to 1989, and the period of attempted reconciliation and reconstruction in the 1990s. At no time during its first half century of existence, even in the best of times, was Lebanon free from tensions caused by ethnic and religious strife or the volatile and unpredictable political storms of the Middle East.

Prior to the outbreak of the civil war, Lebanon was a major Arab intellectual and cultural center. Beirut had some of the Arab world's outstanding academic institutions, including the French-Catholic University of St. Joseph (founded 1875), the American

University of Beirut (founded 1860), and the University of Lebanon (founded 1951). After the Nasser regime in Egypt silenced the Egyptian press, Beirut had the only free press in the Arab world. While many of these institutions have survived the civil war, Lebanon's standing as an Arab intellectual center has declined along with the rest of the country's fortunes.

POLITICS FROM 1946 TO 1975

Lebanon's politics during its first three decades was dominated by maneuvering among the leading families and clans of its four main ethnic-religious communities: the Maronite Christians, the Shiite Muslims, the Sunni Muslims, and the Druze. Although Lebanon sent an army to invade Israel in 1948, it was not deeply involved in the fighting. After the 1949 truce that ended the war, Lebanon in fact coexisted with the Jewish state. The Lebanese-Israeli border was Israel's only quiet frontier until the late 1960s, when Palestinian guerrillas based in Lebanon began launching terrorist raids into Israeli territory. Alone among Israel's immediate neighbors, Lebanon stayed out of both the 1967 and 1973 wars.

The most serious domestic crisis of the first two decades occurred in 1958. The precipitating issue was the Muslim community's mistrust of Lebanon's Maronite leadership and its pro-Western policies. The Muslims wanted a closer alignment with the Arab world in general and Egypt and Syria in particular. When the crisis erupted in the summer of 1958, the Lebanese government requested U.S. assistance and Washington sent fifteen thousand U.S. Marines to restore order. The American presence helped bring about a compromise that held into the 1970s.

The growing Palestinian presence eventually was decisive in fracturing Lebanon's fragile political structure. The PLO was firmly established in the country by the late 1960s, but its activities and power increased dramatically after 1970, when thousands of Palestinians fleeing King Hussein's crackdown on the PLO took refuge there. The Palestinian influx helped upset Lebanon's Christian-Muslim numerical balance. It deepened the political fault line between conservative Christians (mainly

Maronites) defending Lebanon's political system and leftist Muslims (including Palestinians) who wanted to overthrow it. The increased Palestinian presence in southern Lebanon also drew the country into conflict with Israel when Palestinian raids led to Israeli retaliation. Lebanese civilians were caught in the middle of the fighting. By 1975 the Palestinian presence had so inflamed local ethnic-religious and political conflicts that it plunged Lebanon into civil war.

THE CIVIL WAR

The Lebanese civil war was a kaleidoscopic affair involving all of Lebanon's major ethnic-religious groups in shifting alliances. Christians fought Muslims, Christians fought each other, Druze fought both Muslims and Christians, Shiite and Sunni Muslims fought each other, Palestinian factions fought each other, and so on. At one point more than forty militias and armies were active in Lebanon. Several Lebanese political leaders were assassinated, among them two presidents and one prime minister. This was compounded by direct Syrian intervention on behalf of one faction or the other, depending on Syrian interests. At one point, in 1976, the Syrians prevented a complete Christian defeat; at another, in 1981, the Syrians fought the Maronites. Eventually Syrian troop strength in Lebanon peaked at fifty thousand.

Further complicating matters in Lebanon were two Israeli invasions. In both cases, PLO-Israeli fighting forced hundreds of thousands of Lebanese from their homes. The first invasion in 1978 ended with the United Nations sending troops to police southern Lebanon near the Israeli border and protect northern Israel against further PLO raids. That UN effort failed. The second invasion in 1982 drove most PLO forces out of Lebanon, although by 1990 they had returned. It also led to an Israeli occupation of southern Lebanon until 1985 and Israel's creation of a 9-mile-wide (14-km) security zone north of the Israeli-Lebanese border. The second zone was patrolled by Israeli troops and an Israeli-financed and Israeli-equipped Christian militia called the South Lebanese Army (SLA).

The international community also was dragged into the war. The UN peacekeeping force sent to southern Lebanon in 1978 failed to stop the fighting there. A multinational force of American, French, British, and Italian troops sent to Beirut in 1982 fared no better. In October 1983, Shiite suicide bombers sent by Hezbollah killed 241 U.S. Marines and 59 French soldiers. In early 1984, the multinational force withdrew from Lebanon.

In September 1989, the Arab League arranged a meeting of Lebanese leaders in Saudi Arabia. They produced the Taif Agreement, which finally set the stage for peace. The agreement, in reality dictated by Syria, balanced the parliament evenly between Muslims and Christians and increased the powers of the Sunni prime minister at the expense of the Maronite president. It also sanctioned the presence of Syrian troops in Lebanon but stipulated that Syrian troops would leave Lebanon's major cities by 1992. The Lebanese civil war had cost billions of dollars and claimed 150,000 lives.

In effect, Lebanon became a Syrian satellite where the Syrians kept an occupation army of thirty-five thousand. In November 1989, Syria stage-managed the election of Lebanon's first post–civil war president. When he was assassinated eighteen days later, Syria arranged the election of Elias Harawi. A new government of national reconciliation was formed in 1990. The next year, the government disbanded the country's ethnic militias. The only exception was the Shiite Hezbollah militia, which was allowed to keep its weapons to continue attacking the twenty-five-hundred-man SLA and Israeli troops in Israel's security zone in the south. In 1992 Lebanon held its first parliamentary election in twenty-one years. By 1995 the Lebanese army was built up to a force of forty-five thousand. In 1996, however, the south was disrupted by serious Israeli-Hezbollah fighting. Harawi served two four-year terms as president, the second term being extended for three years to 1998 by a one-time-only constitutional amendment. In the fall of 1998, the Syrians selected General *Emile Lahoud* to succeed Harawi, and the Lebanese parliament dutifully elected him.

The new century brought both significant change and new trouble to Lebanon. In May 2000, Israel withdrew from the security zone it had occupied since the 1980s. However, Syrian troops remained, and Syria continued to dominate Lebanese political life. In 2004 President Lahoud's term was about to expire, and he was barred by the constitution from seeking a second term. Syria responded by forcing the Lebanese to amend their constitution and extend Lahoud's term by three years. Many Lebanese, anxious to restore their country's sovereignty, bitterly objected. They included Rafik Hariri, who eventually resigned his post as prime minister in protest. Meanwhile, the UN Security Council passed a resolution calling for Syria to withdraw its troops and stop interfering in Lebanese political affairs.

Nothing happened until February 2005, when an enormous explosion on a downtown Beirut street killed Hariri and twenty other people. All the evidence clearly pointed to Syria as being responsible for the murder, and international pressure quickly mounted on Syria's President *Bashar al-Assad*. By April, the Syrians were forced to withdraw their troops from Lebanon, ending three decades of occupation. Shortly thereafter, Lebanon's first free parliamentary election in decades was won by a political alliance headed by Saad Hariri, Rafik Hariri's son.

By 2005 Lebanon was finally free of occupation by foreign troops. However, its government was not sovereign over all its territory. In the south, the Shiite Hezbollah militia, heavily armed and supplied and controlled by Iran, controlled territory along the Israeli border. By 2006 Hezbollah had an arsenal of more than twelve thousand rockets, some of which had the range to reach Tel Aviv. Even more menacing in the long term, Syria's exit and Hezbollah's rising strength together increased Iranian influence in Lebanon. That unstable situation led to war on July 12, when Hezbollah bombarded Israeli border communities and raided Israeli territory. Israel responded by attacking Hezbollah forces and rocket-launching sites in the south and other Hezbollah facilities and supply routes throughout the country. The fighting went on for almost five weeks, leaving many parts of Lebanon, especially in the south, with extensive damage. Iran was directly involved in the war. It supplied Hezbollah with its most effective and deadly weapons, and military experts from its Revolutionary Guards helped direct Hezbollah forces in the field.

The fighting finally stopped on August 14 after the UN Security Council passed resolution 1701, which called for a ceasefire and for the Lebanese army and a greatly enlarged UN force to police southern Lebanon to make sure the region was free of all armed militia forces. The resolution specifically called for the implementation of resolution 1559, which required that Hezbollah be disarmed. Israel was to withdraw completely from southern Lebanon.

The goal of the resolution 1701 was to promote peace in the region by finally restoring to the Lebanese government control of all its territory, something that could be done only if Hezbollah in fact was completely disarmed. Whether the international community would show the will to bring this about was doubtful. In the months immediately after the passage of resolution 1701, Israel withdrew its troops from Lebanon, but neither the Lebanese army nor the new UN force in Lebanon took any steps to disarm Hezbollah. In fact, Iran and Syria continue to smuggle arms to Hezbollah forces in southern Lebanon. All of this casts a menacing shadow over the region. While Lebanon's future looks a little better than during the dark days of the country's civil war and occupation by Syria, it still is far from bright.

SYRIA

Syria is a Greek term that once referred to the eastern Mediterranean region between Egypt and Asia Minor. It included modern Syria and Lebanon, most of Israel and Jordan, and bits of northern Saudi Arabia and western Iraq. Syrian nationalists often call the area Greater Syria. Foreign powers ruled the region for much of its history, from the ancient Hittites and Egyptians to the Persians, Greeks, Romans, and Byzantines to the Ottoman Empire and France.

Modern Syria has been independent for more than sixty years but is substantially smaller than Greater Syria. It is a chunk of the defunct Ottoman Empire that after World War I was turned over to French rule under a League of Nations mandate. Formal independence came in 1941 during World War II, but actual independence was delayed until French troops left Syria in 1946. Since then Syria has aggressively tried to assert its power in its immediate neighborhood and also play a significant role in the politics of the entire Middle East and Arab world. Its official name is the Syrian Arab Republic.

GEOGRAPHY, ECONOMY, AND PEOPLE

GEOGRAPHY

Syria borders the eastern shore of the Mediterranean Sea between Turkey and Lebanon and extends eastward into Asia. It looks something like a tank rumbling toward the northeast. Its area of 71,467 square miles (185,100 sq. km) makes it slightly larger than Virginia. Syria's Mediterranean coastline is about 110 miles (180 km) long. The rest of its western border is with Lebanon and Israel. Jordan lies to the south, Iraq to the southeast and east, and Turkey to the north. After the 1967 Six-Day War, Israel first occupied and then annexed a 500-square-mile (1,295-sq.-km) border region called the Golan Heights. Syria still claims the region and its status remains in dispute.

Syria has four geographic zones. Its Mediterranean coastal plain is fertile and densely populated. Latakia—Syria's main port and fourth-largest city (population 312,000), as well as its most cosmopolitan and least politically and socially conservative urban area—is at the northern end of the coastal plain. The narrow plain itself extends inland only to the Jebel an-Nusariyah (*jebel*

means "mountain" in Arabic) mountain range, which merges in the south with the Anti-Lebanon Mountains to form Syria's border with Lebanon. The Anti-Lebanon Mountains are capped by 9,232-foot-high (2,814-m) Mount Hermon, the highest point in the region and a point of contention with Israel. East of the mountains is a fertile valley where four of Syria's five largest cities are found. The southernmost is Damascus (population 1.4 million), the capital. In the middle of the valley are Homs (population 540,000) and Hama (population 264,000). Farthest north near the Turkish border is Aleppo (population 1.6 million), Syria's largest city. The Orontes River flows northward toward Turkey through this lowland, which is Syria's part of the Great Rift Valley.

Syria's easternmost and largest region is an arid plateau bisected by a low range of mountains that runs diagonally northeastward from the Anti-Lebanon Mountains to the Euphrates River. South of the mountains is the stony Syrian Desert, which stretches into Iraq. Cutting through the plateau on another diagonal, this one running southeastward from the border with Turkey, is the Euphrates, by far Syria's most important river. It supplies the country with 80 percent of its water. The irrigated area northeast of the Euphrates known as al-Jizirah (Arabic for "island") is Syria's largest fertile region. It is also the area where discoveries of small but not insignificant oil deposits have given Syria its most important natural resource and main export.

Coastal Syria has a Mediterranean climate with hot, dry summers and mild, wet winters. Snow falls in the mountainous regions. Farther inland the climate becomes progressively dryer; about three-quarters of Syria is semiarid. Syria's southeast has a desert climate.

ECONOMY

Although the Syrian government has been promoting industrialization since the 1950s, agriculture still is the dominant sector of the economy. Major crops include wheat, barley, cotton, olives, sugar beets, potatoes, tomatoes, and grapes. Sheep, goats, and camels graze in the country's pastures. Oil is by far the country's most important natural resource and accounts for more than 60 percent of its export earnings. Major industries include refined petroleum products, cement, textiles, and processed foods. Two oil pipelines, one running from Iraq and one from Saudi Arabia, once provided Syria with valuable revenues. However, because of political disputes, Syria closed the pipelines in 1982.

Syria has enjoyed several periods of impressive economic growth since the 1950s, but several factors have hurt the economy in recent years. Excessive state interference, especially over the industrial sector, limits progress. The state still directly controls about 30 percent of the economy, including the petroleum industry and most manufacturing. Foreign investment has been limited because so much of Syria's economy is subject to government planning. Enormous military expenses are another burden, made even heavier by Syria's long-term intervention in Lebanon. Those expenses are an important reason for Syria's large foreign debt, another drain on the economy. Rapid population growth, currently higher than 3 percent per year, also makes development and raising the standard of living difficult. The largest development project in modern Syria is the Tabaqa Dam on the Euphrates. It was completed in 1978 with Soviet aid. The dam enabled Syria to expand both its irrigated farmland and production of electrical power, but it has not eliminated daily power cuts of up to four hours. The government will have to change its policies if Syria is to realize its economic potential.

PEOPLE

Syria's population of about 18.8 million is about 90 percent Arab and 85 percent Muslim. Most, but not all, of the Muslims are Sunnis. However, about 10 to 12 percent of the total population (12 to 14 percent of all Muslims) belongs to the Alawite sect, an offshoot of the Shiite branch of Islam. While the Alawites are generally considered Muslims, most Sunnis, and even most Shiites, consider them heretics. The Alawites are concentrated along Syria's Mediterranean coast and in the mountainous northwest. Syria's Druze, another offshoot of the

Shiite branch of Islam, comprise 3 percent of the population. They live mainly in mountains in the south. Christians, primarily Arabs and ethnic Armenians, account for about 10 percent of the population. The largest single denomination is the Greek Orthodox. About 6 to 7 percent of the population are ethnic Kurds, who are Sunni Muslims but not Arabs. Most Kurds live in the Jazira region of the northeast.

Syria's ethnic mix has political implications. The Alawites, and to a lesser extent the Druze, have long played a role in Syrian politics far out of proportion to their numbers. *Hafez al-Assad*, Syria's dictator from 1970 to 2000, was an Alawite, as is his son and successor, Bashar. This sect has run the country for over thirty years. One of Bashar's major problems is that Muslim fundamentalists, including the powerful Muslim Brotherhood, have opposed the Assad regime on religious grounds. Another problem is the country's lack of deeply rooted national traditions. Most Syrians generally identify first with their city or region. This tendency is intensified because different ethnic groups generally are concentrated in one or two distinct regions.

MODERN SYRIAN HISTORY

Modern Syrian history is divided into two major and sharply contrasting periods: an era of instability marked by frequent coups and intermittent military rule and the brutal but stable dictatorship of Hafez al-Assad. The first period lasted from 1946 to 1970. It began with a civilian regime that was overthrown in a military coup in 1949. The coup resulted in part from Syrian military failures in the unsuccessful 1948–1949 Arab war against Israel. Military rule, punctuated by two more coups, lasted until 1954, when yet another coup restored civilian rule. The next few years saw the development of several political parties, including an active Communist Party and, most important, the Arab Socialist Renaissance Party (Baath). Baath ideology combined a commitment to socialism and an intense devotion to Arab nationalism and unity. Its secular outlook appealed to military

Druze faiths. Syria's Baathists took Syria into its ill-fated union with Egypt from 1958 to 1961. Instability and several more coups, as well as feuds and splits in the Baath Party, followed during the 1960s. In 1967 Syria joined with Egypt and Jordan in the Six-Day War against Israel. That war cost the Syrians the Golan Heights, from which they had regularly bombarded Israeli settlements since 1949. By 1970 there had been at least a dozen successful and unsuccessful coups. That turmoil ended in November 1970 when Baath military officers led by air force general Hafez al-Assad seized power.

SYRIA UNDER HAFEZ AL-ASSAD

Assad consolidated power quickly. In 1971 he was elected to a seven-year term as president in a plebiscite in which, as the only candidate running, he received 99.2 percent of the vote. He would be reelected in similar plebiscites in 1978, 1985, and 1991; in the 1991 election, he received 99.98 of the vote. A new constitution in 1973 declared Syria to be a "popular-democratic and socialist state" as well as a "part of the Arab nation, struggling for the realization of its total unity." The constitution also required that Islamic law be the basis of legislation and that Syria's president be a Muslim. These clauses were designed to satisfy Syria's Sunni majority and powerful Sunni fundamentalist forces headed by the Muslim Brotherhood. They did not. The clause on legislation did not go far enough for Islamic fundamentalists, who wanted Syria to be a full-fledged Islamic state. In addition, many Sunnis did not consider Assad, an Alawite, to be a Muslim. By 1973, the year that Syria joined Egypt in launching the Yom Kippur War against Israel, there already were Sunni demonstrations against Assad and his largely Alawite regime. The war began with a Syrian attack and advances on the Golan Heights. It ended, after very heavy losses on both sides, with an Israeli military victory and the Israelis still in control of the strategic heights.

Assad bitterly opposed Anwar Sadat's peace initiative in 1977 that led to the Egyptian-Israeli peace treaty in 1979. After the treaty, the Syrian leader led the effort that isolated Egypt from the Arab world for much of the 1980s. Syria also was on poor terms with Iraq—the two countries were led by rival wings of the Baath Party. The Syrians therefore supported non-Arab and Shiite Muslim Iran against Iraq in the Iran-Iraq War of 1980 to 1988. Meanwhile, at home the regime's conflict with the Muslim Brotherhood intensified and turned violent. Muslim Brotherhood attacks on government officials increased and were met by savage government reprisals. In 1979 Muslim Brotherhood terrorists murdered sixty-three military cadets, most of them Alawites. Further waves of government reprisals and attacks followed, reaching a state of near civil war. In early 1982, the Assad regime struck with overwhelming force against the Muslim Brotherhood's main base in the city of Hama. The government pounded the city for a week with aircraft and artillery. The city was leveled—its ruined center later became a park—and an estimated twenty thousand people were killed, but Assad achieved his goal by breaking the back, for many years, of the most serious threat to his regime.

Assad needed quiet at home because by 1976 Syria was deeply involved in its expensive and unending intervention in Lebanon. Although the cost was high, by the late 1990s Assad had achieved his main goals there. Lebanon was a Syrian satellite, with Syria acting as the essential power broker between Lebanon's many factions. Syrian troops occupied about half the country, including the Bekaa Valley. That region served a variety of Syrian purposes. It was in effect the largest terrorist base in the world, a safe haven and training center for groups whose activities served Syrian interests. It also was a major center for the processing and trafficking of heroin, which the Syrian government condoned and from which it profited. Much of that heroin was destined for customers in the United States. In addition, southern Lebanon remained a base for terrorist attacks on Israel, all part of Assad's strategy of forcing Israel to give up the Golan Heights. Assad, meanwhile, gave a cold shoulder to the Israeli-Palestinian peace process. He insisted that separate agreements undermined the overall Arab cause against Israel. These agreements also did not serve Syria's interests. Syria's on-again, off-again discussions with the Israelis yielded no serious progress.

On another front, after years of following pro-Soviet foreign policy and sponsoring acts of terrorism in both the Middle East and Europe, Assad tried to improve relations with the West. The opportunity arose when Iraq, long a Syrian rival, invaded Kuwait in 1990. Syrian troops participated in the 1991 Gulf War, in which a U.S.-led coalition of Western and Arab nations drove Iraqi troops from Kuwait. Syria's participation, however, did not secure its removal from the U.S. State Department's list of countries that support international terrorism.

As the 1990s drew to a close, Syria was nearing a changing of the guard. President Assad, the unchallenged dictator for almost thirty years, was in poor health. At seventy years old, he had been suffering from heart disease and diabetes for many years and was rarely seen in public. He was elected for a fifth seven-year term as president, but few observers expected he would serve it out. Instead, Assad's most important agenda item, as one diplomat put it, could be summed up in one word: succession. "It has become the filter through which everything is filtered." Assad's original choice as successor, his oldest son Basel, was killed in an automobile accident in 1994. Assad's new choice was his second son, Bashar, a British-trained physician. After his brother's death, Bashar suddenly began a belated military career. Not surprisingly, he advanced rapidly and in 1999 reached the rank of colonel. Still, Bashar was inexperienced. A Western diplomat in Damascus observed that "I don't think anyone thinks he's ready."

There were other ambitious sharks in Syria's political waters to challenge Bashar. The most formidable was the president's younger brother Rifaat, a hardened and ruthless political veteran unlikely to accept being pushed aside in favor of his untested young nephew. As head of an elite force of fifty-five thousand men equipped with tanks, artillery, and helicopters, Rifaat for years was a key enforcer guarding the Assad regime. However, in 1984 the Assad brothers had a falling out, and Rifaat thereafter spent much of his time abroad, essentially living as an exile. Rifaat nonetheless made it clear that he considered Bashar al-Assad unfit to rule Syria and saw himself as Hafez al-Assad's legitimate successor. In September 1999, determined to prepare the way for his son to succeed him, an increasingly ill and frail Hafez al-Assad ordered the arrest of about one thousand of Rifaat's supporters. The next month, security forces closed down a port in the city of Latakia that had been under Rifaat's control, a measure that led to violent clashes in which, according to some reports, hundreds of people died.

SYRIA SINCE HAFEZ AL-ASSAD

In June 2000, having ruled Syria with an iron fist for three decades, Hafaz al-Assad died. But he left behind a well-oiled political machine, and its wheels turned quickly to assure Bashar al-Assad's succession to the presidency. The constitution was amended to lower the minimum age for the presidency from forty to thirty-four, the age of Bashar al-Assad. Then, in rapid succession, Bashar was nominated to be commander in chief of the armed forces, promoted to the military rank of lieutenant-general, named head of the Baath Party, endorsed by the party leadership for the presidency, nominated for president by Syria's parliament, and then duly elected to the post with more than 97 percent of the vote. The entire process was completed by mid-July.

Once in office, Bashar al-Assad took a few small steps to ease the suffocating dictatorship Syria had lived under for thirty years. The government relaxed a few controls on the economy and released several hundred political prisoners. Assad also, albeit ever so slightly, relaxed controls on the press. In March 2001, Syria's first independent newspaper since 1963 sold out within hours. At the same time, most things remained the same. The younger Assad made it clear he had no use for democracy, and the country remained under martial law, as it had been for four decades. Any political meeting of more than five people required a permit. A permit could be obtained only after providing government security services with two weeks' notice, the name of the speaker, and a complete list of everyone planning to attend.

Syria's most important foreign policy development during Bashar al-Assad's first years in power was its debacle in Lebanon. In 2004 Syria forced Lebanon to amend its constitution to allow Emile Lahoud, the current president and a Syrian puppet, to extend his term for three years. After widespread protests, in early 2005 Syria engineered the murder of Rafik Hariri, a leading politician who had opposed that measure. The international community then responded by demanding that Syria comply with UN Security Council Resolution 1559, passed in September 2004, which called on Syria to end its occupation of Lebanon and its interference in Lebanese affairs. Faced with growing international pressure, Syria withdrew its troops from Lebanon in April, ending an occupation that dated from the 1970s. However, in 2006, as a result of the war Israel and Hezbollah fought in southern Lebanon, Syria was able to bolster its influence in Lebanon by serving as the main conduit for resupplying Hezbollah with Iranian weapons during and after the fighting.

By mid-2006, Bashar al-Assad had very little to show for his first six years in office. He heads an oppressive regime in a country with an economy hobbled by government regulations. His regime has a long list of opponents, ranging from the Muslim Brotherhood and other Islamic fundamentalists to exiled Baathists who had once supported his father. Overall, the future does not look bright for Syria or its dictator.

IRAQ

Iraq is Mesopotamia, the land between the Tigris and Euphrates rivers, where more than five thousand years ago the Sumerians' mastery of agriculture and invention of writing gave birth to the world's first civilization. Mesopotamia was where Sargon of Akkad forged the world's first empire, where Babylon's King Hammurabi issued the world's first systematic code of law, where the biblical patriarch Abraham had his first inspiration about a single God before leaving for Canaan to found the Jewish religion, and where a succession of ancient civilizations added to the fund of human knowledge as they rose and fell. In A.D. 750, the newly founded Arab Abbasid dynasty established its capital in Baghdad, at that time a village on the banks of the Tigris not far from ancient Babylon. The Abbasids turned their new city into the Arab world's cultural and intellectual center during the eighth and ninth centuries, the period known as the Golden Age of Islam. Decline then set in, and by 1000 the Seljuk Turks held real power in Baghdad. In the thirteenth century, the Mongols destroyed what was left of the Abbasid Caliphate and sacked Baghdad. Three hundred years later, Mesopotamia fell to the Ottomans. Not until the twentieth century would an independent state, which would be called Iraq, exist again in the land between the rivers.

GEOGRAPHY, ECONOMY, PEOPLE

GEOGRAPHY

Iraq is a triangular-shaped country in southwestern Asia at the northwestern edge of the Persian Gulf. It has an area of 167,924 square miles (434,923 sq. km), slightly larger than California. Iraq is almost entirely landlocked. Its only outlet to the open sea is a 30-mile (48-kilometer) stretch of coastline squeezed between Iran and Kuwait. The geography and oil resources of the Persian Gulf have been at the core of Iraq's last two wars. The first began with Iraq's attack on Iran in 1980 and lasted until 1988. The second, the Gulf War of 1991, resulted from Iraq's invasion of Kuwait in 1990. In the first case, Iraqi dictator Saddam Hussein attacked Iran to win full control of the Shatt-al-Arab (the "river of the Arabs"), a tidal river 120 miles (193 km) long, formed by the confluence of the Tigris and Euphrates rivers. Basra, Iraq's main port and second-largest city (population 407,000), stands at the northern end of the Shatt al-Arab. In the second case, the stakes were much higher, as

IRAQ

- ✪ Capital city
- ○ City
- — International border
- --- Unofficial border
- — River

Hussein sought to annex Kuwait and take control of its enormous oil reserves. Hussein failed to achieve his goals in either war. Between 1980 and 1988, he was stymied by ferocious Iranian resistance, while in 1990–1991 the United States put together a coalition of Middle Eastern and Western nations that drove Iraq from Kuwait.

Iran is Iraq's neighbor to the east, and Kuwait borders Iraq on the southeast. Iraq borders Saudi Arabia in the south, Jordan in the west, Syria in the west and northwest. Turkey lies in the north.

Iraq is made up of four geographical regions. Its southeastern corner is a huge delta marshland formed as the Tigris and the

Euphrates approach each other near the Persian Gulf. The marshland reaches into Iran and originally covered 6,000 square miles (15,500 sq. km). The marshes once were a world of high reeds, lakes, shallow lagoons, and narrow waterways, a natural refuge for many species of waterbirds such as pelicans, herons, and flamingos. Humans have lived there for more than six thousand years. The Marsh Arabs, as the local people are called, were semi-nomads who herded water buffalo and hunted waterbirds. They lived in elaborate houses built on arches woven from reeds. However, the Marsh Arabs and the marshes themselves became victims of Saddam Hussein's determination to destroy any opposition to his brutally repressive regime. In the early 1990s, the Iraqi government began draining the marshes to force the Marsh Arabs out of their wetland sanctuaries. By the middle of the decade, the Marsh Arab way of life and the natural environment that had sustained it for thousands of years were well on their way to being destroyed. Throughout much of the former marshland where water once stood 5 feet (1.5 m) deep, cracking mud lay exposed to a hot sun. Only a fraction of a community that once numbered half a million survived with its traditional way of life. Tens of thousands of Marsh Arabs lived in refugee camps, mostly in Iran.

The core region of Iraq is the plain between the Tigris and the Euphrates that extends from the marshland northwestward to the Syrian border. Despite problems with high soil salinity, it is a fertile region laced with irrigation canals and dotted with small lakes. This region receives very little rain, and agriculture depends on irrigation. It also is subject to serious flooding. Successive Iraqi governments have built dams on both the Tigris and the Euphrates to control the flooding and produce electricity. Baghdad, Iraq's capital and largest city (population 3.9 million), is in this region. Closer to the Syrian border, the land rises and becomes hilly. This area receives enough rain to grow grains and vegetables without irrigation. Summers in the land between the rivers are very hot and humid. Winters are also humid but considerably cooler.

Northeastern Iraq, the country's third geographic region, begins as a hilly upland and turns into mountains near the Turkish and Iranian borders, where some snowcapped peaks reach 12,000 feet (3,660 m). Iraq's richest oil fields are in this region, whose population is primarily Kurdish. The Kurds—Iran's largest minority group, who also live in neighboring parts of Iran and Turkey—have long sought their own independent state. Mosul, Iraq's third-largest city (population 665,000), and Kirkuk are the northeast's main urban areas. Iraq's fourth region, west of the Euphrates, is a desert that extends into Syria, Jordan, and Saudi Arabia.

Iraq's arid climate means that its survival depends on the water of the Tigris and Euphrates rivers. Both rivers rise in Turkey. The Tigris forms a very short section of the Turkish-Syrian border before entering Iraq, while the Euphrates cuts through Syria before reaching Iraq. Both Iraq and Syria are deeply concerned with Turkish damming, irrigation, and hydroelectric projects. Iraq must also worry about Syrian plans for the Euphrates River. Water is one of several issues that have contributed to tensions between Iraq and its two upstream neighbors.

ECONOMY

Iraq has the world's second-largest reserves of oil, about 112 billion barrels, or 10 percent of the world's total. Only Saudi Arabia has greater reserves. Oil dominates the economy and for decades has provided about 95 percent of Iraq's export earnings. The country is also a leading exporter of dates. Other important crops include cotton and wheat. Iraq's small industrial sector produces a variety of products, including textiles, cement, food products, fertilizers, and electronics products.

The economy suffered enormous damage as a result of three recent wars and their aftermath. Economic damage from the war with Iran exceeded one hundred billion dollars. The 1991 Gulf War added to Iraq's economic hardship. Allied bombing destroyed much of Iraq's infrastructure. After the war, Iraq's interference with UN inspections of its nuclear, chemical, and biological weapons facilities—inspections designed to ensure Iraq had stopped its *nonconventional weapons* programs—caused the United Nations to impose economic sanctions. Because of those sanctions, which limited Iraqi oil exports to the value of what the country needed for vital food and medicines, Iraq was able to earn from its oil sales only about one-third of what it earned prior to the war. Between 1990 and 1997, its agricultural production dropped at an average of 2.5 percent per year. In 1999 the worst drought on record cut crop yields by 50 percent. The scarcity of goods caused severe inflation. While the elite upon whom Saddam Hussein depended continued to live well, the country's overall standard of living plunged to what it had been in the late 1950s.

The war of 2003 that led to the overthrow of Saddam Hussein left a rebuilding bill of between fifty billion and one hundred billion dollars. The war itself did not cause that much destruction. However, postwar looting, sabotage, and attacks by various groups either loyal to Hussein or opposed to American and British efforts to establish a new democratic government in Iraq undermined rebuilding efforts. In particular, hostile actions delayed efforts to restore oil production to the levels reached before the 1991 Gulf War. In 2004 alone, insurgent attacks on oil facilities cost Iraq an estimated six billion dollars.

PEOPLE

Approximately 75 to 80 percent of Iraq's 26.7 million people are Arabs. About 97 percent are Muslims. Iraq's small Christian minority accounts for about 3 percent of the population. The Muslim Arab majority is divided, often bitterly, by the gulf between Sunni and Shiite. Although Shiites account for 60 to 65 percent of the total population, the country has long been dominated by Sunni Arabs. The Shiites are concentrated in the central and southern parts of the country, including the border region with Iran. Slightly less than 20 percent of Iraqis are Kurds, an ancient Middle Eastern people who speak an Indo-European language related to Farsi. The Kurds are Sunni Muslims. Most live in the northeastern mountain region and in the cities. The Kurdish northeast also happens to contain many of Iraq's largest oil fields.

For decades the tension between the dominant, but minority, Sunni Muslim Arabs and the majority Shiite Arabs on the one hand and the Kurds on the other has been Iraq's most serious internal problem. The Kurdish revolts against the government in Baghdad first took place in the 1920s, before Iraq achieved full independence, and have recurred periodically after independence. The Kurds came closest to success in the mid-1970s when they had Iranian help, but they were defeated when Iran withdrew its support in a deal with Baghdad in 1975. The Shiites endured discrimination for centuries at the hands of the Sunni Turks and decades more after independence from the Sunni Arabs. Unlike the Kurds, who seek independence, Iraqi's Shiites want to replace the country's Sunni-dominated government with one of their own. In the 1980s and 1990s, the Hussein regime used extremely brutal methods to repress both communities. In what was perhaps the most infamous incident, the Iraqi army in 1988 attacked the Kurdish village of Halabje with poison gas, killing five thousand people.

HISTORY OF MODERN IRAQ

Iraq is yet another state carved out of the former Ottoman Empire after World War I. The British, who governed Iraq under a League of Nations mandate, made the Hashemite prince Faisal ibn Hussein king of Iraq at the same time as they made his brother Abdullah emir (prince) of neighboring Transjordan. Iraq achieved full independence in 1932, although British influence remained strong as long as the Hashemites remained on the Iraqi throne. With British help the dynasty survived a rebellion by nationalist military officers, who also were pro-German, during World War II. The British then remained in Iraq until 1946. In 1948 Iraq joined the Arab war against Israel, sending a combat force that eventually became the largest Arab army in the war. When the fighting ended in 1949, the Iraqis withdrew, refusing to sign even an armistice with the Jewish state. In the aftermath of that war, rising anti-Semitism in Iraq caused virtually the entire Iraqi Jewish community of more than one hundred thousand to leave their homes, forfeit their property, and flee to the safety of Israel. It was the end of a Jewish presence in Mesopotamia whose roots reached back twenty-five hundred years, the oldest Jewish community in the Middle East outside Israel.

During the early and mid-1950s, the Iraqi monarchy followed conservative policies at home and took a pro-Western approach to foreign affairs. In 1958 King Faisal II, grandson of Iraq's first king, and the Hashemite dynasty were overthrown in a bloody coup led by General Abdul Karim Kassem. The victors executed the entire royal family and many of its supporters. The Kassem regime introduced social reforms at home and followed a pro-Soviet foreign policy. However, it was opposed by other factions, including military officers who admired Egypt's President Nasser and the Iraqi wing of the Baath Party. The regime's opponents attempted several unsuccessful coups. Then, in 1963 the Baath Party seized power in another bloody coup, in which Kassem was murdered. Nine months later a group of pro-Nasser military officers seized power. They managed to hang on until 1968, when a new coup put the Baath Party back in control.

The Baathists, determined to crush all opposition, carried out a series of political purges and established a harsh and efficient dictatorship. Syria also was ruled by the Baath Party, but when a rival wing of the party seized power in Damascus in 1970, Syria and Iraq became bitter rivals. By the early 1970s, the strongman behind the scenes of Iraqi's Baath regime was Saddam Hussein. He controlled both the secret police and the Baath Party's armed militia. In 1979 Hussein took power directly as president. A new and turbulent era in the country's history was about to begin.

IRAQ UNDER SADDAM HUSSEIN

Saddam Hussein came to power with a reputation for utter ruthlessness. He was a Baath Party executioner in his early days; one of his many victims reportedly was his pro-Communist brother-in-law. Saddam was a master of tactical alliance building and the double-cross when the alliance no longer served his purposes. As he demonstrated many times in the decades to follow, he would stop at nothing to keep his iron grip on power. War, murder, mass executions, international terrorism, the use of poison gas against civilians, and the willful destruction of the environment were all part of his stock in trade.

Iraq's new dictator immediately set about making himself the center of a worshipful personality cult. Every city in the country was blanketed with his 30-foot (10-m) portraits. Stadiums, hospitals, and other public places were named for him; he was praised in songs, books, and films. Statues of him sprouted up everywhere, and the media praised his every move. Anyone who opposed him, or who Hussein suspected might oppose him, was arrested or executed.

THE IRAN-IRAQ WAR

Hussein meanwhile turned to his goal of making Iraq into the most powerful state in the Persian Gulf region and the Middle East. His first objective was complete control of the Shatt al-Arab. In 1975, in return for Iran ending its assistance to the Iraqi Kurd rebellion, Baghdad had agreed to divide the Shatt al-Arab in the middle. In September 1980, Hussein repudiated the agreement and immediately launched a full-scale military assault on Iran. He calculated that the Islamic fundamentalists who had come to power less than a year earlier in Iran would be too disorganized to mount a defense. Hussein was terribly wrong. After quick early advances the Iraqi offensive bogged down. By 1982 the Iranians, often using human wave tactics, drove the Iraqis from their territory and crossed into Iraq. At this point, Iran rejected Hussein's attempt to end the war, demanding $150 billion in compensation from the invaders and Hussein's ouster. The war settled into a bloody stalemate. Iraq ran up huge debts to fight the war, mainly in the form of loans from Saudi Arabia, Kuwait, and other Persian Gulf states. Finally, savage Iraqi attacks on Iranian cities and poison gas attacks against Iranian troops brought the Iranians to the negotiating table. At least five hundred thousand soldiers on both sides were dead, and another two million were wounded. After eight years, the Shatt al-Arab remained divided at its median point exactly as before the war.

Hussein suffered another defeat during the war. During the 1970s, Iraq had begun a program to build nuclear weapons, and a nuclear reactor was being constructed with French help. In 1981 the reactor was about to become operational with nuclear fuel that would have enabled the Iraqis to build nine nuclear bombs. They already had aircraft and missiles that could deliver the weapons hundreds of miles away. Israel considered the program a direct threat to its survival. In June 1981, Israeli bombers destroyed the reactor. Because the Israeli planes destroyed the reactor before it was operational, no radiation was released. The only damage was to the building and equipment—and to Hussein's ambitions. The Israeli raid meant that in his next war, Hussein did not have nuclear weapons to use against his opponents, which included the United States.

THE GULF WAR

The results of the war with Iran did not reduce Hussein's ambitions and recklessness. If anything, it increased them, for Iraq emerged from the war with enormous foreign debts totaling eighty billion dollars. Hussein also had an experienced and battle-hardened military at his fingertips. He decided to use his armed forces to seize one of the biggest strategic prizes in the world: the oil reserves of Kuwait. Kuwait was a tempting target. The small country had a tiny population ruled by a reactionary royal family. Its oil reserves only slightly smaller than Iraq's. By annexing Kuwait, Iraq would control almost 20 percent of the world's oil supplies, giving Saddam Hussein incalculable international influence.

The Iraqis struck on August 2, 1990, and overran Kuwait in a matter of days. The UN Security Council reacted immediately, passing Resolution 660 on August 2, demanding that Iraqi forces withdraw from Kuwait and imposing a trade embargo on Iraq on August 6. Formal annexation of what Hussein called Iraq's nineteenth province came on August 8. There was panic in neighboring Saudi Arabia, which saw itself as Hussein's next target. By August 7, at Saudi King Fahd's request, American troops were on their way to Saudi Arabia. When Iraq did not withdraw, the Security Council responded in November with Resolution 678, authorizing all necessary means to force Iraqi troops out of Kuwait. A majority of Arab nations also condemned the invasion. Iraq's main support came from the PLO and the governments of Libya, Algeria, Sudan, and Jordan. Despite that narrow base, Hussein's defiance of the West and the wealthy Persian Gulf states made him the most popular Arab leader in many parts of the Arab world.

The United States brought Western nations and twelve Arab states into a military coalition to enforce the UN resolution. In January 1991, Operation Desert Storm began with air attacks on Iraq that lasted a month. In February, in a fast-moving campaign lasting only one hundred hours, Iraqi forces were routed and driven from Kuwait. Before they left, however, they sabotaged and set on fire hundreds of Kuwaiti oil wells, causing an environmental disaster in the Persian Gulf region.

THE 1991 GULF WAR TO THE OVERTHROW OF SADDAM HUSSEIN

The end of the war did not bring real peace to Iraq. The most important reason for this was that UN war aims were limited to driving Iraqi forces from Kuwait and did not extend to driving Saddam Hussein from power. Still, Hussein was almost immediately faced with revolts by the Kurds in the north seeking independence and the Shiites in the south seeking to overthrow him. Both groups were encouraged by the United States and other Western powers to rebel in the hope that they could drive Hussein from power. But they received no military aid, and Hussein was able to crush both rebellions by the spring of 1991. More than one million Kurds—remembering how Hussein had used poison gas against them in 1988 and fearing genocidal reprisals this time—fled to Iran and Turkey. Some of those who remained in Iraq found protection under the umbrella of two no-fly zones, one in the Kurdish north and the other in the Shiite south, from which Iraqi aircraft were barred and which were patrolled by U.S. and British warplanes. Those who lived beyond the protection of the no-fly zones had no security at all. For example, between 1991 and 2001, the Iraqi government drove at least two hundred thousand Kurds living in the oil-rich region around the city of Kirkuk from their homes in an attempt to Arabize that Kurdish-populated area. Members of other non-Arab minorities were displaced for similar reasons.

Meanwhile, Hussein conducted periodic purges and mass executions to crush all opposition to his regime. Given both the secrecy under which the regime operated and the scope of its activities, it is possible to provide only a partial list of its political murders. In 1992 eighty military officers were executed for an attempted coup, along with seventy-six demonstrators against the regime. Several civilian and military officials were executed in August 1993 for allegedly planning a coup. After an assassination attempt against Hussein's son Udai in December 1996, Hussein executed almost two hundred political prisoners in March 1997. In late 1997, several senior military officers were executed, as were an estimated eight hundred people suspected of belonging to opposition groups. In April 1998, the UN Human Rights Commission reported that fifteen hundred people had been executed in Iraq in 1997 for political reasons. Two senior Shiite religious leaders were murdered in 1998 and one more, this time the community's overall leader, in February 1999. The regime continued to execute hundreds of political prisoners every year. It was not necessary to be a political prisoner or even to be convicted of a crime to be subject to the death penalty. In October 2000, dozens of women accused of prostitution, never having received any sort of trial, were executed in Baghdad and several other cities, as were some men suspected of seeking their services. The executioners used swords to behead the victims, who met their fate in front of their homes.

The Hussein regime had a more difficult time imposing its will on the United Nations. During the course of the Gulf War, the world was shocked to find out the extent of Iraq's programs to develop biological, chemical, and nuclear weapons. As part of the agreement with the United Nations that ended the fighting, Iraq accepted a UN Security Council Resolution requiring that all of its chemical and biological weapons, as well as its materials for developing nuclear weapons, be destroyed. A UN task force called the UN Special Commission on Iraq (UNSCOM) was set up to find and destroy Iraq's capacity to make these weapons. The United Nations also continued economic sanctions against Iraq, including a ban on oil sales, to force it to cooperate with UNSCOM. However, the United Nations offered to allow Iraq to sell a limited amount of oil in order to buy food and medical supplies. These oil revenues would be controlled by the United Nations, and one-third of them would be set aside to compensate victims of Iraq's invasion of Kuwait. Hussein at first rejected that arrangement, but he finally accepted the oil-for-food plan in 1996, five years after it was offered to him, in order to improve the country's dreadful economic situation.

The establishment of UNSCOM began a cat-and-mouse game that lasted for most of the decade. Despite Iraqi attempts to interfere with its work and deny it access to key facilities, UNSCOM discovered evidence of massive biological, chemical, and surprisingly advanced nuclear programs and destroyed vast amounts of material. More evidence became available in 1994 when the former head of Iraq's nuclear program defected to the West. In 1995 additional important information emerged with the defection of the head of Iraq's weapons program, who also was one of Hussein's sons-in-law. By 1998 UNSCOM had found twenty-one nuclear facilities whose existence Iraq had not admitted, warheads loaded with anthrax and other deadly biological agents, huge stores of chemical agents, missiles, and much more. At the same time, it reported that there had been no progress in verifying Iraq's disarmament and that the destruction of its chemical and biological weapons was incomplete. The concern was that Iraq was still hiding both information and materials to make weapons of mass destruction (WMDs). Periodic bombing attacks by U.S. and British aircraft, including a four-day salvo in December 1998 that hit one hundred targets in Iraq, failed to get Hussein to honor commitments to allow UNSCOM to work without interference.

As their leader sparred with the United Nations, most Iraqis suffered. Few people had much hope. As one theater professor, who doubled as a taxi driver to make ends meet, observed:

> Once we had fulfilling lives, but now we have dropped out of the world. Everything has changed, and we really don't understand why. All we can do is accept it. There is no alternative.

Meanwhile, Hussein slowly appeared to be gaining the upper hand. By 1999 UNSCOM had left Iraq, without prospects of returning. In December of that year, the UN Security Council created a new inspection force—the United Nations Monitoring, Verification, and Inspection Commission (UNMOVIC)—to replace UNSCOM. But Iraq refused to allow UNMOVIC to enter the country. The deadlock continued into 2001. Meanwhile, many Iraqis were suffering from difficult economic conditions, but not because of UN sanctions. The oil-for-food program was earning enough revenue for food and medicine. Iraq had sold more than thirty-five billion dollars worth of oil under the program by the middle of 2000. But the Hussein regime was not using those funds to meet the people's needs. The regime also was smuggling large amounts of oil out of the country and using the illegal revenue it gained for its own purposes. While ordinary people suffered, the governing elite loyal to Saddam Hussein continued to live well. In May 1999, the government even announced the opening of a luxurious lakeside resort west of Baghdad. In the capital itself, while poverty stalked the neighborhoods, the government built luxurious new palaces and state guesthouses, as well as an assortment of new statues of Saddam Hussein.

The tension between Iraq and the international community, and especially the United States, increased dramatically after the September 11, 2001, al-Qaeda attacks on New York City and Washington, D.C. In November 2002, the UN Security Council Resolution 1441 demanded that Iraq allow UNMOVIC into the country and give it free access to all potential WMD sites. By the end of the month, Iraq had agreed, and inspectors arrived and began their work. But serious problems continued, as the UN inspectors did not get the cooperation they required from Iraq. In December the United States declared that Iraq was not meeting its obligations to the United Nations. The United States was convinced that the Saddam Hussein regime, with its record of aggression and possession and use of weapons of mass destruction, was a threat to the region and basic American interests.

As a result, in March 2003 the United States and Britain (Australia and Poland also sent small numbers of troops) attacked Iraq and drove Saddam Hussein from power. Baghdad fell to coalition forces in April. Since Iraq had no government, the coalition set up what it called the Coalition Provisional Authority (CPA) to administer the country. In July a twenty-five-member Iraq Governing Council (IGC) began meeting. Its task was to prepare the way for a new democratic government. Hussein was captured in December and surrendered to American soldiers without a fight.

IRAQ AFTER SADDAM HUSSEIN

Although Saddam had been overthrown, it turned out that the most difficult times and the hardest work lay ahead, both for coalition forces and for Iraqis who wanted to see their country become a democracy. It quickly became clear that the damage done to Iraqi society by the Saddam regime during its twenty-four-year reign of terror was worse than what had been known before the war. Evidence of mass murder was documented with the discovery of mass graves, some containing dozens and others thousands of bodies, as was the widespread and systematic use of torture. The issue of WMDs turned out to be more complicated. Before the start of the war, American and other Western intelligence agencies were convinced that Iraq still had WMDs. Indeed, even months after the fall of Baghdad, some senior Iraqi officials believed that there was WMD capability hidden somewhere in Iraq. However, American inspectors after the war were unable to find those weapons. They did find numerous laboratories able to produce chemical nerve agents, other poisonous chemicals, and biological agents on a small scale. The inspectors also found evidence that Iraq intended to restart its WMD programs once UN sanctions were lifted. There also were unconfirmed reports that stockpiles of Iraqi WMDs were moved to Syria and possibly also Lebanon just before the war began.

By far the greatest challenge for the United States and Great Britain was to help the Iraqis establish a democratic government that could unify the country. Deep divisions and hostility between Sunni Arabs, Shiite Arabs, and Kurds slowed that process. Making matters much worse was an insurgency that spread a wave of terror across the country. The terrorists struck coalition troops as well as Iraqi civilians in markets, mosques, and other public places. Thousands of Iraqi civilians died. American soldiers also suffered heavily. By early 2007, more than thirty-two hundred American soldiers had been killed in Iraq.

Two main groups are involved in the insurgency: diehard Sunni supporters of the fallen regime and foreign Islamic militants who came to Iraq to wage jihad against the United States and set up an Islamic state based on Sharia. By far the most effective and deadly of the foreign insurgents was Abu Musab al-Zarqawi, a high-ranking member of al-Qaeda. His string of deadly attacks and his ability to avoid capture demoralized Iraqis working to rebuild their country and frustrated the Americans and British trying to establish order in Iraq.

Yet there was progress. In June 2004, American authorities in Iraq officially turned sovereignty over to Iraq's interim government. In January 2005, Iraq held its first free elections in decades for provincial parliaments and a national assembly charged with writing a new constitution. In December 2005, Iraqis elected a national parliament to govern the country, and in June 2006, after many delays and feuding between Sunnis and Shiites, the parliament finally completed the formation of a cabinet to govern the country. Iraq's new prime minister was Nuri Kamal al-Maliki, a member of the Shiite group of parties that had captured the most seats in the December 2005 elections.

That same day, American forces finally succeeded in killing Zarqawi.

Meanwhile, Iraq had another important matter on its agenda—holding Saddam Hussein accountable for his crimes. In October 2005, the government put Saddam on trial for the murder of 148 men and boys in 1982, after an unsuccessful assassination attempt against him. The actual trial dragged on until July 2006. In November, a five-judge panel handed Saddam a death sentence. By then a second trial was in progress, with Saddam in the dock for the murder of 50,000 Kurds—men, women, and children—in 1988 during the notorious Anfal campaign, when he tried to crush all Kurdish opposition to his regime. In late December, an appeals court upheld the sentence, and Saddam Hussein was hanged on December 30, 2006. His execution did not stop the Anfal trial, which was expected to continue until it produced a verdict.

Where this left Iraq was uncertain. Shortly before completing his cabinet, Prime Minister Maliki announced, "The government has drawn up a program to preserve the unity of the Iraqi people." In light of the deep divisions between Iraq's major ethnic and religious communities, that alone will be an enormous achievement. Preserving unity within a democratic framework would be a historic milestone not only for Iraq but for the Middle East and the entire Arab world. However, in early 2007, the continuing turmoil and bloodshed in Iraq underscored how enormously difficult it would be to attain those goals.

THE NORTHERN TIER: TURKEY AND IRAN

Turkey and Iran are the Middle East's two non-Arab but Muslim countries. They have large populations and are major regional military powers. However, as societies they have been moving in diametrically opposed directions in recent decades. Since the 1920s, Turkey has been attempting to modernize as a secular state, with religion being a personal, private choice as in the West. In fact, most Turkish leaders consider the West to be the model they want their country to follow. Turkey has belonged to the North Atlantic Treaty Organization (NATO) since the early 1950s. The country wants to join the European Union (EU) and is friendly with Israel. Iran appeared to be on a course similar to Turkey's until the Islamic Revolution of 1979. Since then Iran has become an Islamic theocracy, bitterly anti-Western, a supporter of international terrorism, and committed to Israel's destruction. Far from seeking to emulate the West, Iran has militantly rejected everything Western and sought an Islamic alternative on which to build its future.

TURKEY

The Turks originated in central Asia and are relative newcomers to the Middle East. The earliest written account of Turkic-speaking tribes comes from China, where records first mention them around 1300 B.C. The first Turkic group to arrive in the Middle East were the Seljuks, who set up a state in Iran in the eleventh century. In 1071 Seljuk horsemen dealt the Byzantine army a devastating defeat at the Battle of Manzikert in what is eastern Turkey, after which they took over much of Anatolia. Seljuk power lasted only about one hundred years. The Seljuks were overwhelmed and disappeared from history in the wake of the Crusades in the twelfth century and the Mongol invasion of the thirteenth century. This cleared the way for the rise of the Ottoman Turks, who in the thirteenth century had a tiny state in western Anatolia. Over the next two centuries, expanding from the same core region that gave birth to the ancient Hittite Empire and that for centuries was the nucleus of the Byzantine Empire, they built one of the largest empires the Middle East had ever seen. When their empire gradually corroded and finally collapsed in 1918, the Turks rebuilt their national life in Anatolia as a modern nation-state.

GEOGRAPHY, ECONOMY, PEOPLE

GEOGRAPHY

The Republic of Turkey is a rectangular-shaped country occupying a region of southwestern Asia known as Anatolia, or Asia Minor, and a tiny corner of Europe called Eastern Thrace. It has an area of 300,948 square miles (779,452 sq. km), about 12 percent larger than Texas. Turkey straddles one of the most strategic points in the world, where two narrow straits, the Bosporus and the Dardanelles, separate Europe from Asia. The Bosporus, on whose shores stands the city of *Istanbul*, links the huge inland Black Sea to a smaller inland sea, the Sea of Marmara. The Dardanelles, in turn, connect the Sea of Marmara to the Aegean Sea, really a bay of the Mediterranean Sea. Ninety-seven percent of Turkey is in Asia. However, the 3 percent that lies in Europe includes most of Istanbul. For more than one thousand years before it became Istanbul, the city was known as Constantinople, the capital of the Byzantine Empire and for many centuries one of the major centers of European culture. Turkey's small but important piece of European real estate makes it one of only three countries—Russia and Kazakhstan are the others—that boast territory in both Europe and Asia.

Turkey has about 5,800 miles (9,300 km) of borders, almost three-quarters of which are seas. The Black Sea forms most of Turkey's long northern frontier. Its western tip, in the Balkans, fronts on Bulgaria, while its eastern edge, in the Caucasus, touches Georgia. Turkey's neighbor directly to the west is Greece, its longtime enemy. The Aegean Sea forms the rest of Turkey's western border. However, Greek islands just a few miles off the Turkish shore run the length of Turkey's coastline from Thrace to the Mediterranean Sea like a line of watchtowers. The Mediterranean Sea forms about half of Turkey's southern border. The remainder, moving eastward from the Mediterranean, fronts Syria and Iraq. Due east of Turkey are Iran, Azerbaijan (with which Turkey shares a scant 5.5-mile (9-km) frontier and to whose inhabitants the Turks are closely related), and Armenia, another longtime enemy.

Anatolia, the heart of the Turkish homeland, is a broad plateau bordered by narrow coastlines and ringed by several mountain ranges. The plateau averages about 3,000 feet (915 mm) in altitude. Its main lowlands are along the Aegean and Marmara coasts, a narrow coastal area on the Black Sea, a strip along the Mediterranean coast, and valleys along the banks of several rivers that flow into the Black, Aegean, Mediterranean, and Marmara seas. In the south, the plateau region is separated from the Mediterranean coast by the Taurus Mountains. In the northeast, the Pontic Mountains ring the Black Sea coast. Farther west are the Koroglu Mountains. Anatolia rises in the east into a range of mountains that eventually merges with the lofty Caucasus range. Turkey's highest peak, and the most dramatic sight in this region, is the gigantic snowcapped cone of Mount Ararat, an extinct volcano rising 16,945 feet (5,168 mm) above sea level. It was here, according to the Bible, that Noah's ark came to rest after the great flood inundated the world. For two hundred years, explorers have been combing Ararat's slopes in what thus far has been an unsuccessful search for remains of the ark. South of Ararat is Lake Van, a vast salt lake (1,419 square miles, or 3,675 sq. km) that is the largest in Turkey. The rain and snow that fall in the eastern mountains feed the upper reaches of the Tigris and Euphrates rivers, both of which rise in Turkey and flow southward, the Tigris into Iraq and the Euphrates into Syria. The Kizil Irmak, the longest river inside Turkey, also rises in the eastern part of Anatolia. It then heads due west before pivoting toward the northeast and flowing into the Black Sea.

The interior of Anatolia is a vast semiarid grassland. Summers are dry and hot, while winters are cold and snowy. *Ankara*, Turkey's capital city of 3.2 million people, stands near the center of this region. A Mediterranean climate of mild, rainy winters and hot, dry summers predominates the Aegean and Mediterranean coasts. The Black Sea coast gets rain during both its chilly winters and its mild summers. That coast, in particular its eastern section, is a lush well-watered region, with Turkey's only dense forests. Rainfall here reaches almost 100 inches (250 cm) per year. In some places, where it generally rains every other day, the forest takes on the look of a jungle. A rich agricultural region, it is the source of almost all of Turkey's valuable tea crop and fully 70 percent of the world's hazelnuts.

Turkey's tiny European section is a fertile landscape of rolling plains with a Mediterranean climate. Most of Istanbul, Turkey's largest city (population 8.8 million), stands on its eastern edge, overlooking the Bosporus. The rest of the city is on the Asian side of the strait.

ECONOMY

Turkey began its modern history after World War I as a poverty-stricken, backward, agricultural nation where 80 percent of the people earned their living working the land. Turkey has a growing industrial base and a standard of living that has risen significantly in the last generation. About 60 percent of the population lives in cities and towns. Sustained economic growth began in the 1930s when the government took control of many industries and used central planning to accelerate industrial development. State controls are being scaled back in order to increase efficiency and attract private investment. Although the state still owns many large enterprises, Turkey has a strong and rapidly growing private industrial sector. Textiles and clothing, which are almost entirely in private hands, are the leading industries and Turkey's most important exports, accounting for about 40 percent of Turkey's total exports. Other important industries are food processing, iron and steel, petroleum, and construction materials. Tourism has expanded and is a significant earner of foreign currency. Another critical source is the money sent home by several million Turks working abroad. Most work in Western Europe; two million Turks live in Germany alone. The Turks are also justly famous as manufacturers of beautiful carpets, a tradition that predates their arrival in Anatolia to their days as nomads in central Asia.

Turkish agriculture has lagged behind industry in modernizing. The lack of arable land, poor irrigation, and inefficient methods have limited production. Nonetheless, Turkey exports much of what it grows on the land. Cash crops such as cotton, tobacco, hazelnuts, sultanas (grapes grown for raisins and wine), and tea account for about a fifth of Turkey's total exports. Other important crops include corn, rye, wheat, barley, olives, and citrus fruits. Turkish farmers also raise large numbers of sheep, goats, and cattle. The country is a major producer of wool.

Turkey's natural resources include coal, chromium, lignite, iron, and a small amount of oil. It also has an abundance of the rarest resource in the Middle East: water. Turkey is modernizing its agriculture by expanding irrigation and providing the entire country with a clean and cheap source of electricity. The vehicle for these ambitions is the mammoth thirty-two-billion-dollar Southeastern Anatolia Project, or GAP (from the initials of its Turkish name). In one of the largest public works projects in the world, the waters of the Tigris and Euphrates rivers are being harnessed by a network of twenty-one dams and seventeen hydroelectric plants. The project's largest structure and centerpiece, the Ataturk Dam on the Euphrates, is already completed. When the entire GAP project is completed in 2010, it will supply water to more than 9 percent of Turkey's land area, expanding the country's irrigated land by 40 percent, and pro-duce one-fourth of the country's electrical power needs. One goal is to provide better opportunity on the land and keep some of Turkey's growing rural population in the countryside and out of its overcrowded cities. While all this sounds good for Turkey, Syria and Iraq are worried that Turkey's new dams will deny them water they badly need for development and to feed their growing populations. These conflicting national needs are a source of continual tension between Turkey and its southern Arab neighbors. In fact, between 1984 and 1998, the Syrian government, to pressure the Turks to provide Syria more Euphrates River water, allowed Kurdish rebels from Turkey to use bases in Syria.

PEOPLE

More than 99 percent of Turkey's 70.4 million people are Muslims, the vast majority of them Sunnis, with small numbers of Shiites and Alawites. Turkey's tiny Christian and Jewish com-munities account for about 0.2 percent of the population. The Armenian community of perhaps fifty thousand is the country's largest Christian group. About twenty-five thousand Jews still live in Turkey, one of the largest Jewish communities remaining in the Islamic world. However, despite its overwhelmingly Muslim population, modern Turkey is a secular state, the only Muslim country in the Middle East where Islam is not the state religion. Perhaps the single most important change that took place in Turkey with the collapse of the Ottoman Empire and the estab-lishment of the modern Turkish national state was secularization. Since the 1920s, the government has promoted the idea of a sec-ular Turkish identity. Islam ceased to be the official religion of the state, and civil law replaced Islamic law. The government took control of education and made it strictly secular, and a wide vari-ety of other policies were introduced to limit the influence of Islam in public life. The growth of fundamentalist Islam in recent years has become the single most divisive issue in Turkish life.

The other deep division in Turkey is ethnic, and it has been the cause of serious and continuing trouble. About 20 percent of Turkey's population is Kurdish. The Kurds are an ancient Middle Eastern people who are related to the Persians and speak an Indo-European language. Turkey's twelve million Kurds occupy an awkward position in Turkish life. Most live in southeastern Turkey near the Syrian and Iraqi borders and adjacent to the Kurdish populations of those countries. Kurds constitute about 90 percent of the population of this section of Turkey, which is part of a larger region the Kurds call Kurdistan. At the same time, many Kurds also live in cities throughout Turkey, where they have assimilated into Turkish life and achieved success in a broad range of professions. However, there is a strong Kurdish nationalist movement in Turkey. It has deep roots that reach back to the founding of modern Turkey and the Kurdish rebellions against the Turkish government in the 1920s and 1930s. Kurdish nationalists have a range of demands. There are many who would be satisfied with local and cultural autonomy. As one woman told a Western reporter, "What we demand is our identity. We want to say on our identity cards that we are Kurds. We want schools and television stations in our language."

That demand has been rejected by the Turkish political establishment, which fears that any concession to Kurdish demands for autonomy will quickly lead to secession. For many years, the Turkish government refused to even admit that Kurds existed as a distinct ethnic group, calling them mountain Turks. In 1981 a member of parliament received a year in jail for proclaiming, "There are Kurds in Turkey. I am a Kurd." It still is illegal even to use the word Kurdistan or to suggest that Kurds deserve autonomy. By the 1980s, Kurds in increasing numbers saw independence as the only escape from Turkish oppression, and in 1984 the government's ironfisted attempts to suppress Kurdish nationalism led to open rebellion. The rebellion was waged by the Kurdistan Workers' Party (PKK). In fifteen years of bitter fighting, more than twenty thousand Kurds died and many more were driven from their villages. The PKK in turn killed hundreds of government officials and several thousand Turkish soldiers. The best guess is that more than thirty thousand rebel Kurds, Turkish soldiers, and civilians lost their lives in the fighting. The stakes in this bitter dispute were raised even higher because Turkey's GAP hydroelectric project is being built entirely in the Kurdish part of the country. By 1999 the rebellion had been militarily defeated, and the PKK declared a cease-fire. But the basic issues between the two sides remained unresolved. As a result, in 2004 the PKK ended the cease-fire and resumed attacking Turkish military and civilian targets.

THE OTTOMAN ERA

The Ottoman Empire began as a small state in western Anatolia and began to grow after the Mongol invasion of the thirteenth century. Its first expansion took place at the expense of the greatly weakened Byzantine Empire during the first quarter of the fourteenth century. The Ottomans were strengthened when many former Byzantine peasants in Anatolia converted from Christianity to Islam, their main incentive being to escape the crushing tax the Islamic Ottoman state imposed on non-Muslims. By the end of the century, the empire extended deep into the Balkans. A key to Ottoman expansion was the army. Its elite core was the Janissaries, a force that in its heyday prior to 1600 was made up of Christian boys who had been kidnapped at a young age and converted to Islam. Completely cut off from their origins and heritage, the Janissaries were totally loyal to the Ottoman ruler, or sultan. Only after 1700 did they become corrupted; they then became less of a threat to the sultan's enemies and more to the sultan himself and the Turkish state.

The Ottomans suffered a crushing defeat in 1402 at the hands of the Mongol chieftain Tamerlane but recovered after Tamerlane's death in 1405. A new era of dramatic expansion followed. In 1453 the Ottomans shocked the Christian world when they conquered Constantinople and ended the thousand-year history of the Byzantine Empire. The majestic Hagia Sophia, for nine hundred years the largest Christian church in the world, was turned into a mosque. Constantinople, the former center of Greek Orthodox Christianity, became the capital of the Islamic Ottoman Empire. Expansion into Europe and across the Middle East continued into the sixteenth century. Eventually, the Ottoman Empire sprawled from North Africa, the Arabian Peninsula, and the borders of Persia across the Fertile Crescent and Anatolia. It reached to Cyprus and other islands of the Mediterranean Sea, the northern shores of the Black Sea, and the western fringes of the Balkans.

The Ottoman Empire reached both its political and cultural peak during the reign of Suleyman the Magnificent (1520–1566). His reign saw the construction of some of the Islamic world's most beautiful mosques; outstanding craftsmanship in gold, textiles, and other materials; and significant poetic and literary achievements. Suleyman also issued his famous Codex Suleymanicus, a synthesis of Islamic and secular law. At the same time, however, the seeds of decline were being planted. Endless court intrigues resulted in the murder of able princes to eliminate them from the line of succession. Even more damaging in the long run was Ottoman complacency regarding European technological progress.

The first serious European challenge to the Ottomans took place in 1571, five years after Suleyman's death, when naval forces from Spain and Venice defeated the Turkish navy at the Battle of Lepanto. Still, the Ottoman military remained a formidable force. As late as 1683, a huge army surrounded and threatened Vienna, in present-day Austria. The city held, and the Ottoman defeat at Vienna became the beginning of the long period of decline that lasted for more than two centuries. By the early nineteenth century, large pieces of the empire had been lost on all fronts, including the Balkans, where the Greeks finally won their independence. By the mid-1800s, the Ottoman armies clearly were no match for modern European forces, and the empire, wallowing in corruption and decadence, had seriously weakened. The attempt of army officers, called the Young Turks, to reverse the decline in the early twentieth century failed. The First Balkan War of 1912 reduced the Ottoman presence in Europe to the small slice of Thrace around Constantinople.

In 1914 the Ottoman Empire entered World War I on the side of Germany. Its lone major military victory of the war came in 1915 when it thwarted the British-led landing at Gallipoli and thereby defeated the Allied attempt to seize the Dardanelles. The hero of that battle was Colonel Mustafa Kemal, who after the war became the founding father of modern Turkey. Turkey's low point in the war also came in 1915 when its forces deported the Christian Armenian population from several eastern provinces to prevent them from aiding Christian Russian forces. While no exact figures exist, the best estimates are that at least one million Armenians were murdered or died from disease and starvation during that dreadful operation. The Armenian deportation is widely considered the first act of genocide of the twentieth century. (Turkey denies the genocide.) Three years later, the war ended in defeat and dissolution of the Ottoman Empire.

MUSTAFA KEMAL ATATURK AND THE BIRTH OF MODERN TURKEY

The end of the war left the Turks, bereft of their empire, in a struggle for national survival. The Treaty of Sèvres in 1920 gave them control of little more than northern Anatolia. Constantinople, still officially the capital, and the Bosporus and Dardanelles were under British occupation. It was at this point that Mustafa Kemal (later known as *Mustafa Kemal Ataturk*) emerged as a national leader. Between 1920 and 1923, Kemal abolished the Ottoman sultanate and declared Turkey a republic. He defeated Armenian and Georgian forces in the east and forced Italian and French troops out of Anatolia. He signed a treaty of friendship with the Soviet Union that restored some territory to Turkey. In addition, in climactic battles fought in 1922, Turkish forces defeated Greece's attempt to annex western Anatolia. In the aftermath of the Turkish victory, about 1.5 million Greeks were uprooted from western Anatolia and resettled in Greece, ending a Greek presence there that dated from the eighth century B.C. Their forced migration was mirrored by that of eight hundred thousand Turks who were forced from their homes in Greece and Bulgaria and resettled in Turkey. Kemal's victories were confirmed by the Treaty of Lausanne in 1923, which with minor subsequent adjustments established Turkey's current borders.

Mustafa Kemal had one overriding goal—to turn Turkey into a modern secular nation copying the Western model. That required breaking the grip of Islam on Turkish life and confining it to the realm of the private and personal. Kemal's energy and determination and the scope of his reforms were extensive. In 1923 a national assembly Kemal had convened three years earlier abolished the Ottoman sultanate and declared Turkey a republic. Kemal became Turkey's first president. He would be reelected three times and rule the country with dictatorial powers until his death. For most of that time, Turkey was a one-party state run by Kemal's Republican People's Party (CHP according to its Turkish initials). The new regime also moved the country's capital from Constantinople to Ankara, a city in central Anatolia, yet another symbol of Turkey's fresh start. In 1924 the national assembly abolished the caliphate, the Islamic office left over from Ottoman times that made the sultan Turkey's religious as well as temporal ruler. The assembly also introduced a new constitution. It provided for a parliament elected by universal male suffrage.

Kemal broadened his battle against religion in 1925 when the government abolished all religious orders and Muslim courts. It made secular primary education compulsory for all children. Even the fez, the traditional Turkish cylinder-shaped hat, was forbidden as part of Kemal's determination to Westernize Turkey. In 1926 the government adopted the Swiss code of civil law. Civil marriage became mandatory. In 1928 Islam lost its status as the official state religion. Kemal also took the difficult step of banning the use of the Arabic script for writing Turkish and substituting the Latin alphabet, yet another effort to turn Turkey toward the West. The new system was, in fact, better suited to the Turkish language, but Kemal was taking no chances. A new law required all Turks under the age of forty to go to school to learn the Latin-based writing system. In

1930 Constantinople's name officially was changed to Istanbul, a name thought to be derived from two Greek words, *stin poli*, meaning "in the city."

Under the Ottoman regime, women had few rights; women were given the vote in 1934 and full legal equality with men in 1935. Another change implemented in 1934 required all Turks to follow the Western example and adopt surnames. The national assembly honored Kemal by giving him the name Ataturk, Turkish for "Father of Turks."

Westernization also meant economic development. Impressed with what he saw in the Soviet Union, Kemal was convinced that rapid growth was most quickly achieved by direct state intervention in the economy. In the 1930s, the government began a program of central planning and state ownership of major industrial enterprises. Following the Soviet model, but avoiding its disastrous extremes, Turkey introduced its first five-year economic plan in 1934.

In 1938, at the relatively young age of fifty-seven, Mustafa Kemal Ataturk died of liver disease. He was succeeded as president by his longtime second-in-command, Ismet Inonu. Under Inonu's leadership Turkey remained neutral for most of World War II, despite Allied pleas to join the desperate struggle against Nazi Germany. Turkey declared war on Germany and Japan in February 1945, only when the fighting in Europe was almost over. While the decision to remain neutral was questionable from a moral point of view—some Turks consider it shameful—the country did emerge from the most destructive war in history physically undamaged.

TURKEY AFTER WORLD WAR II

Turkey took two major steps in the immediate postwar era to link itself even more closely with the West. The first involved foreign affairs. Faced with pressure from the Soviet Union over control of the Black Sea straits, Turkey quickly chose sides in the Cold War, aligning itself with the Western democracies in their

forty-five-year struggle against the Soviet Union. Turkey came
under the mantle of American protection in 1947, when the
United States proclaimed the Truman Doctrine. It stated that
the United States would protect countries threatened by
Communist aggression or subversion. In 1950 Turkey sent soldiers to Korea to fight with American and other UN forces in
defense of South Korea. In 1952 Turkey became a member of
NATO, the American-led defensive alliance formed in 1949 to
protect Western Europe from Soviet aggression. More difficult,
and still only partially completed, was the second step, in which
Turkey attempted to move toward genuine democracy. That
step ran against stumbling blocks from the start. These included
authoritarian attitudes among Turkey's political leaders, economic instability, the Kurdish rebellion, and the resurgence of
Islamic fundamentalism.

Turkey's one-party system ended in 1946 when Celal Bayar
and Adnan Menderes were allowed to form the Democratic
Party. Other new parties followed. Nonetheless, the first postwar
election, won by the CHP in 1946, was rigged. In 1950 the
Democratic Party won Turkey's first free election. It governed for
the next ten years with Bayar as president and Menderes as prime
minister. However, in the wake of accusations of corruption and
repressiveness, the military in 1960 overthrew the government.
Bayar was imprisoned, while Menderes and two other ministers
were hanged in 1961. That year the military returned Turkey to
civilian rule under a new constitution designed to prevent the
concentration of too much power in the executive branch. The
Democratic Party was banned but came to life again in the form
of the Justice Party, led by Suleyman Demirel, who throughout
the 1960s and early 1970s was Turkey's leading politician.

Turkish political life, rocked by waves of economic hardship and social unrest, lurched through a series of crises during
those years. In the early 1970s, Bulent Ecevit, at the head of a
revived CHP, emerged as a rival to Demirel. In contrast to the
centrist Demirel, Ecevit became the leader of Turkey's moderate political left. During the 1970s, each man served several
terms as prime minister. Meanwhile, by the late 1970s

increasing domestic turmoil and ineffective government brought the country to the brink of civil war. In 1980 the military again stepped in with a coup, banning all existing parties and arresting both Ecevit and Demirel. Reversing its 1961 position, the military wrote a new constitution that in the interest of maintaining order vested more power in the presidency. In 1983 the military permitted civilian political life to resume, but only under its tight supervision. A series of newly organized and named parties ran in parliamentary elections in the fall. The winner, led by former deputy prime minister Turgut Özal, was the conservative Motherland Party (ANAP), which ran with the generals' support. Özal served as prime minister until 1989 and as president from 1989 to 1993. He was responsible for far-reaching economic reforms that promoted free enterprise and economic growth.

Amid seemingly endless political maneuvering, Ecevit and Demirel returned to the political arena after a 1987 national referendum ended a ban the military had imposed on 200 politicians. Demirel headed the conservative True Path Party (DYP), while Ecevit led the leftist Democratic Socialist Party (DSP). Although several new politicians became significant figures in Turkish political life, Ecevit and Demirel would remain central players throughout the 1980s and 1990s. In fact, as the 1990s drew to a close, Ecevit and Demirel, by then the two old men of Turkish politics, were respectively the country's prime minister and president.

Perhaps the most interesting new player on Turkey's political stage in the early 1990s was Tansu Ciller, the country's first prominent woman politician. Ciller became leader of the True Path Party in 1993 when Demirel, then prime minister, was elected Turkey's president. Ciller replaced Demirel as prime minister, thereby becoming the first woman to hold that office in Turkey's history and the first woman to do so in a Middle Eastern Muslim country.

The other important, and militant, new face was Necmettin Erbakan, leader of the Islamic fundamentalist Welfare Party. Erbakan rose to prominence during the first half of the 1990s as

Turkey's most anti-Western major politician. During the municipal elections of 1994, in which his party was victorious in more than a dozen cities and towns, including Istanbul and Ankara, he warned that the Christians of Europe wanted to oppress Turkey and likened them to infidels. While campaigning during the parliamentary elections of December 1995, he again bitterly attacked European influences as a threat to Muslims and said he wanted to abolish Turkey's secular constitution. The Welfare Party stunned most observers by finishing first in the parliamentary elections of December 1995, with 21.4 percent of the vote, riding a wave of sentiment among conservative Turks that modernization and secularism had brought to Turkey crass materialism and moral decay. At the same time, its electoral victory, even though it amounted only to a narrow plurality, caused immediate rumbling in the military, which considered itself the guardian of Ataturk's secular revolution. After a swirl of political maneuvering, which included a failed attempt by the True Path and Motherland parties to work together, Erbakan cobbled together a coalition that included Ciller and the True Path Party. It survived for just over one stormy year. The military immediately criticized Erbakan's government for permitting schools to teach religious courses. An Islamic rally in a small town near Ankara caused further trouble when the local mayor said Turkey should adopt Islamic law. The guest of honor at the rally, the ambassador from fundamentalist Iran, urged the crowd to stand up to the enemies of Islam.

In February 1997, the military demanded Erbakan enforce eighteen measures to protect secular state institutions from Islamic influence. These included closer supervision of Islamic financial institutions and the removal of Islamic fundamentalists from public offices. Erbakan temporarily defused the tension by agreeing to the military's demands, but soon the military and the government again were at odds about Islamic influence in Turkish state institutions. In June 1997, the Welfare Party's coalition fell apart, and Erbakan was forced to resign.

The new government, built around the Motherland Party, was a fragile coalition. During the next eighteen months, tension continued to build between secular and Islamic forces in Turkey. The government pushed antireligious policies that ranged from expelling seventy-three members of the armed forces for membership in Islamic organizations to strictly enforcing laws banning Islamic dress in public institutions, especially schools and universities. To cut down on the number of students attending religious schools, the government raised the minimum age for admission to Islamic schools from eleven to fourteen. In January 1998, a ruling dissolved the Welfare Party and banned Erbakan from politics for five years. Many of its members then joined the newly formed Virtue Party, a clone of the dissolved party. Islamic forces responded with several demonstrations, including one in Istanbul in February attended by ten thousand people. As for Erbakan, by then in his late seventies, he briefly was imprisoned for corruption and in effect was pushed to the political sidelines.

Turkey's struggle to define itself inevitably extended into the realm of foreign affairs. The basis of its foreign policy was alignment with the Western democracies, formalized in 1952 with membership in NATO. At the same time, Turkey's place in the alliance was complicated by its strained and often hostile relations with Greece, its old adversary and a fellow NATO member. The most serious flash point in the 1960s and 1970s between the two countries was the status of the Turkish minority on Cyprus, a Mediterranean island-nation near the Turkish coast with an 80 percent Greek majority. In 1974, with Greek-Turkish relations on the island deteriorating, Turkey invaded Cyprus and occupied 40 percent of the island. Local Turks then proclaimed a Turkish Republic of Northern Cyprus, which has received no international recognition besides Turkey's. Turkey and Greece also have territorial disputes in the Aegean Sea, where oil has been discovered.

Since the 1980s, Turkey has attempted to cement its ties with the West by gaining membership to the European Union. For a long time it was unsuccessful. A major disappointment came in 1997 when Turkey was not one of the five countries invited to begin the admission process. Turkey's rejection came in part because of economic concerns but mainly for political reasons. The most important political issues were Turkey's role in the forceful partition of Cyprus and its human rights record, especially toward the Kurds.

Turkey was more successful in another arena farther to the east: the world of the newly independent Turkic states of the former Soviet Union. These states—Azerbaijan, Turkmenistan, Uzbekistan, Kazakhstan, and Kyrgyzstan—looked to Turkey as a model for nation building. The leaders of several of them also were concerned about Islamic fundamentalism and looked to Turkey for help in dealing with that problem.

If Turkey in many ways stood between Europe and the Middle East, within the Middle East it stood between Israel and the Islamic countries of the region. Turkey and Iran, both Muslim but non-Arab, were the only states in the region to recognize Israel shortly after the founding of the Jewish state. In the decades that followed, those relations periodically cooled and warmed, as Turkey sought to remain on good terms with both Israel and the Arab world. In part because of its problems with Syria and Iraq, Turkey in the late 1990s established a close political and military relationship with Israel that included joint military exercises. In foreign affairs, as in domestic matters, Turkey's leaders based their policies on a secular view of their country's national interests. They joined NATO, opposed Islamic fundamentalism in central Asia, and aligned Turkey with Israel as opposed to Syria and Iraq.

A secular orientation remained the bottom line in the late 1990s, as it had been in the early 1920s. The fragile government installed after Erbakan's fall in mid-1997 collapsed at the end of 1998 in the wake of a corruption scandal. Its fall created the opening through which Bulent Ecevit returned to power. The military, which in 1980 had arrested Ecevit and charged him with acts of treason, welcomed the return of the venerable leftist politician, who like the military itself was militantly anti-Islamic. He made this clear upon assuming the post of prime minister in January 1999 by telling parliament, "To all the problems we face, we shall seek solutions in the enlightened past of timeless leader Ataturk." Another quality Ecevit brought at a time when Turkey was plagued with corruption scandals was a rare and unquestioned reputation for honesty.

Ecevit's immediate tasks were to crack down on Islamic activity and to prepare his divided country for national elections. In February 1999, Ecevit received an enormous boost when Turkish commandos secretly went to Kenya and captured Abdullah Ocalan, the leader of the Kurdish rebellion in Turkey and the country's most wanted fugitive. Two months later, Ecevit's Democratic Socialist Party won with a plurality of 24 percent of the vote in the parliamentary elections. All the other major parties lost strength. The Virtue Party took only 15 percent of the vote versus 21 percent won by Welfare in the 1995 election.

Although Ecevit appeared to have won a victory for secularism, the immediate aftermath of the election provided yet more proof that Turkey's secular-religious combat was far from over. When parliament met to take its oath of office on May 2, 1999, a thirty-one-year-old member of the Virtue Party named Merve Kavakci arrived wearing the traditional Islamic woman's head scarf. An uproar ensued. As part of the effort to keep Turkish public life secular, the government had long forbidden female university students, lawyers, civil servants, and judges from wearing head scarves. Prosecular members of parliament denounced Kavakci. Among them was Ecevit, who told his colleagues:

> No one may interfere with the private life of individuals, but this is not a private space. This is the supreme foundation of the state. It is not a place in which to challenge the state.

When she refused to remove her scarf, Kavakci was not allowed to take the oath of office, which includes a vow to uphold the principles and reforms of Ataturk. It was difficult to imagine Kavakci adhering to that vow in light of what Ataturk said about head scarves in 1925:

> In some places I have seen women who put a piece of cloth or a towel or something like it over their heads and hide their faces. Can the mothers and daughters of a civilized nation

adopt this strange manner, the barbarous posture? It is a spectacle that makes the nation an object of ridicule. It must be remedied at once.

The day after she was barred from taking the oath of office, Kavakci defiantly announced her determination to take her place in parliament, head scarf and all. "I will cover my head in accordance with my religious beliefs," she said. "It is my personal choice." Several days later, the government stripped Kavakci of her Turkish citizenship, using a rarely enforced clause in Turkey's legal code.

While Kavakci's political career appeared over, at least in the short run, the bitter and growing debate over the place of Islam in Turkish life continued. Whereas Kavakci claimed her struggle was for all women and to push for more democratic rights, secular Turks did not see it that way. As a philosophy professor at Istanbul University said of Kavakci and other Islamic politicians, "Their dream is to use democracy to bring an Islamic state." While that statement probably was accurate, it could hardly be said that Turkey was entirely democratic. The country still had laws against terrorism that put people who spoke out on a variety of issues on the wrong side of the law and special state security courts to put them in jail. In April 1999, Turkey's highest-ranking judge boldly criticized the limits on free speech in his country:

> Although everyone knows that freedom of thought is vital to democracy, we have not been able to overcome obstacles that keep us from establishing it. Allowing people to hold opinions is not enough. They must be able to speak freely. The freedom to express one's thoughts is the basis on which all other freedoms are built.

On no issue was debate more restricted than on the Kurdish rebellion, which by 1999 was fifteen years old. The rebels belonged to the Kurdistan Workers' Party (PKK), whose leader was Abdullah Ocalan. The Kurds began their rebellion in the face of restrictions on their cultural expression that went so far as to ban them from speaking their language on the streets and playing their music. By 1999 those restrictions had been removed—the law against speaking Kurdish was repealed in 1991—but the Kurds still lived under oppressive conditions. Education in the Kurdish language was still forbidden. The government kept a tight military rein on the Kurdish region in the country's southeast. As one young Kurd told a Western journalist, "We speak with our eyes." An elderly man added, "You can see us, but you can't hear us. Our lips are sealed."

During fighting that raged for more than fifteen years, Turkish soldiers destroyed three thousand villages, as well as forests where the Kurdish guerrillas tried to hide, and killed more than twenty thousand Kurds. The Turks insisted that the Kurds had engaged in terrorism and that Ocalan was guilty of ordering thousands of murders. Aside from more than thirty thousand victims on both sides, by 1999 the war was costing Turkey eight billion dollars a year—the total cost of the war was one hundred billion dollars—and tying down more than two hundred thousand soldiers. In February of that year, Ocalan was captured. He was charged with treason and put on trial at the end of May. At his month-long trial, Ocalan surprised most observers by calling for peace between the two sides. He accepted blame for some of the violence but also justified the Kurdish struggle. He said Kurds would be satisfied with cultural autonomy within a democratic Turkey. Finally, he asked that his life be spared so he could work toward the goals he had outlined.

Ocalan's appeal fell on deaf ears. In June the court found him guilty and sentenced him to hang. The United States and many European governments immediately urged the Turks not to carry out the sentence. Several Turkish intellectuals, including people close to the government, also publicly opposed the death sentence, which in 2002 was commuted to life in prison. One newspaper columnist made perhaps the strongest case against carrying out the sentence when he wrote:

> Let us not hang him because he will become a symbol; because Turkey will then be isolated; because a democratic

country does not act with vengeance; because terror then will
never end; and because Turkey, to remain part of the democratic world, must realize that Kurds are living on their soil
and respect their demand to protect their identity.

More than a plea for mercy, the statement was an articulate
summary of Turkey's eighty-year struggle to find its place as a
member of the modern democratic world. Turkey took a step
toward that place in 1999 when it at last was invited to join the
European Union (EU). But that invitation was strongly conditional, requiring major economic and political reforms, especially with regard to human rights. Those reforms came slowly,
and in 2004 the EU warned Turkey that membership negotiations would be suspended if any backtracking occurred. In any
event, membership probably was ten years away, assuming it
came at all.

TURKEY SINCE 2000

The new century and millennium began with a new crisis involving Islamic fundamentalism. The government launched an
offensive against a fundamentalist terrorist group called
Hezbollah (not connected to the group with the same name in
Lebanon). It killed its leader and captured two of his top aides.
Then, in several Hezbollah hideouts police discovered dozens of
bodies, many mutilated by torture. One of the victims, a woman
named Konca Kuris, was a well-known author described by her
supporters as a Muslim and feminist. Kuris had challenged many
traditional Muslim practices requiring the subjugation of women
as being distortions of what is written in the Koran. A Hezbollah
videotape revealed she had been tortured for weeks before her
death. The news about Hezbollah went from bad to worse when
evidence came to light that, during the late 1980s and early
1990s, the government had used Hezbollah forces to fight
Kurdish rebels. Those forces had killed thousands of people,
including many intellectuals and businesspeople.

Turkey's November 2002 parliamentary elections brought another Islamic fundamentalist challenge when the newly formed Justice and Development Party (AKP) won a plurality of the vote. Like the defunct Welfare Party, the AKP had deep Islamic roots. It was led by *Recep Erdogan*, the former mayor of Istanbul. A leading member of the Welfare Party before its dissolution, Erdogan was controversial because in 1998 he was convicted and briefly sentenced to jail for promoting religious hatred. Because of peculiarities in Turkey's proportional representation law, the AKP, despite winning only about 34 percent of the vote, wound up with 65 percent of the seats in parliament. At first Erdogan was banned from holding office because of his criminal conviction. However, the AKP-dominated parliament quickly changed the law, and Erdogan became prime minister in March 2003.

The AKP election victory immediately raised concerns among Turkish secularists, who were concerned with protecting the legacy of the Ataturk revolution. The AKP and Erdogan said they were committed to democracy, economic reform, and having Turkey join the EU. Erdogan himself disavowed the hardline Islamic views he had expressed in the past. At the same time, both the AKP and the new prime minister clearly backed moves to increase Islamic influence in Turkish life. To be sure, this was done cautiously so as to avoid a reaction from the military and criticism from abroad, especially the EU. AKP leaders criticized Turkey's constitutional definition of secularism, and Erdogan himself questioned a decision by one of Turkey's high courts that upheld secular values.

Concerns about the AKP increased in 2004 when the AKP-dominated parliament passed a law to end restrictions in university admissions to graduates of strict religious schools that train imams and preachers. Leading Turkish secularists worried that the law would allow Islamic fundamentalists to increase their influence in the government and judiciary. As one leading educator put it, "Secularity is the guarantee of a modern, European Turkish republic. Otherwise it can turn into an Islamic fundamentalist country." Ultimately, the law was vetoed by Turkey's president, Ahmet Secdet Sezer, a former chief justice of Turkey's highest court known for his support of democracy and free speech. In another incident that worried secularists, in 2005 the government jailed the rector of a major university who had opposed Islamic activities at his school. Meanwhile, observers pointed to an upsurge of anti-American and anti-Semitic articles in Turkey's Islamist newspapers.

As of mid-2006, Turkey seemed to be divided about the direction in which it wanted to move. Even with the AKP in power, Turkey is still following the path blazed by Ataturk more than eighty years earlier. But it is far from certain that it will continue to do so.

IRAN

Iranians are the descendants of the ancient Persians, builders of one of the greatest of all Middle Eastern empires more than twenty-five hundred years ago. Persian roots in the Middle East go back another one thousand years, to about 1500 B.C., when the Aryans, a nomadic Indo-European people, first settled on the Iranian plateau. According to the Bible, Persian king Cyrus the Great allowed the Israelites to return to their homeland in the middle of the sixth century B.C. His successors Darius and Xerxes tried and failed to conquer the Greeks in the Persian Wars. In the fourth century B.C., the Persians were conquered by the Greek king Alexander the Great. Greek rule lasted less than a century. Beginning in the third century B.C., the Persians were ruled by the Farsi-speaking Parthians, who for several centuries managed to stand firm against the legions of the mighty Roman Empire. In the third century A.D., the Persians regained control of their country under the Sassanid dynasty. Centuries of warfare with the Byzantines weakened the Sassanids and left them vulnerable to conquest by the Muslim Arabs by 650. After the Arab conquest, the Persians gradually abandoned Zoroastrianism, their ancient native religion, for Islam, the religion of their conquerors.

In the centuries that followed the Arab conquest, Persian scholars, scientists, writers, poets, and artists contributed enormously to the development of Islamic civilization. However, unlike the cultures of many other Middle Eastern peoples, Persian culture and the Farsi language survived Arab rule. They also survived the subsequent conquest and rule by the Seljuk Turks and Mongols. In 1502 the native Safavid dynasty took control of Persia. A vigorous Persian cultural revival followed. The Safavids made the Shiite version of Islam Persia's official state religion. Ever since then, the country has been the main bastion of the Shiite faith in the Islamic world. After a brief period of Afghan rule in the eighteenth century and two short-lived native dynasties, the Qajar dynasty ruled Persia from 1794 to 1925. During that period, European powers increasingly intruded into the Middle East, and Persia became a pawn in the competition between the Russian and British empires. The main positive political development of that era occurred, when the weakened monarchy was forced to grant Persia a constitution and a parliament, or Majlis. The establishment of the Pahlavi dynasty in 1925 by a military officer named Reza Khan marked the beginning of modern Persian, or Iranian, history. A change in the country's name from Persia to Iran in 1935 was symbolic of that transition.

GEOGRAPHY, ECONOMY, PEOPLE

GEOGRAPHY

Iran is a rhombus-shaped country east of Anatolia, with an area of 636,292 square miles (1,646,000 sq. km), about a tenth larger than Alaska. Turkey and Iraq lie to the west, and Pakistan and Afghanistan are to the east. Iran borders Turkmenistan in the northeast and Azerbaijan and Armenia in the northwest. In between, separating Turkmenistan and Azerbaijan, is Iran's long (about 440 miles, or 700 km) Caspian Sea coastline. The Caspian Sea, the world's largest landlocked salt lake, is a rich fishing ground.

RUSSIA

KAZAKHSTAN

UZBEKISTAN

IRAN

EORGIA

Caspian
Sea

ARMENIA

AZERBAIJAN

TURKMENISTAN

Talkheh R.

Ardabil

Tabriz

Bandar-e Anzali

Lake
Urmia

Safid River

Bandar-e
Nowshahr

Gorgan

Atrek

Mashhad

Sabzevar

Elburz Mountains

Tehran

Mt. Damavand

IRAQ

Islamshar

Hamadan

Qum

Dasht-e-Kavir
(Salt Desert)

Z
a
g
r
o
s

Arak

Kashan

Khoramabad

AFGHANISTAN

M
o
u
n
t
a
i
n
s

Isfahan

Karun
R.

Ahvaz

Khuzestan

Khorramshahr

Kerman

Dasht-e-Lut
(Barren Desert)

Abadan

Bandar-e
Khomeini

Zahedan

KUWAIT

Shiraz

Bushehr

Persian
Gulf

SAUDI
ARABIA

Bandar-e
Shahid Rajai

Bandar Abbas

BAHRAIN

Strait of Hormuz

Chah Bahar

QATAR

OMAN

Gulf of
Oman

PAKISTAN

UNITED ARAB
EMIRATES

OMAN

0   100   200 mi

0   100   200 km

IRAN

- ✪ Capital city
- ○ City
- ▲ Mountain
- ── International border
- ── River

N

W   E

S

More important, its waters cover rich oil deposits. To the southeast is the Persian Gulf, the epicenter of the richest oil deposits in the world. Due south, beyond the strategic Strait of Hormuz, through which tankers take Persian Gulf oil en route to the world's industrialized nations, is the Gulf of Oman.

Most of Iran is a rugged semiarid plateau about 4,000 feet (1,200 m) above sea level surrounded by high mountains. Two nearly uninhabited deserts, the Dasht-e-Kavir (Salt Desert) and Dasht-e-Lut (Barren Desert), cover much of the eastern part of the country. The salt swamps of the Dasht-e-Kavir are so treacherous that they remain largely unexplored. The towering Elburz Mountains in the north, which include several active volcanoes, cut off the well-watered but swampy Caspian coastal area from the rest of the country. The northern slopes of the Elburz range are covered by dense forests that are protected by strict government limits on logging. Just south of the mountains, in the shadow of Mount Damavand, a volcano that rises to 18,934 feet (5,771 meters), is *Tehran* (population 6.7 million), Iran's capital and largest city. The Elburz range extends into Iran's northwestern corner, where it shelters Lake Urmia, Iran's largest lake.

The Zagros Mountains cut across southwestern Iran parallel to the Persian Gulf. Southwest of that range is the Karun River, one of the few rivers in Iran that flows all year long. The Karun River basin is Iran's largest fertile lowland. Less than 10 percent of Iran's land area is arable.

Iran has an extreme continental climate. Most of the country is hot and dry in summer and cold and dry in winter. Rainfall occurs mainly in the north along the Caspian coast and nearby mountains, where it falls all year long. In the mountains of the northwest and west, rain is confined to the winter months. Temperatures reach 104°F (40°C) in the summer along the parched Persian Gulf coast. In areas where high altitude moderates the summer heat, winters are bitterly cold and mountain passes are blocked by snow. The snowmelt is a vital part of Iran's limited water supply. Rainfall in Iran ranges from 50 inches (125 cm) in the western mountains to less than an inch (2.5 cm) in the eastern deserts.

Iran experiences occasional volcanic eruptions and severe earthquakes. The most recent major earthquake struck north-western Iran in 1990, killing forty thousand people and injuring sixty thousand more.

After Tehran, Iran's next two largest cities are Mashhad (population 1.9 million), in the northeast, and Isfahan (population 1.25 million), about 200 miles (320 km) south of Tehran. Qum (population 777,000), Iran's eighth-largest city, is more important than its size might suggest. It is Iran's religious center and the birthplace of the movement that in 1979 overthrew Iran's monarchy and established the current Islamic republic. Located about 65 miles (100 km) south of Tehran, Qum is one of the seven cities holy to Shiites and, in effect, is off-limits to non-Muslims.

ECONOMY

Although Iran has a variety of natural resources, they are all overshadowed by oil. Oil first was discovered in Iran in 1908. Most of Iran's oil reserves of about ninety billion barrels, about 9 percent of the world's known supply, are found in a 350-mile-long (560-km) region that begins north of the Persian Gulf and runs about halfway down Iran's Persian Gulf coastline. That region falls largely within Khuzistan province, most of whose inhabitants are Shiite Arabs. Oil accounts for about 90 percent of Iran's export earnings and provides the government with 80 percent of its revenue. Iran also has the world's second-largest reserves of natural gas, trailing only the former Soviet Union. If the modern oil industry provides Iran's most valuable export, an ancient craft provides its number-two export: the world-famous and extraordinarily beautiful Persian carpets. Traditionally, each meticulously woven carpet contains a flaw in its design in deference to the Islamic injunction that only Allah (the Arabic word for God) is perfect. Iran also is the world's largest producer of nuts, and pistachios are its third most valuable export. Other exports include caviar—the tiny but very expensive eggs of the famed Caspian Sea sturgeon—and metal ores.

Iran's main agricultural areas are the Caspian coast, mountain valleys in the northwest, and the Karun River basin. Major crops, aside from nuts, include rice, wheat, barley, hemp, and citrus fruits. Agricultural progress has been held back by outdated methods, overworked soil, and inadequate irrigation. Iran's largest nonoil industry is textiles production, which includes rug weaving. Other major industries produce petrochemicals, weapons, processed foods, and machinery.

PEOPLE

Only 51 percent of Iran's 68.6 million people are Persian, that is, native speakers of Farsi. Most live in cities and towns, as do about 60 percent of the population as a whole, although Persians also live in mountain valleys in central Iran. Turkic-speaking Azerbaijanis account for about a quarter of the population. They are concentrated in Iran's northwest between the Caspian Sea and the Turkish border. In contrast to several other minority groups, the Azerbaijanis are well integrated into Iranian life. There are between four and five million Kurds in Iran, about 7 percent of the population. The Kurds, whose history in Iran, as elsewhere, includes a long tradition of struggling for autonomy, live mainly in the western mountains near the Turkish and Iraqi borders. Their language—actually several dialects that often are not mutually understandable—is related to Farsi. Two distant relatives of the Kurds—the Bakhtiari and the Lurs—live in Iran's southwestern Zagros Mountains and account for perhaps 4 percent of the population. Arabs are about 3 percent of the population, but their importance exceeds their numbers because they are concentrated near the Iraqi border in Khuzistan province, the center of Iran's oil industry. A variety of other ethnic groups whose loyalties are tribal or ethnic rather than national complete Iran's population mosaic. In addition, two million refugees, mainly Kurds from Iraq and people from Afghanistan, currently live in Iran.

About 99 percent of Iran's population are Muslims. Most of them, about 90 percent, are Shiites. Shiite religious solidarity has created a powerful unifying force for Iran, the only large Shiite island in the Sunni Muslim sea that covers most of the Middle East. The remaining 1 percent of the population includes Christians (mainly Armenians and Assyrians), Jews, Zoroastrians—perhaps thirty thousand people still practice Persia's ancient native religion—and Baha'is. While most non-Muslim groups have the legal right to practice their religions, all suffer from some degree of discrimination and persecution. The Jewish community, which numbered eighty thousand prior to the 1979 Islamic Revolution, has shrunk to about twenty-five thousand due to emigration. It is subject to periodic attacks by the government, such as the arrest of thirteen Jews in 1999 for alleged spying. Far worse off, however, are the 350,000 followers of the Baha'i faith. Iran's ruling clerics consider them deserters from Islam and they are denied all religious rights and are regularly subject to severe persecution. In 1999 a report prepared by the U.S. Department of State listed Iran as one of the most religiously repressive countries in the world.

MODERN IRANIAN HISTORY

THE PAHLAVI DYNASTY (1925–1979)

General Reza Khan began a new era in Persian history when he forced the last shah, or emperor, of the Qajar dynasty to go into exile in 1923. He abandoned the idea of turning Persia into a republic because of opposition from religious leaders. Instead, he had the Iranian parliament elect him shah and thereby founded the Pahlavi dynasty.

Reza Shah, as he was called after 1925, was a vigorous modernizer committed to following the example of Mustafa Kemal Ataturk in Turkey. Like Ataturk, Reza Shah ruled with dictatorial powers. Few aspects of Persian life escaped his attention. He reorganized and improved Persia's tax collection system and began construction of a railway to connect Tehran to the Persian Gulf and better tie the country together. He promoted industrialization under state ownership and control, a program that accelerated industrial development but also discouraged private initiative.

Although Islam remained Iran's official religion, Reza Shah introduced secular reforms designed to break the grip of Islamic clerics on Persian life. The state took control of religious schools. Reza Shah established a secular primary education system and in 1934 opened Tehran University, Persia's first university. A new legal system ended the control of religious courts over civil affairs. Other reforms ended legal discrimination against non-Muslims. One of the most important changes was the abolition of the special tax that non-Muslims had previously been forced to pay. Women also were given more legal rights. In 1935 the campaign for modernization was extended to clothing when the government banned the chador, the traditional garment that covered a woman's body from head to toe as well as most of her face. There also was an attempt to rid Farsi of Arabic words and influences.

Reza Shah promoted the development of Persia's oil industry with British help, but he resented British influence in his country. During the 1930s, Reza Shah was strongly pro-German as he tried to counter British and Soviet influence in the region. In August 1941, two years after the beginning of World War II, Britain and the Soviet Union occupied Iran to end the shah's cooperation with Nazi Germany. They forced Reza Shah to leave Iran and abdicate in favor of his son, *Mohammad Reza Shah Pahlavi*. American troops joined the occupation in 1942.

The end of World War II brought unrest rather than genuine peace to Iran. The new shah's first problem was to get the Soviet Union to withdraw its forces from northern Iran, which was achieved in 1946 due to American pressure on the Soviets. The next challenge to the shah came from militant Iranian nationalists led by Mohammad Mossadegh, who became Iran's prime minister in 1951. Mossadegh nationalized Iran's oil industry by seizing control from the previous owners, mainly British (and some American) companies. He also wanted to limit the power of the shah so that parliament, not the shah, would be the real ruler of Iran. Mossadegh's nationalization policies got him into trouble with Western powers whose oil companies had lost property in Iran. In 1953 he was overthrown in a coup organized by the American Central Intelligence Agency (CIA). The shah, who had left the country earlier in 1953, returned to his throne with American backing and increased power. However, part of Mossadegh's legacy lived on when Iran's oil industry remained nationalized. American and European oil companies still made out well when the shah negotiated deals that allowed them to manage Iran's oil industry while earning large profits.

After being restored to his throne, the shah gradually consolidated his power and moved Iran firmly into the Western camp during the Cold War. At the same time, the economic gap between rich and poor grew, as did social unrest and political criticism of the shah. Critics of his rule and the concentration of wealth and power in Iran called it the one thousand family regime. In the early 1960s, the shah responded with a broad program of modernization and social reform he called the White Revolution. The cornerstone of the program was land reform. The government bought millions of acres from Iran's large landlords and distributed them to landless peasants, along with lands owned by the royal family. Within three years, 1.5 million tenant farmers became landowners. There were improvements in education and health care and profit sharing for factory workers. In 1963 women received the right to vote.

While the White Revolution had many supporters, it also had powerful opponents, including landowners and Islamic religious leaders. The Islamic leaders were especially opposed to granting women rights and to other measures, such as the introduction of a secular calendar, that undermined their authority. Leftist groups wanted more radical change and opposed the shah's dictatorial methods. In 1963 there were violent riots against the shah and his policies, led by a militant Islamic cleric, the *Ayatollah Ruhollah Khomeini*. The shah reacted to the riots, and to all other dissent, with force. Khomeini was arrested and eventually exiled from Iran.

The shah meanwhile used his growing oil revenues for a variety of expensive and prestigious projects, such as building a subway for Tehran. He spent billions on modern American weapons to make Iran the most powerful military power in the Persian Gulf region. Iran was a steadfast American ally. Aside from Israel and Turkey, Iran was the most consistently pro-American country in the Middle East. As long as oil revenues grew and the standard of living rose in Iran, despite great inequalities, the shah was able to maintain a strong base of support. Those who did not support his regime were silenced by his dreaded secret police, the Savak. However, after 1975 oil prices fell, government revenues declined, and the shah had to cancel many projects. This hurt businesspeople and the middle class. Rapid population growth meant numerous young people entering the labor force could not find jobs. Peasants who had received their own land often could not make a living on their small farms. Opposition to the shah swelled.

The shah's repressive policies had the effect of channeling much of that opposition into the hands of Islamic militants like Khomeini, who continued to agitate against the shah from outside the country. One reason was that in Iran's oppressive political environment there were few places Iranians could gather for political discussions. Practically the only places Iranians, especially the young, could meet undisturbed were in mosques and religious clubs controlled by Islamic leaders. This was because security forces were reluctant to move against religious institutions.

The shah also offended Iranian nationalist sentiments by inviting thousands of foreign civilian and military experts into Iran. If nothing else, their high standard of living, which few Iranians could match, intensified discontent. So did runaway corruption that extended throughout the government and reached the royal family. By the late 1970s, antigovernment riots and government repression were becoming increasingly violent and bloody. The regime faced a wall of opposition that extended across the political spectrum from the pro-Communist left to the militant Islamic right. Discontent and disorder had reached the point where they had become a threat to the shah's power.

The collapse came with shocking suddenness. The most effective opponents of the regime were supporters of the

Ayatollah Khomeini, who thundered against the shah from his base of exile in France. In late 1978, the shah's regime, once so vigorous and still heavily armed with the most modern weapons, simply crumbled. On January 16, 1979, the shah, who unknown to the public was suffering from cancer, announced he was leaving the country to go on vacation. He never returned.

By February 1, Khomeini was back in Iran. It was the turn of the secular nationalist and radical left opponents of the shah, who had been cheering his departure, to experience their own rapid and bitter defeat. The shah's secular opponents were divided into many groups, ranging from democrats to Communists. None of them had a broad or solid social base. In contrast, the Islamic forces were tightly organized. They could count on the strong religious convictions of millions of Iranians and had a dynamic and charismatic leader in Khomeini. Within ten days of his arrival in Iran, Khomeini was in control of the country. He appointed a provisional government, but real power lay with a fifteen-member Islamic Revolutionary Council that Khomeini had established while in exile. Bands of armed Revolutionary Guards were organized to counter the army, which Khomeini did not control, and intimidate any opponents. It took Khomeini and his supporters only three months to sweep aside anyone who wanted a secular regime. Protests from democratic groups against the perfunctory trials and immediate executions of hundreds of officials of the fallen regime were ignored.

At the end of March 1979, Iranians voted in a national referendum that asked a single question: did they want an Islamic republic? The official figures said that 92.5 percent of eligible voters cast ballots and of those, 92.8 percent voted for an Islamic republic. As of April 1, 1979, a monarchy that traced its roots back twenty-five hundred years to Cyrus the Great was gone. In its place was the Ayatollah Khomeini's newly declared Islamic Republic of Iran, the first Islamic state of that type in history.

THE ISLAMIC REPUBLIC UNDER KHOMEINI (1979–1989)

The year 1979 was one of revolutionary change and continuous turmoil. Khomeini and the Islamic clerics began a process of rapid and thorough Islamization of Iranian society. They banished programs and music from radio and television and closed down newspapers that did not support the Islamic Revolution. Women were forced to wear traditional Islamic clothing, including the veil, that covered their entire bodies. Banks, factories, and other businesses were nationalized. Political parties of all kinds were crippled. The only political organization that managed to survive the onslaught as a viable opposition was the Mujahrdeen Klaq (People's Holy Warriors), a group that was both Marxist and Islamist. It declared armed resistance against the Khomeini regime.

The new constitution, while providing for a parliament and a president to govern the country, placed all power firmly in the hands of Iran's Muslim clergy. The ultimate power was Khomeini himself, who became the country's spiritual leader—or supreme leader—for life. His powers included control of the armed forces and Revolutionary Guard, the right to declare war, and the authority to dismiss the president. His successor after his death would be chosen by the Assembly of Experts, an elected body of about eighty Islamic clerics. A twelve-member Council of Guardians, which included specialists on Islamic law who were appointed by the supreme leader, supervised the work of the parliament. Its job was to make sure all laws were consistent with Islamic teaching. The council also had the power to invalidate laws passed by parliament and determine who could run for president. The Sharia (Islamic law) became the law of the land in personal, criminal, and property matters, and the Shiite version of Islam became the country's official religion. Iran, in short, was being turned into a totalitarian Islamic society, although not without resistance. Tens of thousands of Iranians fled abroad. They included many wealthy people and supporters of the shah but also many of the country's most highly educated citizens. The departure of thousands of educated people and businesspeople helped cripple the economy. Iran continued to be rocked by demonstrations of workers and farmers hurt by economic decline, battles between rival political factions, political assassinations, and executions.

While all this was happening, on November 4, 1979, a group of radical students invaded the U.S. embassy in Tehran and seized sixty-six American hostages. Thirteen were released, but the Khomeini regime, which had labeled the United States the Great Satan and Iran's number-one enemy, refused to secure the release of the remaining captives. The United States broke diplomatic relations and imposed an economic boycott on Iran. A rescue attempt in April 1980 failed, badly embarrassing U.S. president Jimmy Carter. The crisis dragged on for 444 days, until January 20, 1981, when Carter left office and Ronald Reagan was inaugurated as president. Iran then released the hostages, but American-Iranian relations remained in a bitter deep freeze.

The end of the hostage crisis brought Iran little relief. Although the country held presidential and parliamentary elections in 1980, they were tightly controlled and the results were a foregone conclusion. The successful presidential candidate was a former adviser to Khomeini, Abolhassan Bani-Sadr. Bani-Sadr, who had studied economics, sociology, and Islamic law as a university student, was a relative moderate in the context of Iranian politics. He lasted barely eighteen months in office, until Khomeini engineered his removal in June 1981, after which Bani-Sadr fled to France. By 1981 political life was turning increasingly violent. In June a bomb killed seventy-four of Iran's leading Islamic politicians. The next month, another bomb killed the country's president and prime minister. The Khomeini regime responded with a full-scale attack on the Mujahrdeen Klaq, killing between five thousand and six thousand people over the next several years. By 1985 at least seven thousand political opponents of the regime of various stripes had been executed.

The worst crisis of the Islamic Republic's first decade erupted in September 1980 when Iraq invaded Iran. The Iraqi dictator Saddam Hussein feared the Iranian revolution might spread to his country. He calculated that an attack while the Khomeini regime was young and still relatively weak would cause its collapse. Hussein also hoped to use the turmoil in Iran to seize full control of the Shatt al-Arab, a tidal river on the Iran-Iraq border, and the oil-rich province of Khuzistan, a region populated by Arabs. The Iraqis enjoyed early victories, but then the Iranians regrouped. Their soldiers, fired by religious faith, fought with suicidal devotion and in 1981 and 1982 drove the Iraqis back. At that point, Khomeini refused an Iraqi peace offer. He demanded that Iraq first remove Hussein from power and pay Iran $150 billion in war damages. The war continued, turning into a bloody stalemate that dragged on for a total of eight years. Both sides attacked the other's cities, oil production facilities, and even oil tankers of neutral nations in the Persian Gulf. The Iraqi use of chemical weapons against Iranian troops was especially devastating and terrifying.

By 1988 defeats on the battlefield and soaring combat deaths finally convinced Khomeini to make peace. He said having to make peace with Iraq was like being forced "to drink the poison cup." Neither side made any gains in the long war. At least half a million soldiers on both sides were dead and two million people were injured. The war left Iran physically exhausted and financially bankrupt.

Iran's war with Iraq was forced on it by Iraqi aggression. At the same time, Iran could have ended the war in 1982 rather than 1988 had Khomeini not turned it into what amounted to a Shiite religious crusade. That crusade, in fact, dominated Iran's relations with the rest of the outside world. Khomeini denounced the regimes of the Arab states surrounding Iran for betraying Islam and proclaimed the goal of exporting the Iranian revolution to the entire Muslim world. Some of the worst tensions were with Saudi Arabia and the other Arab Persian Gulf states. Relations with Saudi Arabia neared rock bottom in 1987, when 275 Iranian pilgrims to *Mecca*, Islam's holiest city, died during rioting there.

Khomeini, meanwhile, bitterly denounced the West, especially the United States. To drive the point home, Iranian children regularly chanted "Death to America" in elementary schools. Iran became a leading supporter of international terrorist groups, mainly Arab groups in the Middle East, but also radical groups in Europe. Aside from the United States, a special target of hatred was Israel. The Khomeini regime financed a long list of murderous attacks against Israel by various Arab terrorist organizations, as well as attacks against Jewish communities elsewhere in the world. It also violently opposed any attempt, regardless of the source, to promote peace between Israel and the Arab states. Egypt therefore was subject to scathing Iranian denunciations for signing a peace treaty with Israel in 1979. Iran's position did not change after Khomeini's death in 1989. In 1999, twenty years after Egyptian president Anwar Sadat made peace with Israel, Tehran honored one of Sadat's assassins by naming a street after him.

THE ISLAMIC REPUBLIC AFTER KHOMEINI

The Ayatollah Khomeini died on June 6, 1989. Hundreds of thousands of people attended his funeral as the Islamic Republic mourned the passing of its founder and spiritual leader. Khomeini left his successors a revolution that was deeply entrenched, but also a country badly debilitated by war and burdened with a shattered economy. Their urgent task was to restore Iran to physical health, while simultaneously maintaining the dominance of Islamic values and the spirit of the Islamic Revolution.

The day after Khomeini's death, Iran's Assembly of Experts elected the *Ayatollah Ali Khamenei* as the country's supreme leader. A former student of Khomeini, Khamenei served as Iran's president from 1981 until his election as supreme leader. His replacement as president was another cleric, Ali Akbar Hashemi Rafsanjani, until then speaker of the Iranian parliament. Shortly after Rafsanjani's election, the post of prime minister was abolished and its powers transferred to the president.

Although Iran's supreme leader and president were both Islamic clerics, the differences between them reflected a larger division among the Islamic clerics who ruled Iran. Compared to the new supreme leader, Rafsanjani was relatively moderate and pragmatic. He wanted to focus on economic reform. He slightly toned down Iran's militant foreign policy in order to improve relations with Western Europe. Rafsanjani did not, however, intend to forsake the goal of spreading Iran's Islamic Revolution or reduce hostility to the United States or Israel. In any event, while the president generally was more popular with the Iranian people than his archconservative rivals, it was the conservatives who controlled the key levers of power and ultimately determined policy.

Rafsanjani's attempts to reform the economy were thwarted by impersonal and uncontrollable market forces as well as by conservative clerics. The fall in oil prices on international markets reduced government revenues and hurt the Iranian economy. Periodic protests testified to hardships endured by ordinary Iranians who had no other way of expressing their discontent. There were riots in several cities protesting cuts in state subsidies for basic goods in 1994. In 1995 the government, strapped for cash, doubled the price of petroleum products. This led to other price increases and, in April, to serious riots in the poor sections of Tehran.

The gulf between the relative moderates and the archconservatives among Iran's ruling clerics widened as a result of the presidential election of 1997. One of the four candidates approved by the Council of Guardians—it rejected 234—was Sayed Mohammad Khatami, a respected cleric with relatively moderate views. Khatami won the election with more than 69 percent of the vote and received especially strong support from women, young people, and the business community. Khatami's election was clear evidence that the conservative clerics who still held the important reins of power were increasingly out of touch with the people they ruled, especially with the younger generation. A publisher in Tehran explained the appeal that translated into so many votes: "Everybody was depressed. It seemed that laughing was forbidden. Khatami had a huge open smile. He showed he cared about people."

After his election, Khatami spoke openly about the need for economic reform and fewer restrictions on the lives of the people. Yet despite his popularity he could do little of substance because of conservative opposition. Conservatives dominated the 1998 elections to the Assembly of Experts. This was hardly a surprise since the candidates were carefully screened by the Council of Guardians, which disqualified virtually all moderates.

Whatever his problems at home, President Khatami was determined to improve Iran's relations with the outside world and end what, in effect, was two decades of self-imposed isolation. To that end, he traveled abroad. In the fall of 1998, Khatami addressed the UN General Assembly in New York. In March 1999, he became the first Iranian leader in two decades to set foot in Europe when he visited Italy and met with Pope John Paul II at the Vatican. But these and other foreign visits did not allay concerns about Iranian intentions that went far beyond the Persian Gulf.

Iran was known to have extensive programs to develop biological, chemical, and nuclear weapons. It also was developing long-range guided missiles, with ranges as long as 2,400 miles (3,600 km), capable of carrying nuclear warheads. Iran was seeking technological assistance for these programs from various sources, including China, North Korea, and Russia. Russia's eight-hundred-million-dollar deal to complete Iran's unfinished Bushehr nuclear power plant—which was started under the shah but whose construction was abandoned in the wake of Iran's 1979 revolution and the war with Iraq—was of particular concern to the United States. That plant easily could advance Iran's nuclear weapons program. Iran's effort to hire Russian scientists for their weapons programs also was worrisome. There was no doubt that Russian experts, lured by the promise of large salaries, were in Iran working to build weapons of mass destruction and guided missiles. Given Iran's militancy and its extensive support of Islamic terrorist groups, its ambitious weapons programs worried countries throughout the Middle East and beyond it.

THE POST-KHOMEINI GENERATION

In the spring of 1999, three couples in their twenties were strolling along a river high in the mountains overlooking Tehran. Nearby, others were enjoying the lush scenery and clear mountain air that provided a welcome escape from the tension and pollution of Iran's capital city. Suddenly, a stranger walked up to one of the young men and asked accusingly, "What are you doing? Why are you holding that woman's hand? Are you afraid someone will steal her?"

This incident said a great deal about the condition of Iran's twenty-year-old Islamic Revolution as it faced its third decade and a new millennium. The man who accosted the young couples was acting with the approval of Iran's conservative clerics. His actions reflected their determination to make sure all citizens behave according to strict Islamic practices. In this case, the couples, just by holding hands, had violated rules against men and women displaying affection in public. The reaction of the couples showed how difficult keeping behavior under control was becoming. The young people said nothing in public; that would be too dangerous. But in private, they expressed anger and resentment at the Islamic clergy that was interfering in their lives and not allowing them to enjoy themselves.

That attitude was widespread among the two-thirds of the Iranian population that was twenty-five or younger, too young to remember the shah and life before the Islamic Republic. Many were simply fed up with the dreary and humorless life the Islamic authorities continued to impose on them. They secretly went to underground merchants to rent or buy bootleg tapes of banned American movies such as *Big Momma's House* or *Hollow Man* or special television programs such as the annual Academy Awards. As of mid-2000, the going price to rent a tape in Tehran was the equivalent of about one dollar; the same tape could be bought for about eight dollars. Bootleg audiocassettes of music by performers ranging from Britney Spears and Madonna to the Backstreet Boys sold for about a dollar. Also popular were exiled Iranian artists living in places like Los Angeles. They included a famous singer named Googoosh, one of Iran's superstars before the 1979 Islamic Revolution, whose music combined Western styles with Persian traditions. Silent for twenty-one years before she left Iran in 2000, her performances in the United States were smuggled into Iran on audiocassettes and compact discs, where they then reached across the generations. As a political scientist once imprisoned under the shah observed:

> The younger generation has no attachment, no feeling for the revolution. When I teach the revolution, many of my students just look out the window and watch the clock. They say: "What about us? You had your revolution and your war. What's in it for us?" And I can't tell them the answer.

A young man in his late twenties, who had been lashed as punishment for being the lead singer in a rock band, went further. He dared to compare the Islamic Republic to the United States and to Iran before the revolution:

> We have no money and no amusement. I haven't seen America but have heard only good things about it, that you have freedom and an easy life there. Like we hear how it was in the Shah's time—a free and easy life. We loved the Shah. But we don't like this regime. This is not true Islam. . . . I wish we could go back to the old days. If only there could be a disco.

One of the most serious results of this frustration was growing drug addiction. Iran's border with Afghanistan, a major producer of opium, was an open tap for the flow of drugs. By 1999 Iran had at least 1.2 million drug addicts; 60 percent of the country's prison inmates were in jail for drug possession. Many of the drug addicts were jobless young men. In Islamshar, a town just south of Tehran, one young man in his twenties explained to an American reporter why there were so many drug addicts in his town:

> Look at all of us. We're all jobless. We have nothing to do. We try to do a little bit of business here and they arrest us as hooligans. That's why there are so many addicts here. It's the despair.

Throwing people in jail did not improve matters. By 2003 Iran officially admitted to about two million drug addicts, a figure some experts considered far too low, and in 2005 a UN report said that Iran had the highest drug addiction rate in the world.

Many young women also were deeply dissatisfied with life in Iran. The irony of this was that the regime's problems with women were in part the product of a policy that had improved their lives: providing educational opportunity. Under the Islamic Republic, the literacy rate among women more than doubled, rising to 74 percent. Whereas a third of university students were women before the revolution, by 1999 half were. One-third of all Iranian doctors were women, and women were active in many other professions. Yet the regime insisted they cover their entire bodies and their hair in public, live under laws that allow men to have several wives, and endure other forms of legal and social discrimination. Behind closed doors, especially in the cities, it was different. Many women wore makeup, dressed in fashionable Western clothing, and danced to Western music. The Islamic Revolution was kept outside. One twenty-two-year-old student, who prefers to wear T-shirts and jeans indoors, expressed support for President Khatami but also added, "We have an expression: whatever we have woven becomes threads instead of cloth. The Islamic regime has failed to win the loyalty of the children of the revolution."

Khatami himself understood that Iran's Islamic Revolution was in trouble. At the same time, notwithstanding his presumed moderation, he was entirely loyal to it and part of the Islamic power structure. In 1999, in a speech marking the revolution's twentieth anniversary, he warned the Iranian people, "Poisonous winds are blowing inside and outside the country. And enemies are attempting to separate you from the revolution."

Yet disillusionment had reached beyond the young generation to people who remembered the shah and what they considered a better life. While the youth complained about freedom they could only imagine, older people, worn down by two decades of economic privation, bitterly remembered better times. "We haven't had a good meal in 20 years," a thirty-seven-year-old farmer told a Western journalist. "I don't care about the revolution. The problem is we can't live." After twenty years, Iran's ruling clerics still firmly controlled the reins of power. But they no longer controlled what people were thinking.

The dissatisfaction of the young generation burst into the open in the summer of 1999. In July students at Tehran University protested against the slow pace of reform in general and new restrictions on freedom of the press in particular. The government responded with a violent raid on the student dorms by police and militant Islamic vigilantes that left dozens of people wounded and more than twenty people hospitalized. The student demonstrations then spread quickly to eighteen cities, involving tens of thousands of participants, and the regime responded with further violence. The student protesters loudly proclaimed their allegiance to President Khatami and his program of reform and no doubt meant what they said. Yet, in reality, their movement had become the most serious domestic threat to Iran's Islamic Republic in twenty years. When President Khatami finally spoke out five days after the protests began, it was not as a reformer. Echoing the remarks he made a few months earlier, he took pains to distance himself from the students, who he said were led by people with "devilish aims." The protests, he added, were "intended to attack the foundations of the system and lead the country into anarchy."

IRAN SINCE 2000

Khatami's statement underscored that the Ayatollah Khamenei and the Islamic clerical power structure were calling the shots. In the end, the regime's use of force and the threat of severe punishment brought the student protests to an end after nine days. Although reformist candidates won 70 percent of the seats in the parliamentary elections of 2000, conservative clerics continued to hold the key levers of power. One example of this was the campaign by the authorities that closed down more than thirty reformist newspapers and magazines in the months after those elections. Nor did Khatami's reelection in June 2001 with

200

THE

HANDBOOK

OF

THE

MIDDLE

EAST

77 percent of the vote have any noticeable effect on the ultra-conservative clerics who controlled Iran. After his election, the conservatives began a campaign of mass arrests, public floggings, and public executions. Supposedly intended to combat crime, the real goal was to intimidate and silence the reformists. Meanwhile, Khatami's attempts during 2002 to limit the power of the Council of Guardians to control who ran for office and to increase the president's power over the judiciary failed completely. In late 2002, a well-known writer closely associated with Khatami was sentenced to death for giving a speech to a university audience in which he questioned the idea that the Islamic clergy had divine authority. Eventually that sentence was commuted to four years in prison, but the point was made. In local elections held in 2003, the conservative candidates won decisively. The story was the same in parliamentary elections held in 2004. Before the election, the Council of Guardians banned more than two thousand candidates from running, including more than eighty sitting members of parliament and Khatami's own brother. Voter turnout was small, only a reported 51 percent overall and only 28 percent in Tehran. Conservatives won a solid majority of the seats, more than four times as many as the reformers.

The conservatives solidified their monopoly of power in the presidential election of 2005. As usual, the Council of Guardians vetted the field, eliminating hundreds of candidates, including all females. The winner in the June 2005 election was the mayor of Tehran, Mahmoud Ahmadinejad, a militant Islamist known both for his anti-Western, anti-Semitic views and the fiery rhetoric he used to express them. Shortly after his election, Ahmadinejad called for Israel to be "wiped off the map." He also called the Holocaust a myth. In May 2006, Ahmadinejad sent a letter to George W. Bush that, in effect, told the American president to convert to Islam.

These remarks by Iran's new president were not made in isolation. Similar statements commonly were heard from Iran's leaders. What made this language so disturbing to the international community, however, was that it was completely consistent with what Iran was doing. Iran was a country trying to project its power on a global scale. It clearly saw itself as the new leader of the Islamic world in its struggle against the West. According to the U.S. State Department, Iran in 2006 continued to be "the most active state sponsor of terrorism." Iran supported numerous terrorist groups, especially groups attacking Israel, such as Hezbollah in Lebanon—whose weapons and activities it directly controlled—and Hamas in the Gaza Strip. It also provided funding, training, and weapons to Palestinian terrorist groups such as the al-Aqsa Martyrs Brigades and Palestinian Islamic Jihad. In Iraq, Iran was providing weapons and training to violent Shiite groups to attack American troops. By 2006 the advanced rockets it supplied to Hezbollah in Lebanon, which generally were shipped via Syria, had a range of up to 120 miles (193 km) and could reach Tel Aviv. Further, Iran was using Hezbollah to set up monitoring posts along the Lebanon-Israeli border. Iran, which also supplied Hezbollah with a wide range of weapons other than rockets, thus was directly responsible for the 2006 war between Hezbollah and Israel in southern Lebanon that began after a deadly Hezbollah raid into Israel in July of that year.

Far worse, between 2003 and 2006, it also became clear that Iran was secretly developing nuclear weapons. In doing so, Iran was violating international law, since it had signed the Nuclear Non-Proliferation Treaty. Iran was carrying out its work both at known nuclear research facilities and at several secret sites, perhaps as many as thirty or more. In early 2004, it became known that Iran had received help from the head of Pakistan's nuclear program. (Pakistan had secretly built and tested atomic bombs in the 1990s.) In mid-2004, the International Atomic Energy Agency reported that Iran had produced small amounts of plutonium, and in April 2006 Iran announced it had succeeded in enriching uranium. However, the level announced was sufficient only for producing nuclear power, not nuclear weapons. Meanwhile, Iran continued its work on ballistic missiles. By 2006 its most powerful missile had a range of 1,200 miles (1,931 km), but it had missiles under development designed to fly 2,000 miles

(3,218 km) or more. Another potential source of long-range missiles was North Korea, which by 2006 had delivered disassembled missiles to Iran capable of reaching Europe.

Iran unconvincingly claimed its nuclear research was for peaceful purposes only and that it had every right to carry on its work. At the same time, it continued negotiations with various members of the international community, including the EU and Russia. The United States was on record that it would not allow Iran to acquire nuclear weapons. For its part, Iran continued to reject plans from the EU and Russia that would allow it to produce peaceful nuclear power but prevent it from building nuclear weapons. Iran raised the stakes further in August 2006 when it announced the plant it was building near the town of Arak to produce heavy water was operational. This was a clear sign that in addition to enriching uranium, Iran was working on the technology necessary to produce plutonium, which, like enriched uranium, can be used to make nuclear weapons. In March 2007, the UN Security Council passed a new resolution tightening economic sanctions on Iran, but these penalties fell far short of what the United States wanted and what would have a real impact on Iran's economy. The standoff continued and no one involved in the efforts to resolve the intensifying crisis was offering optimistic predictions of how it will end. Countries from the Middle East to Europe and beyond have a vital stake in what happens next.

THE ARABIAN PENINSULA: SAUDI ARABIA, KUWAIT, THE UNITED ARAB EMIRATES (UAE), BAHRAIN, QATAR, OMAN, YEMEN

The Arabian Peninsula is an arid plateau of about 1 million square miles (2.6 million sq. km) that looks like a gigantic boot. It juts out in a southeasterly direction from the Fertile Crescent toward the Gulf of Aden and the Arabian Sea, flanked by the Red Sea on the west and the Persian Gulf and Gulf of Oman on the east. Its enormous oil resources, the largest in the world, make what otherwise would be a barren backwater one of the most valuable pieces of real estate in the world.

As its name suggests, the Arabian Peninsula is the ancient homeland of the Arab people, who form a majority of the population of the Middle East. It is also the birthplace of Islam, the youngest of the world's three major monotheistic religions and the religion of most Middle Easterners. The peninsula has rarely been under the control of a single power. Ancient Middle Eastern empires from the Egyptian to the Persian, daunted by its enormous deserts, stopped their conquests at its northernmost fringe. Alexander the Great, Europe's first empire builder, who conquered the Persian Empire, stayed away completely. Even the mighty Roman Empire was limited to a tiny toehold on the peninsula's northwestern corner. The Ottoman Turks tried to grab it all but failed. The peninsula was unified by the Arabs themselves short-ly after the founding of Islam in the seventh century, but only for a short time. Several parts became independent when the Arabs expanded their conquests and moved their capital from Medina, in the western part of the peninsula, to Damascus, in what became Syria.

Fragile or not, the six monarchies of the Arabian Peninsula are enormously wealthy. They control about half of the world's known oil reserves and in three cases (Saudi Arabia, Kuwait, and the United Arab Emirates, or the UAE) are using up their resources at a slower rate than producers elsewhere in the world. In 1981 Saudi Arabia, Kuwait, the UAE, Bahrain, Qatar, and Oman formed the Gulf Cooperation Council (GCC). The GCC's main purpose was to promote regional security. It also worked to encourage economic cooperation. The GCC's mem-bers often are called the Gulf states.

In three of the Gulf states—Kuwait, Qatar, and the UAE—noncitizens, mainly foreign Arabs and south Asians, make up most of the workforce and the overwhelming majority of the population. All six states were hurt by low oil prices that pre-vailed, aside from a few exceptional years, from the late 1980s through mid-1999. They were forced to cut their budgets, which supported extravagant welfare states for their citizens. In December 1998, Saudi Arabia's Crown Prince Abdullah warned that the boom days were over, but the warning was premature. In March 1999, the Gulf states met their comembers of the Organization of Petroleum Exporting Countries (*OPEC*), the eleven-nation cartel whose member nations control three-quar-ters of the world's known oil reserves. OPEC's members agreed to cut oil production by about 5 percent, and with less oil avail-able on international markets, prices rose quickly, tripling over the next eighteen months. This huge price increase provided a huge income windfall for the oil-producing Gulf states. The surge in world oil prices between 2003 and 2006 brought these states an even greater windfall. Beyond that, their enormous oil reserves remained a guarantee of continued great wealth for a long time to come.

SAUDI ARABIA

Saudi Arabia is a land of contrasts and contradictions. The driest country in the world, its sands hold the world's largest pools of oil. Although it forbids the practice of any religion other than Islam, it depends on non-Islamic countries for protection against its powerful Islamic neighbors. Ruled by a fundamentalist Islamic regime, it nonetheless is threatened by subversion from even stricter fundamentalist movements. Despite billions of dollars spent on the most modern armaments, it is militarily weak. Although its economy has modernized, its political system remains traditional. While it imports Western technology and expertise, it tries to keep out Western ideas and cultural influences. And despite enormous oil revenues and a relatively small population, during much of the 1990s it was unable to balance its budget.

GEOGRAPHY, ECONOMY, PEOPLE

GEOGRAPHY

Saudi Arabia has an area of approximately 865,000 square miles (2,240,000 sq. km), about one-third the size of the United States. It occupies about 80 percent of the Arabian Peninsula, virtually all of it desert. Saudi Arabia's northern neighbors are Kuwait, Iraq, and Jordan. Coastlines along the Gulf of Aqaba and the Red Sea form its western border. To the south are Yemen and Oman, and to the east are the UAE, Qatar, and the Persian Gulf. Saudi Arabia's desert borders with Oman and the UAE remain undefined. Its longstanding border dispute with

Yemen finally was settled in a series of agreements between 2000 and 2006. In 2004 Saudi Arabia began building a security barrier—actually a huge pipe filled with concrete—along the border to prevent infiltration by Islamists it blamed for terrorist bombings and shootings in the kingdom. Saudi Arabia for many years shared two neutral zones, one with Iraq and the other with Kuwait. In 1975 Saudi Arabia and Iraq divided their zone. The neutral zone shared with Kuwait was divided in 1966, but revenues from oil resources are shared.

There are no permanent rivers in Saudi Arabia. Its parched Rub al-Khali (Empty Quarter) desert in the south, an area as large as Texas, can go without rain for ten years. Northern regions get some rain, usually between 4 and 8 inches (10 to 20 cm). Summer temperatures in the interior reach 129°F (54°C); the coastal areas are not much cooler and are extremely humid. Winters are mild, although northern and central regions can see nighttime temperatures drop below freezing.

In addition to the Empty Quarter desert, Saudi Arabia has four other main regions. The largest is the barren central plateau, called the Nejd. It varies in altitude from 2,000 feet (600 m) in the east to about 5,000 feet (1,520 m) in the west. The rugged northwestern region along the Red Sea—there is almost no coastal plain—is called the Hejaz. The Asir region extends down the Red Sea coast from the Hejaz to the border with Yemen. It features Saudi Arabia's highest mountains, gets more rain than any other part of the country, and has a fertile, but narrow, coastal plain. Saudi Arabia's barren Eastern Province along the Persian Gulf is the site of its enormous oil fields.

The two most important cities in Saudi Arabia are Mecca (population 965,000) and Medina (population 608,000). Located in the Hejaz, they are Islam's two holiest cities. Mecca, the birthplace of the Prophet Mohammad, is Islam's holiest site, the place to which every Muslim tries to make a pilgrimage, or hajj, once in his or her lifetime. *Riyadh* (population 2.8 million), in the Nejd, is the country's capital and largest city. Jiddah (population 2 million), on the Red Sea coast about 50

miles (80 kilometers) west of Mecca, is Saudi Arabia's administrative capital.

ECONOMY

When the twentieth century began, Saudi Arabia's economy was based on camel raising by nomads, limited farming, fishing and shipping along the coast, and a little commerce. Taxes on pilgrims making the hajj was an important source of income. Altogether, it added up to a very meager living for most of the population. Everything changed with the discovery of oil in 1938. Large-scale production began after World War II. In 1969 revenues reached one billion dollars. They reached $25 billion in 1975 and hit a peak of $110 billion in 1981, after which they declined along with world demand.

Modern Saudi Arabia's economy is completely dominated by and dependent on oil. After oil was discovered in Saudi Arabia, its resources were developed by the Arabian-American Oil Company (Aramco), a consortium of American oil companies. The Saudi government received a percentage of the profits. Between 1973 and 1980, the Saudi government bought 100 percent of Aramco. In 1988 it changed the company's name to the Saudi Arabian Oil Company.

Saudi Arabia's fourteen major fields contain one-fourth of the world's reserves, almost three hundred billion barrels, and it is the world's largest producer and exporter of oil. Oil revenues make up three-quarters of government revenues—Saudi Arabians pay no taxes—and almost 95 percent of all export earnings. Revenues, however, have fluctuated, depending on the world price of oil. Depending on a variety of economic and political factors, Saudi production of oil in recent decades has ranged from between five and ten million barrels per day. During the second half of the 1990s, the government's annual oil revenues ranged from about thirty-eight to fifty-five billion dollars. Saudi Arabia also has other mineral resources, including significant deposits of natural gas.

Saudi Arabia has played a central role in OPEC. OPEC is dominated by Middle Eastern oil-producing countries and has tried to maintain a high price for its members by controlling production. Usually Saudi Arabia has played a moderating role in OPEC, trying to avoid excessive price increases. Saudi reasons for moderation reflect self-interest. Stable prices are the best way to generate the long-term revenues the kingdom needs for economic development. The Saudis calculate also that moderate oil prices will help ensure that the industrialized nations will not be encouraged to develop alternative sources of energy that might eventually replace oil. At the same time, the Saudis have supported using oil as a political weapon. They played a central role in the Arab oil boycott of the United States after the United States supported Israel in the 1973 Yom Kippur War.

Oil revenues have paid for a generous program of social services that includes free education and medical care for all Saudi citizens. Gasoline and electricity prices are kept low by government subsidies. Oil has made millionaires and even billionaires out of princes in the Saudi royal family and other well-connected Saudi businessmen. It has paid for huge construction projects that have transformed Saudi Arabia's old cities and created entirely new ones. Oil money has paid for building expensive modern factories that produce petrochemicals, steel, and cement.

Oil revenues also have financed the construction of more than thirty plants to desalinize (take the salt out of) seawater. These plants currently supply Saudi Arabia with more than 70 percent of its drinking water.

Oil revenues also pay for an expensive project to extract underground fossil water for use in agriculture. Fossil water is underground water left over from many thousands of years ago when the local climate was wetter. The problem is that, like oil, this water is not renewable. The Saudis are using it to irrigate newly developed wheat fields. They now grow all the wheat they need and even export some. But Saudis are eating and selling wheat that is the world's most expensive to produce. It would be much more economical for the country to import the wheat it needs. Instead, largely as a matter of pride, the Saudi government subsidizes the wheat so it can find customers at home and abroad. Meanwhile, nobody is certain when the irreplaceable fossil water will run out, although twenty-five years is a good guess. Other Saudi crops, grown on oases or on the limited fertile land in the Asir region, include dates, tomatoes, barley, and bananas. With its rapidly expanding population, Saudi Arabia must import about two-thirds of its food.

While the Saudi government has used its oil revenues to develop the country, it has also wasted vast sums of money. Extravagant public projects—the use of fossil water for farming is an example—poor planning, wildly opulent palaces, and other perks for a royal family with four thousand princes have drained the government treasury. Eighty percent of the country's budget regularly has gone to pay salaries of public sector employees. Because the government controls the oil industry and so many other businesses, private enterprise accounts for only 35 percent of the country's gross domestic product. War has been another large expense. The Saudis spent more than twenty-five billion dollars to support Iraq during the Iran-Iraq War. The Gulf War cost them another sixty-five billion dollars. Foreign-made weapons for the Saudi military cost tens of billions more. These expenses, combined with reduced oil revenues in the 1980s and 1990s, led to budget deficits, forcing the Saudi government to cut expenses and undertake other reforms. In 1999 the budget deficit reached almost ten billion dollars and forced the Saudi government to borrow abroad. Higher oil prices wiped out most of the deficit in 2000. Then the surge in oil prices between 2003 and 2006 created a budget surplus while at the same time providing funds for new development projects.

These problems aside, Saudi Arabia is still fabulously rich in oil. It has large investments abroad and a growing industrial base. These assets give it an economic future that most countries would find enviable.

PEOPLE
Saudi Arabia did not take a census until 1974. Current estimates put the total citizen population at about 24.5 million. There also are more than 5.5 million foreigners living in Saudi Arabia, mainly workers who are vital to keeping the economy running.

Some are technical experts from the United States, Western Europe, and various Arab states whose skills are vital to the oil industry and other modern businesses. Most are unskilled or manual laborers, mainly from Egypt, Yemen, South Asia, and Southeast Asia, who do the jobs that Saudis are unwilling to do. Most employed Saudis work for the government.

About 85 percent of Saudi citizens are Sunni Muslims who belong to the ultraconservative Wahhabi sect. The rest are Shiites, including a large percentage of the population of the oil-rich Eastern Province. Ninety percent are ethnic Arabs. Less than 10 percent of the Saudi population follows the traditional Arab nomadic way of life. About three-quarters of the people live in urban areas.

SAUDI GOVERNMENT AND SOCIETY

Saudi Arabia is an absolute monarchy. It has no legislature, and political parties are banned. Since its founding in the 1920s, it has been ruled by its founder, King Abdel Aziz al-Saud (usually called Ibn Saud), and five of his forty-four sons: Saud (1953–1964), Faisal (1964–1975), Khalid (1975–1982), Fahd (1982–2005), and *Abdullah* (2005–present). That Saudi Arabia is the world's only country named for a family is a reflection of the absolute power that family holds.

The king governs by royal decree and appoints all important government officials. However, he does not make his decisions without consulting his cabinet, leading members of the royal family, and religious authorities. The king also must have the support of key members of the royal family. The most important government posts such as minister of defense or commander of the military are held by royal princes. In 1964, after a long struggle, leading members of the royal family forced the woefully incompetent King Saud to abdicate in favor of his brother Faisal. Still, there is no other major country where power is held by so small a group that rules by traditions dating from a tribal past. In 1992 King Fahd issued what is called the

Basic Law of Government, which serves as Saudi Arabia's first constitution. He also established a Consultative Council that began operation in 1993. These measures created some political window dressing for the monarchy but did nothing to alter or limit its power.

Saudi society operates under tight religious control. In the eighteenth century, the House of Saud, ruler of a section of the Nejd, adopted the strict fundamentalist doctrine of the Wahhabi sect. The Wahhabis believed Islam had been corrupted over the centuries and wanted all Muslims to return to what they considered a pure form of worship. They opposed all luxuries, decoration of mosques, and vices such as coffee and tobacco. Wahhabi influence grew along with the power of the House of Saud, which in the 1920s won control over most of the Arabian Peninsula.

In Saudi Arabia, the public practice of any faith other than Islam is forbidden. Non-Muslims may not approach within 15 miles (24 km) of Mecca and may visit only the outskirts of Medina. All forms of public entertainment are banned, including theaters and movies, as are alcoholic beverages. The only exceptions are an annual folklore festival and sporting events such as camel racing and soccer. The special religious police, the *mutaween*, enforces Islamic orthodoxy. Even non-Muslims must be careful not to run afoul of the mutaween, whose official name once was the Committee for the Propagation of Virtue and the Prevention of Vice. Sharia (Islamic law) is the law of the land. This contrasts with the situation in other Arab countries, where Sharia is only the basis of law, a formulation that allows modifications of and alternatives to Sharia's harsh punishments. Those punishments—including death for adultery, amputation of the hand for theft, floggings for various crimes, and public executions—are enforced in Saudi Arabia.

The strict observance of Islamic law, reinforced by tribal and customary law, also severely limits the status of women in Saudi Arabia. In legal cases, a woman's testimony is worth only half a man's, and her share of a family inheritance is only half a man's. Women make up less than 6 percent of the labor force.

Women are strictly segregated from men in business and public life. All workplaces, restaurants, and schools are segregated by gender. City buses have separate sections for women, and women may not travel without a male relative on intercity buses or trains. Women are not allowed to drive.

Women have made some progress in Saudi Arabia. Half of all Saudi women are literate, versus only 2 percent forty years ago, and literacy among women aged fifteen to twenty-four is 95 percent. Girls account for close to half the children in Saudi schools. Educated Saudi women want to work and participate in public life and have said so openly. But they face strong conservative resistance. In fact, the enforcement of public segregation has been stricter in recent years. Saudi Arabia lagged behind the times for many years in yet another important way: slavery was not legally abolished there until the 1960s.

MODERN SAUDI ARABIAN HISTORY

Saudi Arabia was one of the Arab states that emerged from the wreckage of the Ottoman Empire after World War I. Between 1919 and 1926, Ibn Saud defeated a series of rivals to unify about 80 percent of the Arabian Peninsula under his rule in what was called the Kingdom of the Hejaz and Nejd. The last unsuccessful challenger was the leader of the Hashemite family, Hussein Ibn Ali, great-grandfather of Jordan's King Hussein. Saud formally changed the country's name to the Kingdom of Saudi Arabia in 1932. Although Saudi Arabia officially was neutral in World War II, Ibn Saud was one of the few Arab leaders to strongly favor the Allies. His country became a charter member of the United Nations and immediately lined up with the West during the Cold War.

Saudi Arabian history since World War II is primarily a story of the regime's search for security against both internal and external enemies. Internally, the House of Saud has tried to keep the general population quiet by using oil revenues to give them a high standard of living. It has sought the support of prominent Sunni clerics to limit the influence of Islamic fundamentalists critical of the royal family for its friendship with the West and its luxurious lifestyle. It has also tried to keep Western influences from penetrating Saudi society. When all else has failed, it has resorted to force and repression to keep order.

Externally, the Saudis generally have opposed radical Arab regimes. They have resorted to bribery in the form of foreign aid to win the acceptance of countries with secular regimes, such as Egypt, Syria, and Iraq. The Saudis also have tried to settle intra-Arab disputes in order to keep the Middle East stable and to build bridges between conservative Arab regimes. They have sought support and bought weapons from the Western democracies, while keeping them at arm's length to avoid criticism from fellow Arabs, whether nationalist or Islamic. From the 1940s onward, Saudi Arabia lined up with the rest of the Arab world against Israel's right to exist. It joined the rest of the Arab world in denouncing Egypt's 1979 peace treaty with Israel. The Saudis also provided generous aid to the PLO until the PLO supported Iraq after its 1990 invasion of Kuwait. However, after 1993 they supported the PLO-Israeli peace process. At the same time, that support has been qualified by a declaration by the country's chief religious leader that any peace with Israel, in the tradition of the Prophet Mohammad, must be temporary. Meanwhile, during the 1980s and 1990s, the main external threats were its powerful neighbors Iran and Iraq.

THE SONS OF ABDEL AZIZ AL-SAUD (IBN SAUD)

Ibn Saud died in 1953 and was succeeded by his son Saud. During Saud's reign, there was considerable tension between Saudi Arabia and the radical Nasser regime in Egypt. Wasteful and incompetent, Saud was pushed aside in favor of his brother Faisal in 1964. Under Faisal, Saudi Arabia in 1967 strongly supported Egypt, Syria, and Jordan in their unsuccessful war against Israel. While Faisal's reign was relatively stable, there were several rumored coup attempts, the most serious of which occurred in 1969. During 1973 Saudi Arabia led the Arab boycott against the United States for supporting Israel against Egypt and Syria during the Yom Kippur War. The boycott lasted until 1974. The next year, Faisal was assassinated by one of his many nephews and succeeded by his brother Khalid.

Khalid's reign saw the first serious Islamic fundamentalist outburst against the Saudi regime. It occurred in 1979 when several hundred Sunni Muslim fundamentalists seized control of the Grand Mosque in Mecca. It took two weeks and hundreds of casualties before Saudi authorities retook the mosque. In early 1980, sixty-three fundamentalists, including several Egyptians and Yemenis, were publicly beheaded for their part in the incident. Khalid's reign also saw Saudi oil revenues start to decline as world prices fell, a development that marked the beginning of the kingdom's long-term budgetary problems.

Khalid died in 1982 and was succeeded by yet another brother, Fahd. It was during King Fahd's long reign that Saudi Arabia faced its most serious security threats yet. The Iranian revolution, with its militant Shiite fundamentalism, was not welcomed in Saudi Arabia. When Iraq attacked Iran, the Saudis backed Iraq, notwithstanding their fear of Iraq and Baghdad's role as the aggressor in the war. They urged the rest of what they called the Arab nation to do likewise. Saudi-Iranian tensions gradually increased. They reached a deadly flash point in July 1987 when a bloody confrontation took place between Iranian pilgrims making the hajj and Saudi authorities at Mecca's Grand Mosque. More than four hundred pilgrims died, including almost three hundred Iranians. In 1988, the year the Iran-Iraq War ended, Saudi Arabia broke diplomatic relations with Iran.

Soon a new tiger, an Arab one, was at the gate. It was Iraq, the beneficiary of billions of dollars of Saudi aid during the Iran-Iraq War. In 1990 Iraq invaded and overran Kuwait, the small oil-rich state squeezed between Iraq and Saudi Arabia. There was little doubt that Iraqi dictator Saddam Hussein had designs on Saudi territory and oil. Saudi foreign policy lay in ruins. All the aid it had given Iraq had not bought security. Despite billions of dollars of high-tech Western weapons, the Saudi army was no match for Iraq's battle-hardened forces.

King Fahd had to call for Western troops to protect his country from Saddam Hussein and Iraq. Eventually more than five hundred thousand foreign troops, mainly Americans but also Europeans and contingents from Egypt, Syria, and several other Arab states, arrived in Saudi Arabia. In the Gulf War that followed, that coalition routed Iraqi troops from Kuwait. However necessary from a military point of view, the entire operation infuriated the Saudi regime's fundamentalist critics, who feared and loathed the West. It also demonstrated Saudi Arabia's inability to defend itself. In addition, in the wake of the Gulf War, the Saudis broke relations with Yemen, Jordan, and the PLO as punishment for supporting Iraq. They also ended the six million dollar monthly stipend they had been giving the PLO since 1989 and expelled thousands of Palestinian and about eight hundred thousand Yemeni workers from the country.

During the 1990s, the main threats to the Saudi monarchy came from internal Islamic fundamentalist groups. It was to broaden the monarchy's base of support in the face of mounting fundamentalist criticism that King Fahd in 1992 announced a new Basic Law and established a Consultative Council. These steps had no noticeable effect on the fundamentalists, who in 1993 announced the formation of a Committee for the Defense of Legitimate Rights (CDLR). When the government disbanded the organization two weeks later, it moved its operations to London, immediately causing tension between Riyadh and London. In 1994 Osama bin Laden, a billionaire Saudi fundamentalist living in exile and one of the world's most notorious terrorists, announced his support for the CDRL.

King Fahd tried another approach to counter fundamentalist influence in 1994 by appointing a Supreme Council of Islamic Affairs. Its job was to ensure that the country's policies were consistent with Islamic principles. At the same time, the government arrested more than 150 Islamic militants and clerics on charges of sedition. The next year, Fahd reshuffled his cabinet to bring in some younger experts. However, he left the most important ministries, including defense, internal affairs, and foreign affairs, in the hands of royal princes.

These measures did not solve the problem. In November
1995, a car bomb set by Sunni Muslim extremists exploded outside the headquarters of the Saudi Arabian National Guard,
killing seven foreigners, including five Americans. Four Saudis
were executed for the crime in April 1996. Two months later,
another bomb killed nineteen American soldiers and wounded
nearly four hundred at the U.S. military's Khobar Towers housing complex near the city of Dhahran. This time Shiites linked
to Iran were responsible. American officials criticized the Saudi
investigations of both incidents as being designed to withhold
critical information rather than reveal it.

SAUDI ARABIA SINCE 2000

The new century did not begin well for Saudi Arabia, at least not
in terms of foreign affairs and public relations. On September
11, 2001, al-Qaeda terrorists crashed hijacked passenger air-
planes into the World Trade Center in New York City and the
Pentagon in Washington, D.C., killing more than three thousand people. While the Saudi government immediately condemned the attack, it also was true that al-Qaeda's leader was
Osama bin Laden, who came from one of the kingdom's richest
and most prominent families. Fifteen of the nineteen terrorists
who carried out the attacks were Saudi citizens. Beyond that,
Saudi Arabia was one of only three countries (the other two were
Pakistan and the UAE) that until September 11 recognized
Afghanistan's Taliban regime, which had sheltered bin Laden
and al-Qaeda.

That so many of the al-Qaeda terrorists came from Saudi
Arabia could not be considered a surprise, given what young
Saudis are taught. As late as 2006, *after* reforms had been made,
Freedom House reported that "the Saudi public school religious
curriculum continues to propagate an ideology of hatred toward
the 'unbeliever,' that is, Christians, Jews, Shiites, Sufis, Sunni
Muslims who do not follow Wahhabi doctrine, Hindus, atheists
and others." Freedom House cited many examples of this from
textbooks, including the following from a ninth-grade text:
"Jews and Christians are the enemies of the believers, and

cannot approve of Muslims."Meanwhile, some experts pointed out that for years, billions of Saudi dollars had been funding radical Wahhabi ideology, the same thinking that had produced al-Qaeda, in mosques all over the world, from Asia to Europe to America.

Saudi Arabia benefited enormously from the world rise in oil prices between 2003 and 2006 that saw prices top seventy dollars per barrel. In 2005 the kingdom, after many delays, finally joined the World Trade Organization. At the same time, the country still had a serious unemployment problem, in part because of rapid population growth. Because young Saudis either were unwilling or not sufficiently trained to take many jobs, the kingdom's economy depended on the work of millions of foreign workers.

Far more problematic was the combination of Saudi Arabia's outdated and brittle political system and the age of its leaders. In August 2005, King Faud, ill for many years, died. Abdullah, his half brother and the new king, actually had been in charge since the mid-1990s. While in good health, King Abdullah was eighty-two upon officially taking command. The prince next in line was past eighty. Behind them were several brothers in their late sixties or early seventies. After them stood a long line of grandsons. Everything is complicated by a Saudi law allowing the king to name his own successor, which conflicts with the tradition that the eldest surviving brother of the founding king should inherit the throne, as well as the obvious necessity, sooner or later, for a younger generation to begin leading the country. As one Western diplomat noted about the remaining sons of Ibn Saud who might become king, "What you have is a bunch of leaders who, even if they had lots of determination, would just be plain old." Saudi Arabia should have no trouble coming up with another aging leader after King Abdullah dies. The challenge will be to update its political system so it will have effective leadership in a world that shows little mercy to those who lag behind.

GEOGRAPHY, ECONOMY, PEOPLE

Kuwait is a gravelly patch of desert dotted with a few oases and some salt marshes at the northwest corner of the Persian Gulf. Its area of 6,880 square miles (17,818 sq. km) makes it slightly smaller than New Jersey. Kuwait's ten offshore islands include Bubiyan (the largest) and Warba, which sit astride the Shatt al-Arab and until recently were claimed by Iraq. In fact, Iraq at times has claimed all of Kuwait and tried unsuccessfully to annex the country in 1990, an act of aggression that led to the Gulf War. A neutral zone along Kuwait's border with Saudi Arabia was divided in 1969 in an agreement that provided for the two countries to share revenue from the zone's oil deposits. Kuwait has direct borders with only two neighbors: Iraq to the north and west and Saudi Arabia to the south. Its eastern border is the Persian Gulf. Still, its proximity to Iraq means Kuwait must get along in a dangerous neighborhood. Furthermore, not far across a sliver of Iraqi territory and beyond a slice of the Persian Gulf is Iran, whose Islamic Revolution constitutes another serious threat to Kuwaiti security.

Kuwait gets very little rain, and most of that comes in the form of sudden cloudbursts between October and April. It must import or desalinize most of its drinking water. Six huge oil-powered plants desalinize water from the Persian Gulf. Kuwait's desalinated water is expensive, two dollars per cubic meter, about ten times the cost of water in Chicago, but Kuwaiti consumers do not feel the pain because the government absorbs approximately 90 percent of the cost.

Sand and dust storms lash Kuwait throughout the year, especially in the spring. The summers are brutally hot, although not as humid as in other parts of the Persian Gulf region. Winters are mild.

Kuwait is rich because of its geology. Its sands cover almost one hundred billion barrels of oil, more than 9 percent of the world's total resources. Only Saudi Arabia, Iraq, and possibly the UAE have larger oil deposits than Kuwait. Its economy is totally

KUWAIT

- ✪ Capital city
- ○ City
- — International border
- --- Unofficial border

dependent on oil and income from foreign investments bought with oil profits. Oil and refined petroleum products account for almost all of Kuwait's exports and 75 percent of government revenues. Oil refining is the country's main industry. Aside from fish caught in offshore gulf waters, Kuwait must import all its food.

KUWAITIS AND NON-KUWAITIS

A highly unusual and fundamental characteristic of Kuwait's population is the ratio of Kuwaitis to foreign nationals. Since its oil boom, foreigners have done most of the work in Kuwait, especially the difficult or unpleasant jobs. The share of foreigners living in Kuwait passed 50 percent around 1970; soon more than two-thirds of the population was non-Kuwaiti. The largest single foreign group was Palestinians, who in 1990 numbered four hundred thousand, a figure about four-fifths as large as the Kuwaiti population. Additional foreign workers came from other Arab states, Iran, Pakistan, and India, while skilled personnel who came to manage the oil industry generally were Americans or Europeans.

In 1991, after invading Iraqi forces were expelled from Kuwait, the government decided to reduce the number of foreign workers in the country. Most Palestinians were expelled, accused by the Kuwaiti government of supporting the Iraqi occupiers and collaborating with them. Only about twenty thousand were allowed to remain. Workers from other countries also were forced to leave, and restrictions were placed on foreign workers attempting to enter the country. Still, Kuwaitis remained a minority in their own country. As of mid-2006, about 2.4 million people lived in Kuwait. Of those, about 1.3 million, almost 60 percent, were foreigners.

Currently, Arabs—Kuwaiti and non-Kuwaiti—account for about three-quarters of Kuwait's total population. The largest non-Arab groups are South Asians (9 percent) and Iranians (4 percent). Islam is the country's official religion. About 90 percent of Kuwait's inhabitants are Muslims, with Sunnis outnumbering Shiites more than two to one. Christians, Hindus, and Parsis together account for most of the remaining people. Virtually the entire population lives in urban areas, the largest of which is *Kuwait City*, the capital (population 280,000).

One reason such a low percentage of the country's population is Kuwaiti is that it is extremely difficult for outsiders to become citizens. Many descendants of families that have lived in Kuwait for generations are denied citizenship. Once they become citizens, naturalized Kuwaitis may not vote for twenty years; before 1995 the wait was thirty years.

OIL WEALTH AND FINANCIAL PROBLEMS

Kuwait's enormous oil revenues and the additional revenues from foreign investments enabled the government to provide the population with extensive social benefits. All Kuwaiti citizens receive free education, and all residents, including foreigners, enjoy free health care. Most Kuwaiti citizens who work hold government jobs at excellent salaries. Among the many benefits and subsidies Kuwaitis receive is a $230,000 interest-free mortgage when they marry. However, in the 1990s, Kuwait experienced some economic problems. The total damage from the Gulf War and Iraqi occupation was a staggering $170 billion. Furthermore, like the other oil-rich Persian Gulf states, Kuwait was hurt by the decline of world oil prices. Low oil prices reduced government revenue and made it increasingly difficult for Kuwait to maintain its opulent social welfare system. The financial squeeze was made worse by falling income from Kuwait's investments abroad, whose value declined from about one hundred billion dollars to forty billion dollars because of the huge cost of rebuilding after the Gulf War. During the 1990s, Kuwait therefore had a string of budget deficits, although they shrank as oil prices rose after mid-1999 and disappeared as world oil prices surged after 2003.

Still, the financial problems of the late 1990s left some Kuwaitis, especially the rapidly growing segment of the population under twenty, concerned about the future. Most young Kuwaiti citizens had grown up in a world of luxurious entitlements and expected to continue to enjoy them. As one perplexed Kuwaiti youth asked in early 1999, while fellow teenagers raced their expensive sports cars along the seacoast, "With all our oil, why should life be harder for us than it was for our parents?" Since Kuwait still had a per capita income of twenty-three thousand dollars, one of the highest in the world, that complaint probably seemed unreasonable to most non-Kuwaitis.

MODERN KUWAITI HISTORY

Kuwait means "little fort" in Arabic, which is what Kuwait City was into the early 1920s, when it was still surrounded by a mud wall. The city dates from a settlement established in the early eighteenth century by arrivals from the central part of the Arabian Peninsula. The al-Sabah family, which rules Kuwait today, was selected around 1760 by local settlers to manage local affairs and handle their relations with the Ottoman Empire. In this pre-oil era, the local economy was based on pearling, fishing, and trade. In 1899 Kuwait's reigning sheikh put his domain under British protection, mainly to resist Ottoman claims to his territory. Oil exploration began in 1934; the first major strike was made within four years. Full independence came in 1961, at which point Iraq claimed sovereignty over Kuwait. The Iraqis dropped that claim, at least temporarily, in 1963, the year Kuwait joined the Arab League. A constitution adopted in 1962 provided for an elected parliament that has the power to pass laws, an institution unique among the Persian Gulf monarchies. Real power, however, remained with the ruling prince, or emir, who appoints the country's ministers and can dissolve the assembly and suspend the constitution. In 1977 the emir dissolved parliament for the first time. He reinstituted it four years later with reduced powers. The emir also dissolved parliament in 1986 and 1999.

In the decades after independence, Kuwait used its oil wealth to build modern air-conditioned cities, roads, power plants, hospitals, harbor facilities, and much more. In 1975 it took full control of its oil resources from foreign oil companies. Kuwait went through an economic crisis in 1982 when its stock market collapsed amid shady deals, causing billions of dollars in losses. In foreign affairs, it tried to guarantee its security by providing millions of dollars of aid to poorer, but militarily more powerful, Arab states such as Egypt and Syria. Kuwait gave Iraq billions of dollars in aid during the Iran-Iraq War (1980–1988), in part because it feared Iran but also as protection money to Iraq.

The strategy did not work. In August 1990, deeply in debt and tempted by its small neighbor's oil resources, Iraq invaded and annexed Kuwait. The ruling family and much of the Kuwaiti elite fled the country. During the six-month occupation that followed, Iraqi forces carried out a campaign of plunder, murder, torture, and rape. The country was liberated by an American-led coalition of European and Middle Eastern nations in February 1991. Before they retreated, the Iraqis set fire to more than five hundred oil wells, causing devastating environmental destruction.

At enormous cost, Kuwait repaired the physical destruction the Iraqis left behind. During 1991 and 1992, it signed agreements with the United States, Britain, and France to protect itself from foreign aggression. Foreign residents considered potentially subversive, particularly Palestinians, were expelled. But Kuwait remained insecure, largely because of its antiquated political system. There was internal opposition to the absolute power of the emir and the royal family. Some opponents called for democratic reform, most prominently a secular group formed in 1997 called the National Democratic Rally. It was the only political organization in Kuwait whose leadership included a woman. More serious opposition came from conservative Islamic forces. They won a majority in parliament in 1992 and again in 1997, when a majority of the parliament demanded that Sharia become the sole, rather than a source of, Kuwaiti law. Conservative Muslims also opposed a decree issued in May 1999 by Kuwait's ruler, or emir, Sheikh Jaber al-Ahmad al-Sabah, granting voting rights to Kuwaiti women. However, the decree required the approval of parliament, which narrowly rejected it in November. The emir responded the next month by choosing a woman, a member of his family who advocates full political rights for women, to be Kuwait's undersecretary of education. Finally, after complicated maneuvering, in May 2005, the parliament narrowly granted women the right to vote. Islamists who opposed the measure did win one concession: the new law's wording suggested that men and women would vote at separate polling places.

Soon there was more political change. In January 2006, having ruled for almost thirty years, Sheikh Jaber al-Ahmad al-Sabah died. His immediate successor was in very poor health and unfit to rule. After ten days of tense negotiations among members of the al-Sabah family, he abdicated, just after the parliament voted to remove him from office. The new emir was *Sheikh Sabah al-Ahmad al-Sabah*. He ruled over a very wealthy country, but one whose wealth did not necessarily guarantee a secure future.

The UAE is a federation of seven sheikhdoms formed in 1971 when the British withdrew from the Persian Gulf region. It is dominated by *Abu Dhabi*, by far its largest and the richest member. Abu Dhabi has about 85 percent of the UAE's approximately 32,000 square miles (83,600 sq. km) of territory and 40 percent of its population. Most important, it has the bulk of the UAE's estimated ninety-eight billion barrels of oil—almost 10 percent of the world's total reserves—and huge deposits of natural gas. The other two UAE sheikhdoms with oil deposits are Dubai, the second largest in both area and population, and Sharjah, the third ranking in both categories. The other members—Ras al-Khaimah, Ajman, Fujairah, and Umm al-Qaiwain—are smaller, poorer, and largely dependent on the wealthier emirates for protection and support.

The UAE stretches for almost 750 miles (1,200 km) along the Persian Gulf coast. It also has a short coastline beyond the Strait of Hormuz, along the Gulf of Oman. Like its neighbors, it is largely desert, where summer temperatures exceed 120°F (48.9°C). The UAE's southern border with Saudi Arabia remains undefined, and it has a territorial dispute with Iran over several tiny Persian Gulf islands. The UAE's eastern neighbor is Oman, where another undefined border runs through the desert. Abu Dhabi, the capital (population 527,000), and Dubai (population 1 million) are the UAE's largest cities.

The UAE was formed by its members as protection against powerful neighbors, particularly Saudi Arabia and Iran. Its federal structure is rickety, mainly because it was layered over the existing sheikhdoms, which continued to exist under their ruling families. A federal Supreme Council elects the UAE's president, who from independence until 2004 was Abu Dhabi's emir, Sheikh Zayed bin Sultan al-Nahyan. A forty-member Federal National Council appointed by the various emirs is an advisory body. Abu Dhabi and Dubai have veto power over federal policy, but within each sheikhdom the ruling emir's power remains absolute. Since 1971 there has been constant tension between Abu Dhabi, which wants

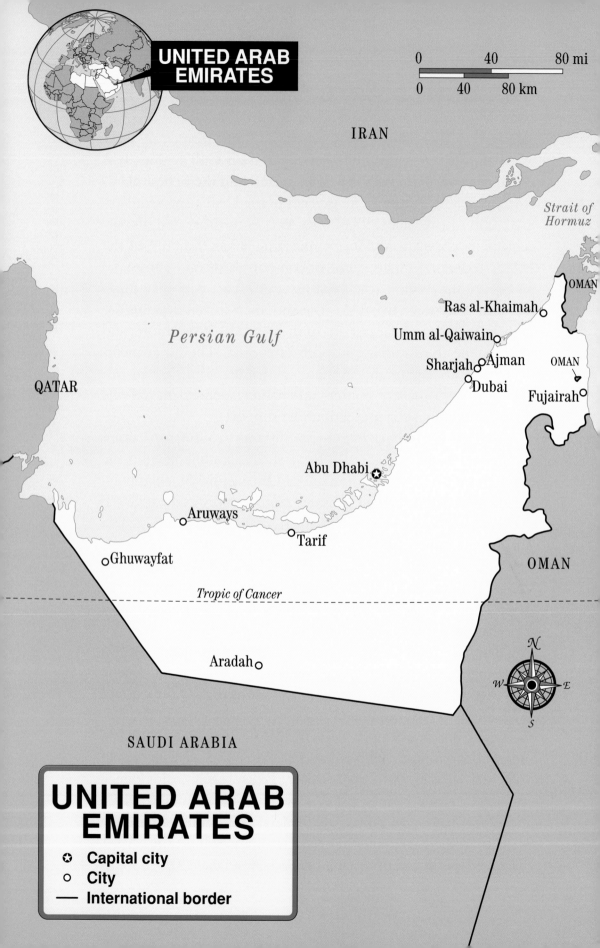

to strengthen federal institutions, and Dubai, supported by several of the smaller emirates, which wants federal powers to remain limited. One result is that the provisional constitution established in 1971 has not been made permanent. Instead, it has been periodically renewed. The federal budget is not financed by taxation but by contributions from the individual sheikhdoms.

If the UAE does not resemble a nation politically, it does so even less demographically. As of 2006, about 79 percent of the total population of approximately 4.6 million was made up of foreign nationals, mainly workers from Pakistan, Bangladesh, Iran, and other Arab countries. Even including foreign Arabs, non-Arab residents outnumber Arabs in the UAE. During the mid-1990s, foreigners made up about 90 percent of the labor force. That percentage may have declined slightly since the passage of a 1996 law designed to force some of them out of the country by limiting their employment opportunities. These workers are terribly exploited. They often live in squalid camps in the desert, cannot form unions, and often must wait for months to collect their low wages. In 2006 about eight hundred workers in the city of Dubai constructing what will be the world's tallest skyscraper staged a protest, something unprecedented in the UAE.

About 80 percent of the total population is Sunni Muslim. Shiites make up about 16 percent. A smattering of Hindus and Christians are found among the foreign workers.

Prior to the discovery of oil, the economy of the UAE sheikhdoms depended on trading, piracy, and pearling. During the nineteenth century, pirating was a major source of income, until the arrival of the British. After their treaties with local rulers, the pirate coast became known as the Trucial Coast. Oil was discovered in 1958 and led to rapid modernization and dramatic improvement in social services provided by the local governments. The oil industry and massive construction also brought in the foreign laborers who today make up the majority of the population.

The UAE suffered a severe financial and embarrassing diplomatic setback in 1991 when the local Bank of Credit and

Commerce (BCCI) collapsed. The bank, owned mostly by Abu Dhabi's ruler, Sheikh Zayed, was linked to international drug dealers, arms merchants, and Third World dictators. Its officers were convicted of extensive fraud and other illegal activities. Billions were lost worldwide, with Sheikh Zayed, who was victimized by his own bank, among the largest losers. The bank itself was liquidated in 1996.

During the 1990s, the UAE's main focus was security. In 1992 Iran began asserting its territorial claims over three disputed Persian Gulf islands, warning the UAE it would have to cross a "sea of blood" to make good its claims. In 1994 the UAE followed the example of several other Gulf states by signing a military cooperation agreement with the United States. That year Sheikh Zayed ordered that a wide range of crimes—including murder, theft, adultery, and drug offenses—be tried according to Sharia in religious courts rather than in civil courts. At the same time, the UAE has called for cooperation among Arab states to combat militant Islamic fundamentalists.

On the economic front, the UAE has broadened its economic base. It has built plants to produce steel, aluminum, and chemicals. It has also established itself as a trading center from which more than 350 companies operate. The country's per capita income, which at twenty-eight thousand dollars in the early 1980s was the world's highest, in 1999 stood at twenty-two thousand dollars, still one of the world's highest. It is politics that remains the problem. In 2004, when Sheikh Zayed died, he was succeeded by his son *Sheikh Khalifa bin Zayed al-Nahyan* in an orderly transition of power. That was a milestone and achievement for a country whose political system seems so unsuited for the demands of the modern world.

BAHRAIN

Bahrain is an archipelago in the Persian Gulf just off the Saudi Arabian coast. Its 273 square miles (707 sq. km) make it about one-fifth the size of Rhode Island, or about three and a half times the size of Washington, D.C. Only six of its thirty-five islands are inhabited. Bahrain, the main island and by far the largest (240 square miles, or 620 sq. km), is connected to two of the other major islands by causeways. An additional causeway 16 miles (25 km) in length connects Bahrain to Saudi Arabia and the mainland. The country's capital, *Manama* (population 135,000), is at the northern end of Bahrain island. More than a third of the country's 698,000 inhabitants are foreign nationals, mainly south Asians, Iranians, and foreign Arabs. Almost all are Muslims, with Shiites outnumbering Sunnis by between two and three to one. The al-Khalifa family, which has ruled Bahrain since the 1780s, is Sunni. The tension between the Sunni-dominated government and Bahrain's Shiite majority has been a constant problem in the politics of the country.

Although Bahrain island has a typical desert climate, its strategic location along ancient trade routes, good harbors, and freshwater springs attracted settlers as far back as the Bronze Age, five thousand years ago. In more recent times, during the seventeenth and eighteenth centuries, it was contested by Persians and Arabs until an Arab tribe expelled the Persians in the 1780s. The island was under British protection from the 1820s until 1971, when the British withdrew from the sheikhdoms of the Persian Gulf. After unsuccessful negotiations with what was then called the Trucial States (the modern UAE) and Qatar, Bahrain chose to become an independent state.

In the 1930s, oil was discovered in Bahrain, which became the Persian Gulf's first oil exporter during that decade. Bahrain's early start enabled it to modernize its economy before its neighbors and develop into a banking center during the oil boom years of the 1970s. The government also provided an extensive network of social services that included free education and medical care. The downside of Bahrain's early start is that its oil deposits are relatively small and are running out. Soon it will not be able to count on oil to sustain its economy.

Currently, oil production and processing produce 60 percent of Bahrain's export earnings and a similar percentage of government revenue. Bahrain's efforts to diversify its economy have included building a large aluminum plant and a shipyard. The government, hoping to expand Bahrain's status as a financial center, has worked hard to attract foreign banks. It also has encouraged tourism as a long-term revenue producer.

Bahrain faces environmental problems. Along with its diminishing oil reserves, groundwater resources, which are nonrenewable, are being depleted. Bahrain, once famous as a green island in the midst of a desert region, has lost much of its vegetation. Desertification is a serious problem. Oil spills have polluted

Bahrain's coastline, offshore coral reefs, and sea vegetation.

Bahrain was ruled from 1961 to 1999 by Emir Sheikh Isa bin Sulman al-Khalifa. He was succeeded at his death in March 1999 by his forty-nine-year-old son *Hamad*, in a smooth transition of power. Like his father, Sheikh Hamad rules as an absolute monarch, even though since Hamad proclaimed himself king in 2002, Bahrain technically has been what he calls a constitutional monarchy. All major political posts are held by members of the ruler's family. Political parties are banned. The tight lid on political life in Bahrain has led to discontent, especially among the Shiite community.

Bahrain's problems intensified after Iran's Islamic Revolution. Iran renewed some of its old territorial claims on Bahrain, and several plots to overthrow the government linked to the Khomeini regime were uncovered in the 1980s. The 1990s brought violent clashes between government security forces and Shiite protesters. Violence in 1996 included several bombings in the capital. That year saw Bahrain's first execution—a Shiite convicted of murdering a police officer in 1995. Shortly thereafter, the government announced it had uncovered yet another Iranian plot to overthrow the government. Adding to Bahrain's problems were long-standing territorial disputes with neighboring Qatar. The most important disagreement concerned the Hawar Islands, just off the Qatari coast in a region believed to contain valuable oil and natural gas deposits.

In order to diffuse political tensions, in 1992 the emir announced the formation of a thirty-member Advisory Council. In 1996 he enlarged the council to forty members. Significantly, at about the same time, the emir expanded his security forces. Overall, these measures were not an adequate response to Shiite demands for a role in the country's political life. Hamad then decided to hold a referendum on the establishment of a two-house parliament. It would have an elected lower house with full law-making powers and an appointed upper house. In mid-February 2001, on the eve of the election, the sheikh announced the freeing of nine hundred political prisoners. The referendum marked another milestone, as it was the first time women were allowed to vote in Bahrain. The vote itself confirmed a foregone conclusion, for more than 98 percent of the electorate support-ed the emir. In February 2002, Hamad declared Bahrain a con-stitutional monarchy with himself as king. Elections to the lower house, held in October, resulted in moderates winning twenty-one of the forty seats, with nineteen going to Islamists. Tension between the government and the Shiite majority continued, and in 2004 King Hamad banned a Shiite advocacy group called the Bahrain Center for Human Rights. Bahrain has sought security in agreements with the United States and Britain and has main-tained close ties with Saudi Arabia. However, it would be a mis-take to take Bahrain's long-term stability for granted.

QATAR

Qatar occupies a thumb-shaped peninsula that juts out from Saudi Arabia for about 100 miles (160 km) into the Persian Gulf. It is a parched landscape of 4,247 square miles (11,000 sq. km) whose highest hills barely rise 130 feet (40 m) above sea level. Beneath the peninsula's barren western hills are 3.7 billion barrels of oil. Just off the northeast coast beneath the shallow waters of the Persian Gulf is the North Field, one of the largest natural gas fields in the world, which holds 4 per-cent of the world's total reserves. The exploitation of oil since its discovery in 1949 has turned Qatar from one of the world's poorest countries into one of the richest.

Qatar borders Saudi Arabia and the UAE in the south. Just offshore is Bahrain, with which Qatar has had several territorial disputes. Less than 100 miles away across the Persian Gulf is Iran, which all the Gulf states, especially the smaller ones, con-sider a security threat. Three-quarters of Qatar's approximately 768,000 residents are foreign nationals who do most of the country's work. They come mainly from South Asia, Iran, and other Arab states. More than 92 percent are Muslims, the overwhelming majority of them Sunnis. Most native Qataris belong to the strict Wahhabi sect. There are some Christians and

Hindus among the foreign residents. About 80 percent of the population lives in and around *Doha* (population 264,000), Qatar's capital and main port.

Oil is the liquid spine of Qatar's economy. It accounts for 70 percent of export earnings and two-thirds of government revenues. Oil production is expected to last at its current level for twenty-five years. While Qatar has tried to diversify its economy by building plants that produce steel, chemicals, and cement, the real guarantor of its future is the North Field. The gigantic field is half the size of Qatar itself. Once Qatar's oil runs out, it will be able to produce natural gas in huge quantities for a century.

Qatar's rulers, the al-Thani family, arrived in the region in the late eighteenth century and became its ruling family about one hundred years later. They signed agreements for British protection in the nineteenth century but lived under Ottoman occupation from 1872 until 1915. New agreements with Britain made Qatar a British protectorate until 1971. When the British left, after failed negotiations with sheikhdoms that ultimately formed the UAE, Qatar declared its independence, in late 1971. Although a new constitution in 2005 provided for a national assembly, two-thirds of whose members would be elected, al-Thanis continue to rule the country as absolute monarchs.

Although one family rules Qatar, the country's politics in the twentieth century has been disorderly. Every ruler has been deposed or forced to abdicate. A year after independence, the free-spending and ineffective ruling emir was overthrown in a bloodless coup by his cousin Khalifa bin Hamad al-Thani. He presided over an era of prosperity and modernization, especially during the oil boom years of the 1970s. At the same time, he focused on security concerns, especially after the Gulf War. In 1992 the emir rejected an appeal by fifty leading citizens for democratic reforms, responding instead by briefly jailing some of them. During 1992 and 1993, he signed a series of security agreements with the United States, Britain, and France.

While these agreements did protect Qatar, they did not keep the emir in power. In 1995 Emir Khalifa was deposed by his son *Hamad bin Khalifa al-Thani*. As soon as he came to power, Hamad made it clear that he intended to make some changes and follow independent policies, some of which have not been popular with the conservative and insecure rulers of the other Gulf states. In foreign affairs, he took the lead in trying to improve relations with Iraq and Iran. He also was involved in on-again, off-again trade discussions with Israel. In April 1996, Israeli prime minister Shimon Peres made an official visit to Qatar. In domestic affairs, the emir announced in 1997 that Qatar would hold municipal elections in which women would be allowed to vote. That precedent-breaking election took place in March 1999.

Emir Hamad's most far-reaching innovation, in the sense that it literally reaches twenty-two Arab countries, was the founding in 1996 of Al Jazeera, the first television station in the Arab world to broadcast news free from government control. The Arabic-language station became a sensation in the Arab world, winning a wide audience among the Arab public but also widespread anger from several Arab governments. At the same time, Al Jazeera adopted a worldview that was strongly anti-American, and it consistently reinforced negative stereotypes of Israel. As one expert observer put it, "Al Jazeera may be more independent—but it is also more inflammatory." Even after September 11, 2001, its reporting portrayed Osama bin Laden in a positive light.

One of the station's reporters added that the station has "put Qatar on the map." Whether that would help or hurt the emir, who has his share of opponents, remained an open question.

OMAN

Thousands of years before anyone cared about petroleum, Oman grew rich as a source of frankincense, a fragrant tree resin used as incense and in embalming that was one of the most valuable products in the ancient world. In the early nineteenth century, Oman was the most powerful state on the Arabian Peninsula. Its rule extended to the island of Zanzibar off the East African coast and to a small part of the South Asian coastline in what later became Pakistan. At the start of the twentieth century, however, Oman's fortunes had declined and it was a poor country that depended on Britain for protection. Oman became independent in 1951, but as late as 1970, three years after oil production began, it had only 6 miles (9.5 km) of paved roads.

Oman's ruling dynasty has held power since the mid-eighteenth century. Its ruler from 1932 until 1970, Sultan Said ibn

Taimur al Said, banned travel and trade and tried to keep the country isolated from the outside world. He even forbade the use of bicycles and sunglasses. A new era began in 1970 when Sultan Said was overthrown by his son *Qaboos*, who still rules Oman. Modern Oman has 3,500 miles (5,600 km) of paved roads, hospitals and health clinics, generous social benefits, a school system with almost five hundred thousand students, a medical school, and a telephone network that allows calls anywhere in the country for ten cents.

Oman faces the Arabian Sea and the Gulf of Oman. It has an area of 199,500 square miles (309,500 sq. km). A tiny part of the country, separated from the main part by about 20 miles (32 km) of UAE territory, is at the tip of the Musandam Peninsula. It overlooks the strategic Strait of Hormuz, through which oil tankers must pass to take Persian Gulf oil to customers worldwide. Altogether, Oman has more than 1,000 miles (1,600 km) of coastline, including a fertile plain along the Gulf of Oman. *Muscat* (population 686,000), Oman's capital and largest city, is on that plain. Immediately to the west and southwest of the coast region are mountains; beyond them to the west and south is a desert plateau that covers the bulk of the country. The Dhofar region in the far south, watered and cooled by summer monsoon rains, has more moderate temperatures than the rest of the country.

Oman has a population of about three million people. That figure includes almost six hundred thousand non-Omanis, the vast majority from South Asia, who make up about half of the labor force. Foreign workers hold most of the nongovernment jobs and do the bulk of the country's unskilled labor. They work long hours at low salaries while native Omanis occupy high-paying government jobs in offices that usually close in midafternoon. About three-quarters of all native Omanis are Muslim Arabs who belong to the small Ibahdi sect. Most of the rest are Sunnis.

Oman's economy is dominated by oil, which provides 75 percent of all export earnings and government revenues. The country has about five billion barrels of oil, which is expected to last for only about twenty more years. Attempts to encourage other industries and diversify the economy before that happens have had limited success. Oman's other natural resources include natural gas, gold, and copper. Agriculture and fishing, the traditional occupations of Oman before the oil boom, are still important parts of the economy. Sur, Oman's main fishing center on the Gulf of Oman, once had another, less savory, business. From the seventh to nineteenth centuries, it was a center of the slave trade that ran from East Africa to the Middle East and India.

Sultan Qaboos has been an effective ruler during the three

decades he has been in power. He defeated a rebellion by radical Arab groups in the 1970s. While retaining his absolute power, he appointed a Consultative Council in 1981 and increased its membership and expanded its range of activities in 1991. He introduced a major reform in 1994 when he announced that women could serve in the council. Two were appointed, out of a total membership of eighty. That same year, the sultan's security forces arrested more than two hundred Islamic militants in an effort to curb the rise of Islamic fundamentalism in Oman. In 2003, for the first time, all Omani citizens over the age of twenty-one, including women, were allowed to vote in Consultative Council elections.

Oman has followed an independent foreign policy under Sultan Qaboos. It was the only Arab state in the Middle East to support Egypt's peace treaty with Israel in 1979. In 1994 Israeli prime minister Yitzhak Rabin visited Oman; his successor, Shimon Peres, made an official visit in 1996. However, at the end of the year, Oman announced it was freezing all ties with Israel because of what it said was lack of progress in the peace process with the Palestinians. Meanwhile, Oman has attempted to ensure its security through cooperation and military ties with the United States. During the Gulf War, American soldiers used weapons the United States had been storing in Oman since the 1980s.

Despite three decades of prosperity and stability, Oman has serious problems. Sultan Qaboos, at age fifty-nine, is very popular but is unmarried and childless, raising the question of succession. Oman's growing population—half of which is under fifteen—means it will be difficult for young Omanis entering the workforce to find the high-paying jobs they want. An increasingly well-educated population is likely to demand political reforms that go beyond advising or consulting and would limit the sultan's absolute power. Islamic fundamentalists are another potential challenge to the regime. In 2005 hundreds were arrested for allegedly threatening national security. In short, like the other Gulf monarchies, Oman faces an uncertain future.

The world's first famous Yemenite was the Queen of Sheba, who, according to the Bible, journeyed from her kingdom in the southern part of the Arabian Peninsula to Jerusalem to visit the Israelite king Solomon about three thousand years ago. The other kingdoms that rose and fell in what became Yemen drew their wealth from trade, especially the export of frankincense and myrrh, fragrant tree resins that were highly valued in the ancient world. By the seventh century A.D., when the population converted to Islam, the region was in decline. After Islam split into Sunni and Shiite sects, many Shiites fleeing Sunni persecution elsewhere in the Arab world fled to the highlands of Yemen. The Shiite Rassid dynasty ruled parts of northern Yemen from 897 until it was overthrown in a revolution in 1962. Foreigners, including the Fatamids of Egypt, Ottomans, Portuguese, and British also controlled different parts of Yemen for varying periods of time. In 1728 a local Sunni dynasty took control of part of southern Yemen, establishing a division of the country between north and south that lasted until 1990.

Yemen has an area of 205,335 square miles (531,869 sq. km). It includes the former Yemen Arab Republic (North Yemen) and the People's Democratic Republic of Yemen (South Yemen). Yemen borders only two countries, Saudi Arabia in the north and Oman in the east. The 1,100-mile border with Saudi Arabia was not defined until a series of agreements between 2000 and 2006. The Red Sea is Yemen's western border, while the Gulf of Aden and the Arabian Sea form its southern frontier. Two African countries, Eritrea and Djibouti, are just across the strategic Bab al-Mandab Strait that connects the Red Sea to the Gulf of Aden.

Yemen has the most varied geography and climate on the Arabian Peninsula. Most of its interior is desert where summer temperatures reach 130°F (54°C); conditions are especially brutal in the east, where the Empty Quarter begins. The country's coastal region is a semidesert about 40 miles (64 km) wide. Aden (population 400,000), the country's main port and second-largest city, whose history dates back twenty-five hundred years, stands on the coast by the Gulf of Aden, astride the major sea route between India and Europe. Yemen's northwestern highlands and mountains between the coast and the interior desert are the wettest part of the Arabian Peninsula, getting as much as 20 inches (50 cm) of rain a year. They are also the highest part of the peninsula, with some peaks rising to more than 12,000 feet (3,660 m) above sea level. Some fertile farmland is found in this region, although farmers must depend on rainfall that often is irregular. *Sanaa* (population 954,000), Yemen's capital and largest city, is in the highlands. Yemen also controls two islands: Perim in the Bab al-Mandab Strait and Socotra in the Gulf of Aden.

Yemen has a population of about 20.7 million, giving it about as many citizens as Saudi Arabia. The Saudis, in fact, were not enthusiastic about Yemen's unification because they feared a united Yemen might someday challenge their dominant position on the peninsula. About 90 percent of all Yemenis are Arabs. A significant Afro-Arab population lives in the western coastal regions opposite Africa. Northern Yemen is almost entirely Muslim; some Christians and Hindus live in the south. The Muslims are approximately equally divided between Shiites, who are concentrated in the north, and Sunnis, most of whom live in the south. This has been a divisive factor in Yemen's history. Tribal loyalties are another divisive force in Yemeni society. An important part of Yemen's population, and its economy, are the hundreds of thousands of citizens who work abroad. Most of them work in the oil-rich Gulf states and regularly send part of their earnings home to help relatives.

Unlike the other countries of the Arabian Peninsula, Yemen is a poor country, one of the twenty poorest countries in the world. It has only begun to exploit its oil deposits, which were not discovered until the mid-1980s. Yemen's per capita income is only about four hundred dollars, and more than half the workforce is involved in agriculture or fishing. Yemen's economy was badly hurt after the Gulf War when Saudi Arabia, in retaliation for Yemen's sympathy for Iraq, expelled about eight hundred thousand Yemeni workers. On the positive side, since the 1980s, oil income has financed new schools, roads, hospitals, and other projects. Along with Yemen's natural gas deposits, Yemen's oil reserves provide the basis for an improved economy in the future.

At the same time, oil money may not be able to over-come the impact of khat, a widely used stimulant drug made from the leaves and buds of a local shrub. Yemenis have been chewing khat for a thousand years. Addiction to khat, in fact, may be Yemen's most serious social problem. About 80 percent of Yemen's men, 60 percent of its women, and a growing percentage of children under ten years of age regularly chew khat. Farmland that once produced cotton, fruits, and vegetables increasingly is used to grow the drug. North Yemenis in particular chew khat on a regular basis. The habit is a serious drain on the incomes of people who cannot afford it. Many Yemenis who make less than one hundred dollars per month admit they spend half their income on khat. The drug induces a state of mind marked by extreme moods that often keeps people away from their jobs and, if they do manage to show up, undermines their ability to work. As one Yemeni economist noted:

> In the West, you work from 9 to 5. We claim to work from 8 to 2, but many people knock off at noon to be sure to get to the khat markets while they can buy the freshest leaves. So we lose at least four hours work every day, and if we continue like that, we'll stay poor forever.

In 1999 Yemen's president, *Ali Abdullah Saleh*, himself a khat chewer for many years, announced a campaign to end khat chewing, which he called a social evil. He is likely to find the job difficult. Many Yemenis seem to agree with a government official who told a Western reporter, "Without khat, Yemen is nothing." Beyond that, few Yemenis believe that President Saleh practices what he preaches. As the speaker of Yemen's parliament put it, "After all those fine words, he's still chewing khat."

If Yemen is to prosper, it must first achieve political stability. So far, that has not been possible. Both of the two independent Yemeni states were unstable while they existed. North Yemen was a backward monarchy until the revolution of 1962. The Yemen Arab Republic (YAR) that succeeded it was rocked by civil war until 1967 and then by military coups and assassinations until Lieutenant General Ali Abdullah Saleh took power in 1978. Meanwhile, a second Yemeni state came into being in 1967 when the British, who had conquered Aden and its surrounding territory in 1839, withdrew from South Yemen. That state, the only Marxist regime in the Arab world, was called (after 1970) the People's Democratic Republic of Yemen (PDRY). South Yemen was no more stable than North Yemen. The two countries fought a border war in 1979 and eyed each other warily thereafter. Unity finally came in 1990, after South Yemen lost its main supporter when the Soviet Union collapsed. General Saleh became the newly formed Republic of Yemen's first president.

Unity brought continued political infighting rather than stability. Yemen's sympathy for Iraq during the Gulf War crisis of 1990–1991 increased tensions with Saudi Arabia and the other Gulf states and cost Yemen foreign aid. In 1994 a civil war broke out when former South Yemen leaders tried to secede. Within two months, General Saleh and the former North Yemen leadership were victorious. Over the next few months, Saleh reinforced his position by having Yemen's legislature reelect him president and revise the constitution to strengthen his powers. Meanwhile, there were growing tensions between Saleh's secular political party, the General People's Congress (GPC), and the main Islamic group, Yemeni Congregation for Reform (YCR). The YCR opposed Saleh's decision to grant women the vote and the right to run for office prior to the 1997 parliamentary elections. Those elections, won by the GPC, appeared to be generally fair, marking a first for the Arabian Peninsula. Saleh then appointed an economist from the former South Yemen as the country's prime minister in an attempt to overcome divisions that did not end with the conclusion of the civil war. In September 1999, Yemen held its first presidential election in which voters cast ballots directly for the candidates. While Saleh won with more than 96 percent of the vote, the opposition, with considerable justification, denounced the election as a sham. The main opposition party, which was not permitted to field a candidate, called for a boycott of the vote. Saleh strengthened his grip on power when the GPC increased its majority in parliamentary elections held in 2003.

Yemen is a country that has generally attracted little attention outside the Arabian Peninsula, but that suddenly changed on October 12, 2000, when a small rubber boat pulled along-side the U.S. Navy destroyer *Cole* as it was refueling in the port of Aden. At least two Islamic fundamentalist terrorists belonging to Osama bin Laden's al-Qaeda organization were on board the rubber boat, and they were on a suicide mission whose goal was to kill Americans. At 12:15 P.M., an enormous explosion tore a huge hole, 20 by 40 feet (6 by 12 m), in the side of the USS *Cole*. Seventeen U.S. sailors died and thirty-nine were injured. It was the worst terrorist attack against American military forces since nineteen airmen were killed in the bombing of their barracks in Saudi Arabia in 1996.

Several months after the *Cole* incident, in February 2001, the citizens of Yemen went to the polls to vote in municipal elections and on a referendum Saleh had put on the ballot. Saleh claimed the referendum was to advance what he called Yemen's democratic experience. In reality, it was on constitutional amendments to extend the presidential term from five to seven years, extend the term of the parliament from four to six years, and create a second house of parliament appointed by the president. Rather than make Yemen more democratic, the amendments were intended to strengthen the power of Saleh and his ruling party. Not surprisingly, the voters approved the amendments by a majority of more than 77 percent. Equally unsurprising was the violence that accompanied the election. Tribal clashes of various sorts that caused the postponement of the voting at 140 polling stations also left more than twenty people dead.

Yemen thus began the new century and millennium as a troubled country. It remains poverty stricken. Its secular government is under a growing challenge from Islamic forces. One radical group, the Aden-Abyan Islamic Army, is disrupting the country with a campaign of violence, including car bombings in cities. The regime itself, despite the parliamentary elections of 1997 and 2003 and some degree of political freedom, at its core is a military dictatorship with a reputation for corruption. Very rapid population growth is certain to be a heavy drain on efforts to promote economic development. So is violence having nothing to do with politics in a country where sixteen million people own a total of fifty million guns. Some of those guns are used to kidnap Westerners working in or visiting Yemen who were then held for ransom. All of these factors add up to a problematic future.

9000–8000 B.C.
- Agriculture develops.

8000 B.C.
- Jericho and Catal Huyuk emerge as world's first cities.

3500 B.C.
- Sumerians in Mesopotamia develop the world's first system of writing.

3100 B.C.
- Egypt unites as the world's first country. The Old Kingdom dynasty lasts from 3100–2258 B.C.

2400 B.C.
- Sargon of Akkad conquers neighboring states in Mesopotamia and creates the world's first empire.

2000–1786 B.C.
- Middle Kingdom era rules in Egypt.

1800 B.C.
- Judaism, the world's first monotheistic religion, begins.

1750–332 B.C.
- New Kingdom era rules in Egypt.

14TH CENTURY B.C.
- Egyptian pharaoh Akhenaton makes religious reforms.

1200 B.C.
- Phoenicians perfect the world's first phonetic alphabet, which has twenty-two letters.

11TH AND 10TH CENTURIES B.C.
- United Israelite kingdom emerges with Jerusalem as its capital.

7TH CENTURY B.C.
- Zoroastrianism begins in Persia.

6TH CENTURY B.C.
- Cyrus the Great rules Persia; he allows exiled Israelites to return to Judea.

334–323 B.C.
- Alexander the Great conquers parts of Europe, Africa, and Asia.

4TH CENTURY B.C. TO 4TH CENTURY A.D.
- Greeks and Romans dominate Middle East.

2ND AND 1ST CENTURIES B.C.
- Rome extends its power to the Middle East. Alexandria's library burns, and 500,000 irreplaceable papyrus scrolls are destroyed.

1ST CENTURY A.D.
- Jesus is born (possibly 4 B.C.). Origins of Christianity begin.

1ST AND 2ND CENTURIES A.D.
- Two unsuccessful Jewish revolts occur against Rome. Romans destroy the Jews' Second Temple after the first revolt in A.D. 70. In the wake of the second revolt (132–135), the Romans either kill or exile most of Judea's Jewish population and rename the region Syria Palestina.

5TH CENTURY
- Coptic Church begins in Egypt.

7TH CENTURY
- Islam is founded. Islamic conquests include Mesopotamia, Persia, and Egypt.

10TH CENTURY
- Fatamids rule Egypt and found Cairo in 969.

11TH
- Crusader era begins.

1071
- Seljuk Turks defeat Byzantines at Manzikert.

1250–1517
- Mamelukes rule in Egypt. They defeat Mongol invaders in Syria in 1260.

14TH CENTURY
- Ottoman Empire begins.

1453
- Ottoman Turks conquer Constantinople.

16TH CENTURY
- Safavid dynasty makes Shiite version of Islam official religion in Persia.

1520–1566
- Ottoman sultan Suleyman the Magnificent reigns.

1571
- Spanish and Venetian navies defeat the Turks at Lepanto.

1728
- Yemen divided into two countries.

1798–1801
- French occupy Egypt; Rosetta Stone found in 1799.

1840s
- Baha'i faith begins in Persia.

1861

- French intervene in Lebanon to save Christians from massacres by the Druze. Lebanon Mountain district is established for Lebanese Christians.

1869

- Suez Canal opens.

1881–1903

- First large wave of Jewish immigration to Palestine arrives from Russian Empire.

1882

- Great Britain occupies Egypt.

1897

- First Zionist Congress is held.

1899

- Kuwait goes under British protection.

1904–1914

- Second large wave of Jewish immigration to Palestine arrives from Russian Empire.

1908

- Oil is discovered in Persia.

1911

- Italy seizes Libya from Ottoman Empire.

1914

- World War I begins.

1915

- Ottomans, led by Colonel Mustafa Kemal, thwart British invasion at Gallipoli.

- Ottoman Empire commits genocide against the Armenians.

1917

- Balfour Declaration promises Jews a national home in Palestine.

1912

- World War I ends with an Ottoman defeat.

1919–1926

- Ibn Saud conquers most of the Arabian Peninsula and creates Saudi Arabia.

1920

- Supreme Council of the League of Nations, at the San Remo Conference, gives Britain the mandate for Palestine. It defines Palestine as including land on both sides of the Jordan River.
- Treaty of Sèvres limits Turkey's territory to northern Anatolia.

1922

- Egypt officially becomes independent.
- Turks defeat the Greeks and drive them from Anatolia.
- Britain detaches all territory west of the Jordan River, three-quarters of Palestine's total area, from its mandate and creates Transjordan.

1923

- Under Treaty of Lausanne, Turkey achieves current borders.

- Kemal has Turkish national assembly abolish the Ottoman sultanate and declares Turkey a republic.

1924
- Turkish national assembly abolishes the Ottoman caliphate.

1925
- Pahlavi dynasty takes power in Persia.

1927
- Oil is discovered in Iraq.

1928
- Islam is disestablished as Turkey's official religion.

1930
- Turks rename Constantinople Istanbul.

1932
- Iraq becomes independent.

1933–1939
- Large wave of Jewish immigration arrives in Palestine as Jews flee persecution in Nazi Germany.

1935
- Persia's name is changed to Iran. Government bans the chador.
- Turkish women receive full legal equality with men.

1936
- Farouk becomes king of Egypt.

1938
- Mustafa Kemal Ataturk dies.
- Oil is discovered in Saudi Arabia; oil pumping begins in Kuwait.

1939
- World War II begins.

1941
- Britain and the Soviet Union occupy Iran.
- Syria officially becomes independent.
- Lebanon officially becomes independent.

1943
- Lebanese National Covenant sets the basis for the ethnic and religious division of power in the government according to the census of that year.

1946
- United States successfully pressures the Soviet Union to end its occupation of northern Iran.
- Kingdom of Transjordan becomes independent, with Abdullah as king.
- France withdraws from Syria completely.

1947
- Britain announces it will leave Palestine. UN votes to divide Palestine into a Jewish state and an Arab state, a decision the Jews accept and the Arabs reject.

- United States sends aircraft carrier to eastern Mediterranean to back Turkey against Soviet pressure.

1948
- Israel declares independence.
- War of Independence is fought. Israel defeats Egypt, Syria, Jordan, Iraq, Lebanon. War lasts until 1949.

1950
- In Jordan, Abdullah annexes eastern Jerusalem and the West Bank and grants its residents Jordanian citizenship. He changes the name of the country to the Hashemite Kingdom of Jordan. The international community does not recognize the annexations.
- Turkey sends soldiers to Korea to help the United States defend South Korea against North Korean aggression.

1951
- In Jordan Abdullah is assassinated by Islamic fanatic opposed to the king's peace talks with Israel.
- Libya becomes independent.
- Mohammad Mossadegh becomes prime minister of Iran.

1952
- Military officers overthrow King Farouk and declare Egypt a republic.
- Hussein ibn Talal is named king of Jordan.

- Turkey joins the North Atlantic Treaty Organization.

1953
- In Iran Mossadegh is overthrown by U.S.-sponsored coup. Shah returns from exile.

1954
- Nasser emerges as Egypt's undisputed leader.

1956
- Nasser officially becomes Egyptian president after running unopposed in election.
- Nasser seizes Suez Canal.
- Egypt fights Suez War with Britain, France, and Israel.

1958
- The United Arab Republic (UAR) is established in Egypt and Syria.
- U.S. Marines land in Lebanon to protect government from pro-Nasser Muslim forces.
- Military coup in Iraq overthrows King Faisal and abolishes monarchy. Entire royal family is executed.
- Oil is discovered in Abu Dhabi, United Arab Emirates.

1960
- Military coup in Turkey ends civilian rule.

1961
- Civilian rule in Turkey is restored under a new constitution.
- Kuwait becomes independent.
- UAR dissolves.

1962

- Nasser intervenes in civil war in Yemen with 50,000 soldiers. Egyptian troops fight in Yemen for more than five years.
- Baath Party seizes power in Iraq for the first time.
- Kuwait adopts constitution with parliament.
- North Yemen monarchy overthrown; Yemen Arab Republic is established.

1963

- Women in Iran receive the right to vote.
- Baath Party is overthrown.

1964

- Palestine Liberation Organization is founded.

1967

- Nasser orders UN peacekeeping force out of the Sinai Peninsula, blockades Israeli port of Elat, moves troops and tanks to Israeli border, signs military alliances with Syria and Jordan, and proclaims intention to destroy Israel.
- Six-Day War is fought. Israel defeats its opponents and occupies eastern Jerusalem, the Sinai Peninsula, the West Bank and Gaza Strip, and the Golan Heights.
- Britain leaves Aden colony (South Yemen), which becomes People's Democratic Republic of Yemen.

1968

- Baath Party again seizes power in Iraq. Saddam Hussein starts his rise to power.

1969

- Golda Meier becomes prime minister of Israel.
- Yasser Arafat becomes head of the PLO.
- Military coup in Libya ends the monarchy and brings Muammar Qaddafi to power.

1970

- Nasser dies; Anwar Sadat becomes president of Egypt.
- King Hussein's army crushes the PLO during Black September fighting and drives Palestinian militias from Jordan.
- Palestinian militias reestablish themselves in southern part of Lebanon.
- Qaboos bin Said overthrows his father and becomes ruler of Oman. Oman begins economic development.
- Hafez al-Assad takes power in Syria.

1971

- Assad is elected president of Syria with 99.2 percent of the vote.
- Qatar becomes independent.
- The UAE is formed.

1973

- Yom Kippur War; Israel again defeats Egyptian and Syrian forces but at extremely high cost in casualties.

- In Libya Qaddafi declares cultural revolution against non-Islamic thinking.

1974

- Arab League officially recognizes PLO as sole representative of the Palestinian people.
- Turkey invades Cyprus and sets up Turkish Republic of Northern Cyprus.

1975

- Civil war begins in Lebanon.
- Iraq and Iran agree on division of the Shatt-al-Arab waterway.
- King Faisal of Saudi Arabia is assassinated.

1976

- Yitzhak Rabin elected prime minister of Israel.
- Rescue of Israeli and Jewish hostages at Entebbe, Uganda.
- In Libya Qaddafi publishes first part of his Green Book.

1977

- Egyptian president Sadat declares willingness to make peace with Israel, and he visits Jerusalem.
- Menachem Begin becomes prime minister of Israel.

1978

- Camp David Accords are negotiated.
- Israeli army invades southern Lebanon to attack PLO bases.

1979

- Israel-Egyptian peace treaty is signed.

- Arab League suspends Egypt; most Arab countries sever diplomatic relations with Egypt; Egypt ousted from several Arab economic and financial institutions.
- Saddam Hussein openly takes power as president of Iraq.
- Shah flees Iran.
- Ayatollah Khomeini comes to power in Iran as leader of Islamic Revolution.
- Iranian monarchy is abolished; Iran declared an Islamic Republic.
- Iranian students overrun U.S. embassy and seize hostages.

1980

- In Iraq Saddam Hussein repudiates the 1975 agreement on the Shatt al-Arab waterway and invades Iran, launching Iran-Iraq War.
- Turkish military again seizes power and installs new constitution with more powerful presidency.

1981

- Egyptian president Anwar Sadat is assassinated by Islamic fundamentalists for making peace with Israel.
- Hosni Mubarak becomes president of Egypt.
- Israeli air raid destroys Iraqi nuclear reactor before it is operational.
- American and Libyan warplanes clash over the Gulf of Sidra.

- In Iran opponents of the regime kill seventy-four leading Islamic politicians in bombing attack.

1982

- Israel sends its army into Lebanon to destroy PLO bases. PLO forced to leave Lebanon and relocate headquarters in Tunisia. Beginning of Israeli military presence in Lebanon.
- Christian Lebanese militia forces allied with Israel murder hundreds of Palestinians in two refugee camps near Beirut.
- Assad has Syrian army destroy Hama, the stronghold of the Islamic fundamentalist Muslim Brotherhood, killing an estimated 20,000 people.

1983

- In Turkey, civilian rule is restored under tight military supervision.
- Motherland Party, with military support, wins parliamentary elections in Turkey; Turgut Özal becomes prime minister of Turkey.
- Shiite suicide bombers attack U.S. and French military bases in Lebanon, killing 241 U.S. Marines and 59 French soldiers.

1984

- In Egypt, Sadat's murderers are tried and executed.

- In Israel, Operation Moses begins.

1985

- Israel withdraws from most of southern Lebanon to narrow security zone along the Israeli-Lebanese border.

1986

- American warplanes bomb Libya after its agents are tied to a terrorist nightclub bombing in Europe that kills several American soldiers.

1987

- More than 400 pilgrims in Mecca, Saudi Arabia, for the hajj are killed during rioting at the Grand Mosque.
- First Palestinian intifada (uprising) starts against Israeli occupation of the Gaza Strip and West Bank.

1988

- Pan American Flight 103 is bombed in midair over Lockerbie, Scotland, with 270 lives lost; Libyan agents are implicated.
- UN imposes sanctions on Libya.
- King Hussein renounces all Jordanian claims to the West Bank.
- Kurdish village of Halabje attacked by Iraqi military using poison gas bombs: 5,000 people are killed and 10,000 injured.

- Iraq-Iran War ends in stalemate, with Shatt-al-Arab divided as before. Iraq uses chemical weapons to get Iran to accept an end to the fighting.

1989

- Egypt is readmitted to the Arab League.
- Jordan holds the first parliamentary elections since the 1950s. Women are allowed to vote.
- Taif Agreement ends Lebanese civil war but leaves Syria in control of the country, with more than 35,000 troops occupying key areas.
- Syria orchestrates the election of Elias Harawi as Lebanon's president.
- In Iran Ayatollah Khomeini dies; Ayatollah Khamenei succeeds him as supreme leader.

1990

- Iraq's Saddam Hussein invades Kuwait and annexes it. Diplomacy fails to get Hussein to withdraw.
- UN imposes trade embargo on Iraq.
- UN authorizes all necessary means to force Iraq from Kuwait.
- Earthquake in the northwest of Iran kills 40,000 people.
- Yemen is reunited for the first time since 1728 as Republic of Yemen.

1991

- Operation Solomon in Israel brings 15,000 Ethiopian Jews to Israel.
- Gulf War involves most countries of the region.
- Iraq's military forces are driven from Kuwait but not before setting hundreds of oil-well fires and causing an environmental disaster in the Persian Gulf region.
- UN Security Council requires that Iraq give up all chemical and biological weapons, as well as all materials for developing nuclear weapons. UN Special Commission on Iraq (UNSCOM) is formed to find and destroy Iraq's capabilities to make these weapons.
- Hussein regime begins removing Kurds from city of Kirkuk and surrounding territory in order to Arabize that oil-rich region.
- Islamic fundamentalists in Egypt begin attacks on Coptic Christians.
- BCCI bank scandal in the United Arab Emirates leads to billions of dollars in losses for investors.

1992

- Islamic fundamentalists in Egypt begin attacks on foreigners, government officials, and intellectuals.
- Egyptian Boutros Boutros-Ghali becomes UN Secretary-General.

- Jordan's King Hussein treated successfully for cancer in the United States.
- First parliamentary elections in twenty-one years are held in Lebanon.

1993

- Egyptian Islamic fundamentalist group Islamic Group tries to blow up the World Trade Center in New York City.
- Oslo Accords are signed in Washington, D.C.
- Suleyman Demirel becomes president of Turkey.
- Tansu Ciller becomes Turkey's first woman prime minister.

1994

- Cairo agreement fills in various details of Oslo Accords.
- Palestinian Authority is established according to Oslo Accords.
- Israel hands over control of Jericho and Gaza Strip to the PA.
- Israel-Jordan peace treaty is signed.
- Civil war starts in Yemen.

1995

- Oslo II agreement is signed in Washington, D.C. Israel withdraws from six more West Bank towns.
- Israeli Prime Minister Rabin is assassinated by extremist opposed to the peace process.

1996

- Benjamin Netanyahu is elected prime minister of Israel.

- Palestinian Council is elected; al-Fatah, led by Arafat, wins a majority.
- Arafat is elected president of the PA.
- Saddam Hussein accepts UN oil-for-food program.
- Turkey's Welfare Party, an Islamic fundamentalist group led by Necmettin Erbakan, wins election and takes power.
- Islamic fundamentalists in Saudi Arabia bomb U.S. military residence at Khobar Towers, killing nineteen American airmen.
- Al Jazeera television station is founded in Qatar.

1997

- Hebron Protocol is signed. Israel withdraws from most of that city.
- Sayed Mohammad Khatami is elected president of Iran, with almost 70 percent of the vote.

1998

- Wye River Memorandum is signed. The agreement calls for additional Israeli withdrawals in return for antiterrorist efforts by the PA and amendment of the PLO Covenant to eliminate clauses calling for Israel's destruction.
- Palestinian National Council votes to approve a letter to President Bill Clinton stating that twenty-four articles in the PLO Covenant calling for Israel's destruction have been either nullified or modified.

- Jordan's King Hussein is again ill with cancer.
- U.S. and British warplanes bomb Iraq for four days to force compliance with agreements regarding UNSCOM but without success.
- Turkey's military bans the Welfare Party; it is reorganized as the Virtue Party.

1999

- Egypt's Mubarak is elected to fourth term as president.
- Ehud Barak is elected prime minister of Israel.
- Jordan's King Hussein dies; he is succeeded by his son Abdullah.
- UNSCOM leaves Iraq, having been unable to complete its mission.
- UN Security Council replaces UNSCOM with new inspection group, the UN Monitoring, Verification, and Inspection Commission (UNMOVIC). Hussein refuses to allow it into Iraq.
- Bulent Ecevit returns to power as prime minister of Turkey.
- Commandos in Kenya capture Abdullah Ocalan, leader of the Kurdish rebellion in Turkey.
- Virtue Party member Merve Kavakci is banned from Turkey's parliament for wearing a traditional Islamic woman's head scarf.
- Kurdistan Workers' Party accepts a cease-fire.

- Catastrophic earthquake near the northern town of Izmit, Turkey, kills at least 18,000 people, injures more than 50,000, and leaves 350,000 homeless.
- Turkey is invited to join the European Union, but invitation conditional on major political and economic reforms.
- Kuwaiti emir grants women the right to vote, but parliament refuses to approve the measure.
- In Qatar women are permitted to vote and run for office in municipal elections for the first time.

2000

- Camp David peace talks fail.
- PA launches second intifada.
- Syrian president Hafez al-Assad dies; his son Bashar becomes president.
- In Turkey police discover dozens of bodies of people murdered by the Islamic fundamentalist group Hezbollah.
- Kurdistan Workers' Party formally announces the end of its rebellion.
- Ahmet Secdet Sezer is chosen president of Turkey by the country's parliament.
- Governments of Saudi Arabia and Yemen sign border treaty.

- In Yemen, Islamic fundamentalists sponsored by Saudi citizen Osama bin Laden blow up a bomb alongside the U.S. destroyer *Cole*, killing seventeen U.S. sailors and injuring thirty-nine.

2001
- Ariel Sharon is elected prime minister of Israel.
- Hamas suicide terrorist murders twenty-one Israelis outside Tel Aviv disco.
- Israeli-Palestinian cease-fire designed to end the second intifada fails.
- Khatami reelected president of Iran, with 77 percent of the vote. Conservative authorities launch campaign of arrests, intimidation, and public executions.
- Scottish court convicts one Libyan agent for the midair bombing of Pan American Flight 103 over Lockerbie, Scotland. A second agent is acquitted.
- Kuwait's highest court rejects a suit intended to win women the right to vote.
- Al-Qaeda terrorists, many of them Saudi Arabians, attack the World Trade Center and the Pentagon in the United States.

2002
- Israeli government starts building security fence after a series of deadly terrorist attacks.

- Iraq agrees to allow UNMOVIC inspections in response to UN Security Council Resolution 1441.
- Islamic political party AKP wins parliamentary elections in Turkey and forms government.
- Iranian president Khatami's unable to limit power of the Council of Guardians.
- Emir Hamad declares Bahrain a constitutional monarchy with himself as king.

2003
- Libya agrees to $2.7 billion compensation for families of Pan American 103 victims.
- Libya agrees to give up all WMDs and stop research to develop them.
- In Israel Likud Party wins parliamentary elections.
- Prime Minister Sharon announces disengagement plan, which calls for Israel's unilateral withdrawal from the Gaza Strip and part of the West Bank.
- Jordan holds parliamentary elections.
- United States finds Iraq in violation of UN Security Council Resolution 1441.
- U.S.-led coalition invades and deposes Saddam Hussein regime.
- Recep Erdogan becomes prime minister of Turkey.
- In Iran conservatives win local elections.

- Secret program to develop nuclear weapons is exposed.
- Oman holds elections to Consultative Council on the basis of universal suffrage for all citizens over the age of 21, including women.
- In Yemen parliamentary elections won by ruling GPC.

2004

- Libya's WMD are eliminated under international supervision.
- Arafat dies and is succeeded by Mahmoud Abbas.
- In Jordan Abu Musab al-Zarqawi sentenced to death in absentia for murder of American diplomat.
- Jordan's King Abdullah removes his half-brother from succession and makes his son heir to the throne.
- Syria forces Lebanese parliament to extend President Lahoud's term.
- U.S. turns over official sovereignty to Iraq's interim government.
- Conservatives win parliamentary elections in Iran.
- In the United Arab Emirates, Sheikh Zayed bin Sultan dies; he is succeeded by his son Sheikh Khalifa bin Zayed.
- Saudi Arabia starts building security barrier along border with Yemen to stop infiltration by Islamic terrorists.

2005

- In Egypt Mubarak wins first multicandidate presidential election, with 88 percent of the vote.
- Israeli parliament approves Sharon's disengagement plan.
- Sharon founds Kadima, a new political party, to support his peace plan.
- Former Lebanese prime minister Rafik Hariri is murdered. Syria is blamed.
- International pressure forces Syria to withdraw its troops from Lebanon.
- Iraq holds parliamentary elections. Voter turnout is high.
- Mahmoud Ahmadinejad is elected president of Iran.
- King Fahd of Saudi Arabia dies; he is succeeded by Crown Prince Abdullah.
- Kuwaiti women get the right to vote.
- Sheik Jaber al-Ahmad al-Sabah dies; he is succeeded as ruler after ten days by Sheikh Sabah al-Ahmad al-Sabah.
- In Qatar new constitution provides for national assembly, two-thirds of whose members are elected and one-third appointed.
- In Oman hundreds of Islamic fundamentalists are arrested and accused of subversive activity.

2006

- United States restores diplomatic relations with Libya and removes Libya from its list of state sponsors of terror.
- Israeli prime minister Sharon suffers incapacitating stroke. Ehud Olmert becomes interim prime minister.
- Kadima wins parliamentary elections; Olmert becomes prime minister.
- Israel wages war with Hezbollah in Lebanon. UN Security Council Resolution 1701 ends the fighting after five weeks.
- Jordan provides key intelligence to United States that results in Zarqawi being hunted down and killed in Iraq.
- All cabinet seats in Iraq are filled, completing formation of permanent government.
- Saudi Arabia and Yemen agree to final border demarcation.
- Lebanese army and new UN peacekeeping force take up positions in southern Lebanon but do not stop Iran and Syria from violating resolution 1701 by rearming Hezbollah.
- Saddam Hussein is tried and executed.

2007

- UN Security Council passes resolution tightening economic sanctions against Iran for its refusal to stop its program to build nuclear weapons.

ENCYCLOPEDIA

A

ABBAS, MAHMOUD (1935–)

President of the Palestinian Authority. Also known as Abu Mazan, Abbas became PA president in 2004, after the death of Yasser Arafat, when he won an election with 62 percent of the vote. Abbas became a refugee in 1948 when his family fled to Syria during the fighting of Israel's war of independence. He earned a doctorate in history from a Soviet university. A longtime Arafat associate and founding member of al-Fatah, Mazan became the first PA prime minister when that post was created in 2003. His views and policies have been consistent with those of Arafat.

ABDULLAH IBN ABDEL AZIZ AL-SAUD (1923–)

King of Saudi Arabia. The oldest of the surviving sons of Saudi Arabia's founder, Abdullah became king in 2005. Because his predecessor had been seriously ill for years, Abdullah, in effect, has held the reins of power in Saudi Arabia since 1997.

ABDULLAH IBN HUSSEIN (1962–)

King of Jordan. Abdullah became king in 1999 when his father, King Hussein, passed over his own brother, Crown Prince Hassan, to select Abdullah. British-educated, the new king pledged to continue his father's policies, including promoting peace between Israel and its Arab neighbors. A career military officer for eighteen years, Abdullah could count on the strong support of the army as he began his reign. A few months after ascending the throne, the king showed his determination to be in touch with the pulse of his country when he twice donned disguises—once posing as a television reporter and the other time as a taxi passenger—to travel around Amman and directly experience how ordinary Jordanians lived. Two years into his reign, there was grumbling among many Jordanians that Abdullah was too Western and pushing too hard to modernize a country where traditional values still ruled.

ABU DHABI

Capital of the United Arab Emirates. Abu Dhabi has the same name as the UAE's largest member sheikhdom and the island on which it is located. The city was founded around 1760 and remained a small trading and pearling center until the oil industry developed in the 1960s. It has since become a modern city with sleek office buildings, hotels, and an international airport. Consistent with traditional Muslim attitudes regarding the mixing of the sexes, Abu Dhabi has a government-run beach reserved exclusively for women.

ALEXANDRIA

Former capital of Egypt. Located on the Mediterranean coast just east of the Nile delta, Alexandria was founded by Alexander the Great in 332 B.C. Under the Greek Ptolemaic dynasty, it was Egypt's capital and most important city, as well as a major port and trading center. Its great library of five hundred thousand volumes and its university made Alexandria the intellectual center of the Hellenistic world. (The library, with its priceless ancient knowledge, was destroyed by fire in the first century B.C.) The remains of the magnificent Pharos lighthouse, one of the ancient Seven Wonders of the World, lie underwater just offshore. Beginning in the first century Alexandria was a center of the newly founded Christian religion. The city was reduced to the status of Egypt's second city in the tenth century, when Egypt's Fatamid Arab rulers founded their new capital at Cairo. Alexandria enjoyed a renaissance in the nineteenth century, becoming the cosmopolitan home to large Greek, Italian, French, and British communities. Their departure after the 1952 revolution ended that era of pluralistic vibrancy. Alexandria, still Egypt's second-largest city, is a major port and industrial center.

AMMAN

Capital of Jordan. Amman and its surroundings probably have been inhabited for almost nine thousand years. Just outside the city is one of the Middle East's largest Neolithic (c. 6500 B.C.) archaeological sites. From the third century B.C. until the Arab conquest in A.D. 635, the city was called Philadelphia. The Arabs changed its name to Amman. About half of Jordan's population lives in and around Amman, a far cry from 1948, when it was a dusty town of twenty-five thousand on the edge of the desert. Much of the city's commercial dynamism is due to its Palestinian residents, who came to the city as refugees after the 1948–1949 and 1967 Arab-Israeli wars. After the 1991 Gulf War, hundreds of thousands of Jordanians and Palestinians expelled from Kuwait settled in Amman.

ANKARA

Capital of Turkey. Ankara was a commercial center in Hittite times thirty-eight hundred years ago. Later it was the capital of a Roman province. In 1402 Ankara was the scene of the crushing defeat the notorious Tamerlane dealt the Ottoman Turks. The city was in decline in the nineteenth and early twentieth centuries and had a population of only sixty thousand when Mustafa Kemal Ataturk made it the base of his nationalist movement in 1920. It became Turkey's capital in 1923. It is Turkey's second-largest city as well as an industrial and cultural center. It is also home to the Anitkabir—the mausoleum of Mustafa Kemal Ataturk.

ARAB-ISRAELI CONFLICT

The Arab-Israeli conflict dates from the late nineteenth century, when Arabs began to oppose Jewish immigration into what was then called Palestine. After 1948, when Israel became an independent country, that opposition translated into the Arabs refusing to accept Israel's right to exist and attempting to destroy the Jewish state. The Arab refusal to accept Israel's right to exist remains the core issue of the conflict. The Arab states most directly involved in the Arab-Israeli conflict have been Egypt, Syria, Jordan, Lebanon, Iraq, Saudi Arabia, and Libya. Iran, Muslim but not Arab, has been among Israel's most militant foes since its Islamic Revolution of 1979. The Palestinian Arabs formed several dozen organizations (see Palestinian Organizations) to oppose Israel, mainly through terrorist attacks and guerrilla warfare. The most important of them is the Palestine Liberation Organization (PLO), founded in 1964.

The Arab-Israeli conflict has produced four wars between Israel and one or more Arab states. Israel's War of Independence (1948–1949), which the Arabs call the Palestine War, was fought between Israel and Egypt, Syria, Jordan, Iraq, and Lebanon. The Suez War (1956) was between Israel and Egypt (in which Britain and France also fought against Egypt). In the Six-Day War (1967), Israel fought against Egypt, Syria, and Jordan. In the Yom Kippur War of 1973, which the Arabs call the Ramadan War, Israel fought Egypt and Syria.

The term *war* sometimes is attached to three other large-scale military confrontations. Israel and Egypt also fought a series of battles along the Suez Canal during 1969–1970 known as the War of Attrition. Israel's attempt to drive PLO forces from Lebanon in 1982 is called the Lebanon War. Its five-week campaign during the summer of 2006 against Hezbollah in southern Lebanon is now called the Second Lebanon War. There also have been countless incidents of violence, mainly involving terrorist attacks against Israelis by Palestinian guerrillas and retaliation against Palestinian bases by the Israeli military.

Arab-Israeli peacemaking efforts have been based on two UN Security Council Resolutions—Resolution 242 and Resolution 338—each adopted in the wake of a major war. UN Resolution 242 (November 1967) called for Israel to "withdraw from territories" occupied during the Six-Day War of 1967 and for all countries in the area to be guaranteed the right to live in peace within secure and recognized boundaries. Resolution 242 contained ambiguities, among them a lack of precision about the extent of Israel's withdrawal. However, Israel could point to what the resolution did not say. It did not include the word *the* or the word *all* before *territories*, nor did it call for a withdrawal to the lines of June 5, 1967. These omissions had been deliberate, as several diplomats involved in drafting the resolution pointed out. This enabled Israel, which was determined not to return to its insecure 1967 borders, to maintain that under Resolution 242 it would not be obligated to withdraw from all the territories taken during the war, an interpretation supported by the United States. Israel also insisted that it was not obligated to evacuate any territories except as part of a general peace agreement, since that was the implied goal of Resolution 242. Not surprisingly, the Arab states interpreted the resolution far differently. They insisted that Israel must withdraw from all territories occupied during the war. At the same time, they expressed no interest in peace. (Syria rejected Resolution 242 entirely.) In fact, at a summit meeting the previous September, the Arab League had responded to Israeli peace proposals with what came to be called the three "no's": no peace, no negotiations, no recognition. UN Resolution 338 (October 1973) called for direct negotiations between Israelis and Arabs to implement Resolution 242. However, Arab leaders refused, as they had since 1948, to deal directly with Israel until Egyptian president Anwar Sadat broke ranks and went to Jerusalem in 1977. That visit led to negotiations that produced the Camp David Accords of 1978 and the Egyptian-Israeli peace treaty of 1979.

The first groundbreaking agreement between the Israelis and Palestinians was the Declaration of Principles of 1993, usually called the Oslo Accords. Negotiated by Israel and the PLO, the Oslo Accords set up the Palestinian Authority. That agreement was followed by the Israeli-Jordanian peace treaty of 1994. A second major Israeli-Palestinian agreement, signed in 1995, called the Taba Agreement but better known as Oslo II, expanded on the 1993 Declaration of Principles. During the 1990s, four narrower agreements—the Cairo Agreement (1994), the Hebron Protocol (1997), the Wye River Memorandum (1998), and the Sharm al-Sheikh agreement (1999)—focused on specific Israeli withdrawals from West Bank and Gaza territory in return for Palestinian commitments to Israeli security requirements.

While these agreements represented progress, they fell far short of a comprehensive Middle East peace, and the peace process collapsed in the wake of the failed negotiations in 2000, the second intifada, and the Hamas victory in the 2006 Palestinian elections. As of mid-2006, many of the most difficult issues between Israel and the Palestinians remained unresolved. Most of the Arab world, as well as Iran, continues to be hostile to Israel, and several heavily armed states formally remain at war with the Jewish state.

ARAB LEAGUE (LEAGUE OF ARAB STATES)

The Arab League was founded in 1945 by Egypt, Syria, Lebanon, Transjordan (present-day Jordan), Iraq, Saudi Arabia, and Yemen. Since then more than a dozen new members from the Middle East and North Africa have joined. Its most influential member has been Egypt, with the exception of the decade (1979–1989) when it was suspended from the league for making peace with Israel. The league has tried to promote Arab cooperation in political, economic, and cultural matters. These efforts have enjoyed limited success, largely because of rivalries that divide the Arab states. Various sessions and summit meetings have been boycotted over the years by different members, especially radical states such as Libya, Syria, and Iraq. One of the league's most notable successes was to defend newly independent Kuwait against threats from Iraq in 1961.

The one area where the league maintained unity for decades was in its opposition to Israel. Several member countries jointly attacked Israel in 1948 in an unsuccessful attempt to destroy the Jewish state in its infancy. The league then established an economic boycott of Israel. Aside from banning all trade with Israel, the boycott was extended to companies worldwide that did business of any kind with Israel. This secondary boycott went beyond refusing to do business. It included requiring companies to reveal if they had Jewish shareholders, employees, or directors. The boycott finally began to erode in the mid-1980s, when several Arab states stopped observing some of its provisions, but it has not been ended.

Iraq's invasion of Kuwait in 1990 and the Gulf War in 1991 deepened old divisions in the league and caused some new ones. In March 2001, the league finally held its first summit meeting in more than ten years. The only unifying theme its members could find was hostility to Israel. Yet the bitter rift between Iraq and Kuwait was not bridged, which made it impossible for league members to unify around an effort to lift UN sanctions against Iraq.

ARAFAT, YASSER (1929–2004)

Late president of the Palestinian Authority. Arafat was born in Cairo, where his father had moved from a small town in what today is the Gaza Strip. He became involved in Palestinian Arab student politics while at Cairo University, served in the Egyptian army, and worked as an engineer in Kuwait. In the late 1950s, he cofounded the al-Fatah ("Conquest") guerrilla organization, which began terrorist operations against Israel in 1965. Arafat became head of the Palestine Liberation Organization, which al-Fatah came to dominate, in 1969. Under Arafat's leadership, the PLO became the world's largest and most active terrorist organization, carrying out attacks primarily against Israel but also against Jordanian and American targets in the Middle East and Europe.

After years of calling for Israel's destruction, in 1993 Arafat and the PLO negotiated the Oslo Accords, which became the basis for subsequent Israel-Palestinian peace negotiations. However, when speaking to Arab audiences, Arafat repeatedly has compared the Oslo Accords to Mohammad's peace treaty (the Khudaibiya treaty) with a Jewish tribe on the Arabian Peninsula. The treaty was only temporary. Slated to last for ten years, it was broken by Mohammad after two, at which point he attacked and conquered the Jewish tribe. Arafat also has continued to call for jihad, or holy war, against Israel.

Arafat met face-to-face with every Israeli prime minister from Yitzhak Rabin to Ariel Sharon. In July 2000, Arafat rejected extensive concessions made by Israeli prime minister Ehud Barak during negotiations in the United States, and al-Fatah played a prominent role in Palestinian attacks against Israelis that followed the breakdown of negotiations. Arafat died in 2004.

AL-ASSAD, BASHAR (1965–)

President of Syria. Assad became Syria's president after the death of his father, Hafez al-Assad, in June 2000. An ophthalmologist by training who was not involved in politics, Bashar Assad did not become his father's heir apparent until his older brother was killed in a car accident in 1994. At that point, Assad was called home from London, where he had been studying for two years. He was given an officer's appointment in the army and was set on a course to gather the power he would need to succeed his father. Not surprisingly, he advanced quickly in the army, reaching the rank of colonel in 1999. That same year, he was put in charge of an anticorruption drive that removed a number of high-ranking politicians from office. Unlike his father, Bashar Assad has traveled widely and has an extensive knowledge of the world beyond Syria. He is fluent in both English and French. Assad has been his country's most visible and important advocate of computer literacy as head of the Syrian Computer Society since 1994. Bashar Assad's education and travels do not seem to have made him more tolerant than his father.

AL-ASSAD, HAFEZ (1930–2000)

President of Syria, 1971–2000. Assad was Syria's dictator for three decades, making him among the most durable Middle Eastern leaders. He was born into a prominent family of the minority Alawite sect in a country with a Sunni majority. Trained as an air force pilot, Assad entered politics and served as minister of defense and commander of Syria's air force before becoming president. Once he was in charge, he relied on Soviet aid and military equipment to build up Syria's armed forces, in effect making Syria a Soviet client state until the Soviet Union collapsed in 1991. Assad dealt with Islamic opposition to his secular regime by brutally suppressing the fundamentalist Muslim Brotherhood in 1982. Assad died in June 2000 and was succeeded by his son Bashar.

ATATURK, MUSTAFA KEMAL (1881–1938)

Founder and first president of the Turkish Republic. Mustafa Kemal was a World War I military hero who led Turkey's revival after the war. He was committed above all else to Turkey's becoming a modern secular state based on the Western model, and he fought Islamic influences in public life at every turn. His secularist and modernizing principles are known as *kemalism*. Mustafa Kemal took the surname Ataturk, "Father of Turks," in 1934. He and his principles are still mentioned in Turkey's current constitution.

B

BAGHDAD

Capital of Iraq. Baghdad was founded in the eighth century when the Arab Abbasid dynasty ruled the region. The city originally was built inside circular walls on the west bank of the Tigris River, which explains why it was called the Round City. Eventually the city expanded beyond those walls and to the east bank of the Tigris. Baghdad reached a glorious peak as the Arab world's cultural and intellectual center under the Abbasids in the eighth and ninth centuries. It stood astride major east-west trade routes and was one of the richest cities in the world. The city then declined as Abbasid rule weakened. Centuries of stagnation followed after the Mongols sacked the city and destroyed Baghdad's vital irrigation system. The city started to recover in the twentieth century as the capital of Iraq. Beginning in the 1970s, oil revenues financed extensive building and industrial and business development. Baghdad was hit on and off by Iranian missiles and bombs during the Iran-Iraq War of the 1980s and suffered extensive damage from allied bombing during the Gulf War of 1991. While some rebuilding occurred after the war, the city again suffered extensively destruction in 2003, when U.S.-led military forces invaded Iraq and overthrew the Saddam Hussein regime. As of early 2007, Baghdad was both the headquarters of the Iraq's first-ever democratically elected government and the center of an ongoing terrorist campaign by Sunni insurgents determined to defeat all efforts to establish democracy in Iraq.

BARAK, EHUD (1942–)

Prime minister of Israel, 1999–2001. Barak entered politics after retiring from military service in 1995. In the 1999 election campaign, he pledged to do more than Benjamin Netanyahu to further the peace process with the Palestinians. At the same time, he stressed that he would not compromise Israel's security needs. In 1999 he negotiated the Sharm al-Sheikh agreement with Yasser Arafat. Considered Yitzhak Rabin's political heir, Barak has a bachelor's degree in physics and mathematics from the Hebrew University in Jerusalem, a master's degree in systems analysis from Stanford University in California, and is an accomplished classical pianist. Barak's political fortunes declined after mid-2000, when American-sponsored Israel-Palestinian peace talks failed. Barak had offered the Palestinians unprecedented concessions that most Israelis considered excessive, but Palestinian leader Yasser Arafat nonetheless turned them down. This seriously undermined Barak's standing at home. In February 2001, he was defeated in his reelection bid by Ariel Sharon.

BEIRUT

Capital of Lebanon. Beirut is a major port that stands where the foot of the Lebanon Mountains reaches the Mediterranean Sea. Its history goes back more than three thousand years, to when it was a Phoenician port. The city remained an important port and cultural center under Greek, Roman, and Byzantine rule but declined after the sixth century. Its revival began as European influence in the region grew in the 1860s. In 1920 the French made it the capital of their newly created Lebanon. Beirut then prospered as the Middle East's financial center. Its lively and cosmopolitan cultural life and physical beauty led many people to call it the Paris of the Middle East. The Lebanese Civil War of 1975–1989 physically and economically devastated the city and left it divided into Muslim West Beirut and Christian East Beirut. Since the mid-1990s, Beirut has been the scene of major rebuilding, with the focus on restoring its business and commercial center to regain that the city's position of prominence in the region.

BEN-GURION, DAVID (1886–1963)

First prime minister of Israel. Ben-Gurion served as prime minister from 1948 to 1953 and again from 1955 to 1963. He also served as Israel's first minister of defense. Born in Poland, he arrived in what was then called Palestine in 1906 and spent several years as a farm worker. Ben-Gurion believed in socialist-

Zionism, the dominant form of Zionism during his lifetime, which advocated building a Jewish state that would have a socialist economy. The outstanding Zionist and Israeli leader of his generation, Ben-Gurion supported compromise and acceptance of the UN-sponsored partition of Palestine in 1947. After retiring from politics, he lived on a kibbutz in the Negev Desert until his death.

CAIRO

Capital of Egypt. Cairo is Egypt's cultural, financial, and industrial center. More than sixteen million people live in greater Cairo, making it the largest urban center in the Middle East. Founded by the country's Fatamid rulers in A.D. 969, just a few miles north of Egypt's ancient capital of Memphis, *Cairo* means "the Victorious" in Arabic. Ibn Khaldun, the distinguished fourteenth-century Arab historian, called Cairo the metropolis of the universe. Modern Cairenes, a bit more modestly, still call it the Mother of the World. For most of its history Cairo has been the intellectual center of the Arab world. Since 970 it has been the home to the mosque and Islamic university of Al-Azhar, which continues to attract Muslim students from around the world. Many of Cairo's great monuments were built by Egypt's Mameluke rulers beginning in the thirteenth century. Its modern center, however, is the huge square of Maydan at-Tahrir, which was laid out in 1865. Cairo's Egyptian Museum, built in 1902, contains the world's greatest collection of ancient Egyptian artifacts.

DAMASCUS

Capital of Syria. Damascus may be the oldest continuously inhabited city in the world. It has had the same name for more than thirty-five hundred years. The city exists because of the Barada River, which rises in the Anti-Lebanon mountains. Its waters create an oasis in an otherwise barren region. Damascus was ruled by various ancient conquerors, including the Egyptians and Hittites. Later, Damascus was an important urban center under the Persians, Greeks, and Romans. The apostle Paul was traveling to Damascus, at the time a major commercial center, when he underwent his dramatic conversion to Christianity. Damascus became a Muslim center when the Arab Umayyad dynasty made the city its capital. The Arabs took over the city's large Christian church, originally built by the Roman emperor Theodosius, and rebuilt it as the Great Mosque. The mosque has survived several disasters, including a devastating fire in the nineteenth century. It remains one of the largest and most famous mosques in the Muslim world. Damascus remained an important city even after the Umayyads were succeeded by the Abbasids, who moved the Arab capital to Baghdad. But Damascus declined, as did Baghdad, after being sacked by the Mongols, and it remained a backwater until the 1940s, when it became Syria's capital. A vastly expanded Damascus is Syria's cultural, financial, and industrial center.

DOHA

Capital of Qatar. Doha was once a center of piracy, which led to its being razed in 1867. Prior to the oil boom that started in 1949, Doha was a village whose inhabitants earned their living by fishing and pearling. In recent decades, oil money has turned Doha into a modern city with a deepwater port and an international airport.

ERDOGAN, RECEP (1954–)

Prime minister of Turkey. Although he comes from a poor background, Erdogan graduated from a leading business college in Istanbul. Aside from his interests in business and politics, he also has been a professional soccer player. He joined Turkey's Islamic fundamentalists movement after meeting Necmettin Erbakan during his university days. He became mayor of Istanbul in 1994 but in 1998 was convicted of inciting religious hatred. He and several associates founded the Justice and Development Party (AKP) as a successor to the banned Welfare Party. In recent years, Erdogan has tried to shed his reputation as a hard-line Islamic fundamentalists and take on the image of a moderate conservative. For many Turks who are loyal to the Ataturk tradition, his efforts have not been very convincing.

GAZA CITY

Capital of the Gaza Strip. Gaza City is the main base of the Palestinian Authority. Its roots date back to when it was an Egyptian garrison town thirty-five hundred years ago. Later it was one of the main cities of the Philistines and, according to the Bible, the place where Samson destroyed one of their temples, killing himself as he brought destruction down on the enemies of the Israelites. Since then Gaza City has seen many conquerors. It became the capital of the Gaza Strip when that area fell under Egyptian control after the 1948–1949 Arab-Israeli war and the home to many Arab refugees after that war.

Hezbollah

A Shiite fundamentalist Muslim organization. Hezbollah, whose name means "party of God," is based in Lebanon. It was formed in 1982, after Israel drove the PLO out of southern Lebanon. Hezbollah was started at the instigation of Iran as part of the effort to spread Iranian influence and its Islamic Revolution throughout the Middle East. It is controlled, trained, and largely funded by Iran. Hezbollah pioneered the use of suicide bombings against Israeli and American targets, including the 1983 attack against the U.S. Marine barracks in Beirut that killed 241 troops. Hezbollah is a militantly anti-Semitic organization, uncompromisingly committed to the destruction of Israel. Its leader, Hassan Nazrallah, does not distinguish between Israelis and Jews.

With Iranian and some Syrian help, Hezbollah built a powerful military organization in southern Lebanon. Its advanced weapons included thousands of short-range rockets as well as rockets with a range of up to 120 miles. It also became a major political force in Lebanon, with seats in the country's parliament and ministers in its cabinet. After provoking a war with Israel in July 2006, in less than five weeks Hezbollah hit Israel with about four thousand rockets, almost all of which were aimed at civilian targets. Hezbollah launched many of those rockets from civilian areas inside Lebanon. Many Lebanese civilians became casualties when Israel responded by attacking those launchers as it tried to stop the bombardment of its territory and people. The UN Security Council resolution that ended the fighting in August called for Hezbollah to be disarmed.

Hezbollah is both a terrorist and a criminal organization. Among its numerous criminal activities, it is deeply involved in the international drug trade. It has cooperated with groups involved in a variety of smuggling activities in the United States.

HUSSEIN IBN TALAL (1935–1999)

King of Jordan, 1952–1999. Few people expected Hussein to have a long reign when, as a teenager, he became Jordan's king. Yet he survived numerous internal and external attempts to depose him and eventually took a leading role promoting peace between the Arab nations and Israel. Under Hussein, Jordan fought in the 1967 Six-Day War against Israel, losing control of the West Bank and eastern Jerusalem as a result. In September 1970, the king defeated a Palestinian attempt to overthrow him in a short, fierce civil war. Thousands of Palestinians died during what they have since called Black September.

A moderate in Arab politics and strongly pro-Western, Hussein held the first of many secret meetings with Israeli leaders in 1963. By the time Jordan and Israel finally signed a peace treaty in 1994, Hussein had warm friendships with many influential Israelis, including Yitzhak Rabin and Shimon Peres. King Hussein's death from cancer in 1999 was widely mourned in the West and especially in Israel, where he was trusted and respected.

HUSSEIN, SADDAM (1937–2006)

President of Iraq, 1979–2003. Born into a landless peasant family, Saddam Hussein became the unchallenged dictator of Iraq in 1979. He used purges and murder to retain power. He led Iraq into three disastrous wars: the eight-year war with Iran (1980–1988); the 1991 Gulf War, which pitted Iraq against a broad coalition of nations led by the United States; and the 2003 war that led to his overthrow. Hussein spent billions of dollars to acquire biological, chemical, and nuclear weapons. His ruthless repression enabled him to keep a tight grip on power until an American-led coalition invaded Iraq in 2003 and removed him from power. In 2005 Iraq's newly elected democratic government put Saddam Hussein on trial for murder. He was convicted nine months later and was hanged in December 2006.

ISLAMIC FUNDAMENTALISM

No development in the Middle East in the past two decades is more important than the resurgence of Islamic fundamentalism. This movement is a reaction to Western influences that have been growing since the early nineteenth century. Islamic fundamentalism rejects all Western secular ideas and values as decadent and destructive to Muslim civilization. It maintains that to combat Western influences, Muslim societies must reassert their Islamic heritage. This requires overthrowing all secular or insufficiently Islamic regimes and replacing them with regimes based strictly on Islamic teachings and on Sharia, or Islamic law.

The most successful Islamic fundamentalists are in Iran, where they came to power in a revolution led by the Ayatollah Khomeini in 1979. However, Islamic movements are growing in influence in almost every Arab country in the Middle East, from Egypt to Jordan. Even Saudi Arabia, which has a fundamentalist regime, is not strict enough for certain Islamic groups. In many Arab countries, they are the main threat to the existing government. They frequently resort to terrorism and assassination against the regimes they are trying to overthrow. Aside from opposing Western influences in all their forms, Islamic fundamentalist organizations such as the Palestinian group Hamas have taken an uncompromising stand against all peaceful attempts to resolve the Arab-Israeli conflict. They continue to assert that Israel has no right to exist. Islamic fundamentalist groups also have attacked U.S. targets, including the World Trade Center in New York City and the Pentagon in Washington, D.C. The combined death toll of the 2001 attacks was over three thousand.

ISTANBUL

Major Turkish city. Although Ankara is Turkey's political capital, Istanbul is its industrial, commercial, and cultural center. For sixteen hundred years before its name was officially changed in 1930, Istanbul was Constantinople, one of the world's great historic cities. Constantinople was founded in A.D. 330 at Europe's eastern rim, on the site of the city of Byzantium, by the Roman emperor Constantine, who made it the capital of the empire. The city was built on both sides of the Golden Horn, an inlet of the Bosporus, one of the two straits (the other is the Dardanelles) that separate Europe from Asia.

After the collapse of the western part of the Roman Empire, Constantinople survived as the capital of the Byzantine Empire. In the sixth century, the Byzantine emperor Justinian built the Hagia Sophia, considered the architectural wonder of its day and for one thousand years the largest church in the Christian world. (The Ottoman Turks turned the Hagia Sophia into a mosque after they conquered Constantinople in 1453. In 1930 Turkish president Mustafa Kemal Ataturk made the building a museum.)

Constantinople was by far Europe's largest and richest city during the Middle Ages. Even after it began to decline, it remained the center of Orthodox Eastern Christianity until it fell to the Turks. The city enjoyed a building boom and golden age during the sixteenth and seventeenth centuries, when the Ottoman Empire and Turkish culture reached their heights. The majority of Istanbul's most beautiful mosques date from that period. As the city grew, it expanded to the Asiatic side of the Bosporus. It experienced explosive growth in the 1970s and 1980s, when it tripled in size. In 1973 the Bosporus Bridge, one of the world's longest suspension bridges, finally linked the two parts of the city. The Second Bosporus Bridge was completed in 1988. In August 1999, Istanbul was among the cities battered by the devastating earthquake that struck northwestern Turkey, killing thousands of people. However, the city's

major monuments, including the Hagia Sophia, Topkapi
Palace, and the Blue Mosque, escaped severe damage.

JERUSALEM

Capital of Israel. Jerusalem has been at the center of Jewish identity and spiritual life since King David made it the capital of the ancient Israelite kingdom more than three thousand years ago. Not only specific religious sites but the city itself is also sacred to people of the Jewish faith. For centuries, when they lived outside the city, Jews regularly turned to face Jerusalem in prayer. With a brief interlude in the sixth century B.C., when the Jews were exiled to Babylon, Jerusalem remained the capital of a Jewish state for more than nine hundred years, until the mighty Roman Empire ended Jewish independence. It became the capital of an independent Jewish state again in 1949, a year after the establishment of the modern state of Israel.

Jerusalem also has deep religious significance to Christians and Muslims. Christians revere the sites associated with the preaching and crucifixion of Jesus, while Muslims hold sacred the place where they believe the Prophet Mohammad rose to heaven.

Jerusalem, whose name means "City of Peace," has known both glory and tragedy in its long and tumultuous history. The Jewish First Temple, built by David's son Solomon, was destroyed by the conquering Babylonians in 586 B.C. The Second Temple, completed about seventy years later, was leveled along with much of the city itself by the Romans in A.D. 70. The Temple's only remnant, known as the Western Wall, is the Jewish people's most important religious shrine. After Roman times, Jerusalem passed through the hands of many foreign conquerors, including the Byzantines, Arabs, Christian Crusaders, Egyptian Mamelukes, and Turks. Christians and Muslims both built religious shrines in the city. In the fourth century, the Roman emperor Constantine built the Church of the Holy Sepulchre at the site where it is believed Jesus was placed in his tomb after he was crucified. In the late seventh century, the Arabs, who often built mosques on the holy sites of conquered non-Muslims, built a mosque called the Dome of the Rock on the vast elevated plaza called the Temple Mount where the two ancient Jewish temples once stood. They later built a second mosque, Al-Aqsa, on the Temple Mount.

The Arab-Israeli war of 1948–1949 left Jerusalem divided between Jordan and Israel. Jordan controlled the eastern part of the city, including the Old City where the Western Wall is located and which is surrounded by a wall built by the Turks. The Jordanians expelled all Jews from the Old City, destroyed or desecrated its Jewish holy places, and banned Jews from praying at the Western Wall. Christians faced constant discrimination, and eastern Jerusalem's Christian population dropped by more than half under Jordanian rule. Israel controlled the western and newer part of the city, which grew rapidly during the next two decades.

Jerusalem was reunited under Israeli control as a result of the 1967 Arab-Israeli war. Since then access to religious sites has been guaranteed by Israeli law. The appropriate religious authorities, whether Jewish, Christian, or Muslim, have jurisdiction over the city's religious sites. The city, however, remains a point of intense controversy between Israelis and Arabs. The Palestinian Authority claims the eastern part of the city, which it wants as the capital of a future Palestinian state. Israel, however, considers Jerusalem its permanent capital, and most Israelis insist they will never permit the city to be divided.

KATSAV, MOSHE (1945–)

President of Israel. Although Israel's presidency is mainly a ceremonial post with little power, Moshe Katsav's election to the post by parliament in July 2000 was a landmark because he was the first Sephardic Jew to hold that position. Born in Iran and the oldest of ten children, Katsav immigrated to Israel with his family in 1951 and grew up in a tent camp in the southern part of the country. The camp eventually developed into a small working-class town called Kiryat Malachi, populated mainly by poor Jews who had immigrated from Middle Eastern countries. As a boy, Katsav learned to speak Arabic from Jewish children who were immigrants from Arab countries. He became the first child from Kiryat Malachi to attend a university and continued to live there with his wife and five children even as he rose through Israel's political ranks and became a government minister. After his election, Katsav said he intended to represent all Israelis—religious and secular Jews, Sephardic and Ashkenazic Jews, and Israel's Arab citizens—and hoped they would all see him as their president.

AL-KHALIFA, SHEIKH HAMAD BIN ISA (1950–)

Emir (ruler) of Bahrain. Sheikh Hamad came to power in 1999 at the death of his father, who had ruled as Bahrain's emir since 1961. Sheikh Hamad is a graduate of a British military academy and an experienced military commander. Bahrain's crown prince since 1964, he was in charge of building its military strength. He supports Bahrain's growing cooperation with Western powers in the Persian Gulf region.

KHAMENEI, AYATOLLAH ALI (1939–)

Supreme leader of Iran. Iran's president from 1981 to 1989 and a former student of the Ayatollah Khomeini, Khamenei succeeded his teacher as Iran's supreme religious leader when Khomeini died in 1989. He served in several important posts before becoming the country's president. Although more moderate than his predecessor on issues such as economic reform, Khamenei remains bitterly anti-Western and uncompromisingly opposed to Israel's right to exist. In 1999 his regime used violence and threats of severe punishment to disperse and silence student protesters demanding democratic reforms.

KHOMEINI, AYATOLLAH RUHOLLAH (1902–1989)

Founder of Iran's Islamic Republic and its supreme leader, 1979–1989. Khomeini was only five months old when his father, an Islamic clergyman, was murdered. By the age of six, he reportedly knew the Koran by heart. Trained as an Islamic cleric, he bitterly opposed the secularist policies of Mohammad Reza Shah Pahlavi and was forced into exile in 1963. Khomeini continued his campaign from exile, returning to Iran in triumph in February 1979 following the shah's overthrow. Khomeini then ruthlessly eliminated all opposition to the new Islamic republic and held ultimate authority as Iran's supreme religious leader until his death.

KUWAIT CITY

Capital of Kuwait. Kuwait City was founded in 1710. In 1776 the British East India Company established a base there as a stopover point along the route from Britain to India. The city sustained severe damage during the Iraqi occupation of Kuwait in 1990–1991, but that has since been repaired. Its main land-mark is Kuwait Towers, a Swedish-designed structure made up of three towers, the tallest of which stands 613 feet (187 m) high. Kuwait City's port area contains shipyards and oil refiner-ies. Although Kuwait City is in the desert, Kuwait's desaliniza-tion plants provide water for parks and trees that line many of its streets.

LAHOUD, EMILE (1936–)

President of Lebanon. Lahoud was Syria's choice to become Lebanon's president when the parliament elected him in 1999. Prior to becoming president, Lahoud served as the commander of Lebanon's army for nine years. In 2004 Syria forced changes in the Lebanese con-stitution that extended Lahoud's term for three years. He has studied military science in Britain and speaks English fluently.

MANAMA

Bahrain's capital and commercial center. Founded about 650 years ago, Manama was under Portuguese control for about eighty years before 1602 and under Persian rule from 1602 until 1783. The city is divided into a new area of gleaming modern hotels and office buildings constructed on reclaimed land, and older sections that look much like they did a half cen-tury ago. Manama has a shipyard for building dhows, the tradi-tional Arab boats of the Persian Gulf.

MECCA

The birthplace of the Prophet Mohammad in A.D. 570. Mecca is Islam's holiest city. All Muslims who are able to are expected to make the hajj, or pilgrimage, to Mecca once in their lifetimes, and about one million do so each year. Muslims all over the world say their daily prayers facing Mecca. The Great Mosque stands at Mecca's center. Inside the Mosque is the Kaaba, a cube-shaped shrine covered by a black cloth that houses the holy Black Stone. The Black Stone, which may be a meteor, has been an object of worship since pre-Islamic times. The touches and kisses of uncounted pilgrims over many centuries have worn it smooth.

The hajj has not been without problems, especially in recent years. In 1979 more than one hundred people died when Muslim fundamentalists seized the Grand Mosque and held it for two weeks. In 1987 more than four hundred people died during a confrontation between Iranian pilgrims and Saudi authorities. In 1990 a stampede in a tunnel near the pilgrimage sites caused the deaths of more than fourteen hundred pilgrims.

Prior to Mohammad's birth, Mecca was a commercial and religious center for Arab tribes. The city has changed hands numerous times in its long history, most recently in 1924 when Abdel Aziz al-Saud seized it from the Hashemite clan as he completed his unification of Saudi Arabia.

MEIER, GOLDA (1898–1978)

Israeli prime minister, 1969–1974. Meier was born in Russia but was raised and educated in the United States from the age of eight before immigrating to what was then called Palestine in 1921. She was Israel's first ambassador to the Soviet Union and served as minister of labor and foreign minister before becoming prime minister in 1969. Meier was Israel's first woman prime minister and the first woman to head a

government in the Middle East. She led Israel through the 1973
Yom Kippur War but resigned in 1974 in the wake of a special
commission's report that criticized her government for being
unprepared when Egypt and Syria attacked Israel.

MUBARAK, HOSNI (1928–)

President of Egypt. Mubarak became
president of Egypt after Anwar Sadat's
assassination in 1981. He was trained
as an air force pilot and commanded
the Egyptian Air Force in the 1973
war with Israel. In 1975 he was
appointed Egypt's vice president.
Unlike Nasser and Sadat, his two
charismatic predecessors, Mubarak
has an unemotional and unideological
approach to politics. His policies, both
at home and abroad, stress pragma-
tism and moderation. Mubarak is popular in Egypt, but his government also faces significant opposition, particularly from Islamic
fundamentalists. He has maintained strong ties with the United
States, being especially helpful in mobilizing Arab support for the
1991 Gulf War. A consistent supporter of the Israeli-Palestinian
peace process, Mubarak at the same time has done little to encourage Egyptian-Israeli ties beyond the formal peace that exists
between the two countries.

MUSCAT

Capital of Oman. A port city surrounded by mountains, Muscat's
history as a center for trade with East Africa dates from the thirteenth century. The Portuguese held the port from 1508 until
1648, and it was briefly under Persian control in the early 1740s.
Two sixteenth-century Portuguese forts still overlook the
entrance to Muscat and the city's royal palace. The city's long-
standing trade ties with Asia, Africa, and Europe give it a cosmopolitan atmosphere unmatched in the Persian Gulf region.

There are three types of nonconventional weapons: nuclear, chemical, and biological. Because of their great killing power, they are also known as weapons of mass destruction (WMDs). Several nations in the Middle East have at least one of these three types of weapons.

Israel is the only nuclear power in the Middle East. It has never officially admitted having nuclear weapons but probably developed its first nuclear bomb in the late 1960s. It may have as many as one hundred nuclear bombs. Israel also has developed guided missiles and is one of a handful of nations that has used its own rocket to put a satellite into orbit. Israel has never used its nonconventional weapons.

Iraq began a nuclear program in the 1970s, but its effort to build a nuclear bomb was set back in 1981 when Israeli jets destroyed its French-built nuclear reactor (called the Osirik reactor) just before it was about to be loaded with nuclear fuel. In the aftermath of the 1991 Gulf War, UN inspectors discovered that since the destruction of the Osirik reactor, Iraq had put together an ambitious program to build a nuclear bomb. The UN destroyed the facilities it found in Iraq after the 1991 Gulf War. Under Saddam Hussein, Iraq used chemical weapons on the battlefield against Iran and against Kurdish civilians inside Iraq.

Iran is attempting to build nuclear weapons and the missiles to deliver them, as well as chemical and biological weapons. It has received technical help from Russia in developing both nuclear weapons and long-range guided missiles. Iran also has hired Russian scientists privately, taking advantage of Russia's hard economic times, which left many of its scientists unable to make a living at home. Those scientists are helping Iran develop all three types of nonconventional weapons. Iran's secret nuclear program was revealed to the world in 2003. As of early 2007, efforts by the international community to stop that program had not been successful.

Egypt has had chemical weapons for more than thirty years and used them when it intervened in Yemen's civil war in the

1960s. Syria also has chemical weapons and missiles with ranges up to 300 miles (500 kilometers) to deliver them. Libya probably at one time had the ability to build chemical weapons, but it gave up its WMD program in 2004. The U.S. government is especially concerned about weapons in Iranian and Syrian hands because both nations have been linked to international terrorism. Saudi Arabia, which reportedly has helped finance Pakistan's nuclear program, is also believed to be interested in acquiring a nuclear military capability.

OIL, OPEC, OAPEC

The Middle East has almost seven hundred billion barrels of oil reserves, about two-thirds of the world's total. Most of that is located in five countries: Saudi Arabia, Iraq, Kuwait, the United Arab Emirates, and Iran. Saudi Arabia alone has a quarter of the world's oil reserves. These states are the main powers in the Organization of Petroleum Exporting Countries (OPEC), a cartel established in 1960 that includes oil-producing countries from outside the Middle East. OPEC's main goal is to control production so that oil prices remain high but not so high that oil consumers will seek alternative forms of energy. In 1979 OPEC nations profited enormously when disorder caused by Iran's Islamic Revolution cut that country's production drastically, and world oil prices skyrocketed. From the mid-1980s until 1999, however, OPEC was unable to control production, and therefore prices, in large part because some members with large populations needed to sell as much oil as possible. The result was lower oil prices for importing nations such as the United States. That changed in early 1999, when OPEC and nonmember producing countries such as Russia, Mexico, and Norway agreed to cut production by two million barrels per day. When the countries involved actually adhered to their assigned cuts, oil prices doubled within six months.

The Organization of Arab Petroleum Exporting Countries (OAPEC) includes most Arab oil-producing nations but has been much less active than OPEC. Its most significant act was to proclaim an oil boycott during the Yom Kippur War in October 1973 against Western countries until Israel withdrew from all territories it had occupied in 1967. The United States remained subject to the oil boycott for six months, until March 1974. The Arab oil boycott cost the United States five hundred thousand jobs.

OLMERT, EHUD (1945–)

Prime minister of Israel. Olmert became acting prime minister in January 2006 after Ariel Sharon was incapacitated by illness. He became prime minister in his own right after leading the newly formed Kadima Party to victory in parliamentary elections. Olmert served as a combat infantry unit officer in the Israeli army and then earned a law degree. He was mayor of Jerusalem before being elected to Israel's parliament in 1998. In 2005 Olmert followed Sharon out of the Likud Party into Kadima and was his logical successor when a stroke incapacitated Sharon a few months later.

PAHLAVI, MOHAMMAD REZA SHAH (1919–1980)

Shah of Iran, 1941–1979. Mohammad Reza Shah Pahlavi came to the throne after Britain and the Soviet Union deposed his father, who was sympathetic to Nazi Germany. In 1953, after Pahlavi was forced to flee the country by radical nationalists, the United States intervened to restore him to power. With American support, he launched his White Revolution of social reform and modernization. The reforms, which included emancipation of women, angered Islamic traditionalists. The shah's dictatorial methods made him additional enemies. Although he was America's closest ally in the Persian Gulf region, the United States could do little to help him when opposition mounted in 1979. The shah, already ill with cancer, fled Iran in 1979 and died a year later.

PALESTINE

Palestine's boundaries have shifted over the centuries, although at a minimum they have included the territory between the Mediterranean Sea and the Jordan River. The region has had many different names. It was called Canaan in ancient times prior to the arrival of the Israelites. After the Israelites established themselves in the region, they briefly united most of it under their kings David and Solomon (usually called the Kingdom of David and Solomon). In the tenth century B.C., that kingdom split into two independent states: Judea in the south and Israel in the north. Although Israel disappeared after its conquest by the Assyrians in the seventh century B.C., Judea survived until Roman times.

Palestine, which means "Land of the Philistines," has no historic link with any of the current inhabitants of the region, whether Jewish or Arab. It was the name given to the region by the Romans after they suppressed the second Jewish revolt against their rule in A.D. 135. The Romans chose that name to replace *Judea* in order to blot out any identification of the country with the Jews. *Palestine* had nothing to do with anyone living there at the time. The actual Philistines, who had lived along the region's Mediterranean coast beginning in about 1200 B.C., had long disappeared as an identifiable people.

Between Roman times and the twentieth century, the region again had a variety of names, depending on who was in control. In 1099 the Crusaders conquered the city of Jerusalem. They briefly united as the Latin Kingdom of Jerusalem an area that included most of present-day Israel, the West Bank, Gaza, western Jordan, and southern Lebanon. The Ottomans, who controlled the region from 1518 until 1917, divided it into three different administrative units, none of which was called Palestine. After World War I, the British received a mandate from the League of Nations to govern what the League called Palestine. The mandate, which called for the establishment of a Jewish national home, initially extended eastward to include what became Jordan. The British severed all territory east of the Jordan River—about three-quarters of the original mandate—from Palestine in 1923 to create the Kingdom of Transjordan. The majority of the region known as Palestine from the early 1920s until 1948 is occupied by the state of Israel. The rest consists of the West Bank, where Israel and the Palestinian Authority respectively exercise varying degrees of control, and the Gaza Strip, which is controlled by the Palestinian Authority.

PALESTINIAN ORGANIZATIONS

By far the most important of the dozens of organizations formed by Palestinian Arabs is the Palestine Liberation Organization (PLO). It was founded in 1964, when Jordan controlled the West Bank and eastern Jerusalem, and Egypt controlled the Gaza Strip. Since then it has served as an umbrella organization, bringing together many independent groups, often with sharply conflicting views. The PLO was initially set up by the Arab League and was not really controlled by Palestinians themselves for about five years. Its founding charter—adopted in 1964 and amended in 1968— repeatedly denied Israel's right to exist and called for its destruction. The PLO Covenant, therefore, was a stumbling block in the Israeli-Palestinian peace process until it was amended in 1998. Yasser Arafat became the PLO's chairman in 1969 and proved to be an effective leader. His achievements included winning observer status for the PLO at the

United Nations in 1974 and, by the late 1970s, diplomatic recognition from more than one hundred countries. The funds for the PLO's five-hundred-million-dollar budget came mainly from the oil-rich Arab states.

The largest and most powerful PLO member is al-Fatah ("Conquest" in Arabic), cofounded by Arafat in 1958. Arafat built al-Fatah into the most powerful Palestinian guerrilla group, and it has dominated the PLO since 1969. A large part of its reputation came from terrorist attacks against Israel. But it also made Americans a target, including two diplomats murdered in 1973 in Khartoum, capital of Sudan. At its peak in the 1970s, al-Fatah had an armed force of six thousand to ten thousand fighters.

Other PLO groups generally were even more militant than al-Fatah in rejecting any political solution to the Arab-Israeli conflict. They also carried out terrorist acts against Israel. The largest was the Popular Front for the Liberation of Palestine (PFLP), led by Dr. George Habash, which combined Arab nationalism with Marxist-Leninist ideology. It carried out several airline hijackings and in 1972 murdered twenty-seven passengers at Israel's main airport. A smaller but equally militant group was the Democratic Front for the Liberation of Palestine (DFLP), led by a Jordanian named Naif Hawatmeh. The DFLP is best known for murdering twenty-two Israeli schoolchildren and wounding more than one hundred in the small town of Ma'alot. Both the PFLP and DFLP, along with others both inside and outside the PLO, opposed the Oslo Accords and all peace negotiations Arafat conducted with Israel.

Perhaps the most radical of all Palestinian groups was the Fatah Revolutionary Council, better known after its leader, as the Abu Nidel group. Abu Nidel was a renegade within the Palestinian movement who in the 1970s was condemned to death by al-Fatah for planning to assassinate Yasser Arafat. At various times, his organization was based in Iraq, Syria, and Libya. The United States at one point considered him the most dangerous terrorist in the world, and in 1991 blamed him for more than one hundred terrorist attacks since 1974.

In the 1980s, Palestinians began forming groups with Islamic fundamentalist beliefs. The largest and best known is Hamas (Movement of Islamic Resistance), founded by Sheikh Ahmad Yasin and several other Islamic leaders in 1987. The organization opposes any peace with Israel and has carried out suicide bombings inside Israel in an attempt to stop the peace process. It wants to see Israel replaced by an Arab Islamic state. Another important fundamentalist group is Islamic Jihad, founded in the mid-1980s, which also has opposed the peace process with suicide bombing attacks against Israeli civilians. In 2006 Hamas defeated al-Fatah and took over the Palestinian Authority, the autonomous political entity set up in the Gaza Strip and part of the West Bank as a result of Israeli-Palestinian negotiations in 1994.

PERES, SHIMON (1923–)

Prime minister of Israel, 1984–1986, 1995–1996. Peres was born in Poland, arriving with his family in what was then called Palestine in 1934. Under David Ben-Gurion, Peres played a major role in building Israel's military capabilities, including its program to develop nuclear weapons. From the 1970s until the 1990s, he and Yitzhak Rabin struggled for leadership of Israel's Labor Party. Peres began the peace negotiations that led to the 1993 Oslo Accords while serving as Israel's foreign minister under Rabin. Peres became prime minister for the second time in 1995 when Rabin was assassinated but lost to Benjamin Netanyahu in the 1996 elections. Peres remained active in Israeli politics after that defeat and held several important positions in subsequent governments under both Ehud Barak and Ariel Sharon.

QADDAFI, MUAMMAR (1942–)

Dictator of Libya. Even though he holds no official government post, Muammar Qaddafi still dominates Libya, as he has for three decades. He is known for his ruthlessness and vast ambitions. These range from uniting the Arab world under his leadership to uniting Africa to relieving Libya's water shortage with his Great Man-Made River project. His other passionately held goal is the destruction of Israel. Qaddafi also bitterly detests the United States. He has supported terrorist organizations both in the Middle East and in Europe. In 1999 widespread reports said that Qaddafi had been seriously injured in an assassination attempt. These reports appeared to be confirmed when he was interviewed by a Western news organization sitting in a wheelchair and looking pale and weak. Opposition to his regime appears to be growing, but reports about attempted coups and Qaddafi's declining health only add to the mysteries surrounding one of the most durable and charismatic leaders in the Middle East.

RABIN, YITZHAK (1922–1995)

Prime minister of Israel, 1974–1977, 1992–1995. Rabin fought in Israel's War of Independence of 1948–1949 and rose to become the Israeli army's chief of staff. He became a hero when he led the army to victory over Egypt, Syria, and Jordan in the 1967 Six-Day War. He joined the Labor Party after retiring from the army. During his second term as prime minister, Rabin presided over secret talks with the Palestine Liberation

Organization that led to the Oslo Accords in September 1993. The next year, Rabin's government negotiated a peace treaty with Jordan. Rabin's peace policies, which included turning land over to Palestinian control, were bitterly opposed by right-wing Israeli extremists, and he was assassinated by a religious fanatic on November 4, 1995.

RIYADH

Capital of Saudi Arabia. Riyadh in the early nineteenth century became the center of the Wahhabi fundamentalist religious movement that still dominates Saudi Arabia. It also was the base from which Abdel Aziz al-Saud (Ibn Saud) began his conquest of that country. Riyadh is an oasis town about 240 miles (390 km) inland from the Persian Gulf. In recent decades, it has grown from a medieval town into a modern city. It is Saudi Arabia's business, industrial, educational, and administrative center and the largest city on the Arabian Peninsula.

AL-SABAH, SHEIKH SABAH AL-AHMAD (1929–)

Emir (ruler) of Kuwait. Sheikh Sabah became emir in 2006, ten days after the death of Jaber al-Ahmad al-Sabah, his half brother, who had ruled the country for almost thirty years. Those ten days amounted to something of a political crisis because the sheik in line to become emir was physically unfit to carry out his duties and had to be pushed aside. That took intense negotiations among leaders of Kuwait's ruling Sabah family. Sheikh Sabah is said to be in good health, but he was in his mid-seventies upon becoming emir and was fitted with a pacemaker for his heart in 1999. When he became emir, he already had been in charge of Kuwait for several years because of Sheikh Jaber's declining health.

AL SAID, QABOOS IBN SAID (1940–)

Sultan (ruler) of Oman. Qaboos came to power in 1970 by over-throwing his father, an archconservative opposed to any reform. As Oman's sultan, Qaboos promoted economic and social development. He distinguished himself by following a foreign policy that broke with Arab rejection of Israel's right to exist. Under Qaboos, Oman was the only Arab country that openly supported Anwar Sadat's peace with Israel. After the Israeli-Palestinian Oslo Agreement, Qaboos fostered ties between Oman and Israel and hosted visits to Oman by two Israeli prime ministers, Yitzhak Rabin in 1994 and Shimon Peres in 1996. Qaboos also has strongly supported U.S. policies in the Persian Gulf region.

SALEH, ALI ABDULLAH (1942–)

President of Yemen. Saleh was president of North Yemen from 1978 to 1990 before becoming president of a united Yemen in 1990. In reality he rules Yemen as the head of a military dictatorship. He angered Saudi Arabia by remaining neutral in the Gulf War crisis of 1990–1991, and the Saudis retaliated by supporting a secessionist movement in Yemen in

1994. Saleh's success in defeating that movement boosted his standing in Yemen.

SANAA

Capital of Yemen. Sanaa stands on a high plateau in the interior of Yemen more than one mile (1.6 km) above sea level. Founded in the second century A.D., its name means "fortified city," and much of its ancient city wall still stands. Muslim conquerors in the seventh century destroyed most important pre-Islamic structures and replaced them with mosques. Over the centuries, Sanaa was the scene of many battles, and its fortunes rose and fell according to shifting balances of power in the region. Sanaa became the capital of the Kingdom of Yemen (North Yemen) in 1918 but lost that status between 1948 and 1962. It became a capital again in 1962 with the founding of the Yemen Arab Republic, and in 1990 it became the capital of a united Yemen. Sanaa's population has mushroomed from thirty-four thousand in 1962 to almost one million today. Its Muslim university and other centers of learning make it a center of Islamic culture.

SHARON, ARIEL (1928–)

Prime minister of Israel, 2001–2006. Born in a small Jewish cooperative agricultural village, Sharon joined the Hagana, the Jewish self-defense organization, during the era of the British mandate in Palestine, at the age of fourteen. He remained a soldier and became one of Israel's most brilliant and daring army commanders in a military career that lasted until 1973. Sharon commanded an infantry company during Israel's War of Independence in 1948–1949. After the war, he organized and commanded the special 101 commando unit whose job it was to retaliate for Arab terrorist attacks against

Israeli civilians launched from the Egyptian-controlled Gaza Strip and the Jordanian-controlled West Bank. Sharon commanded a parachute brigade that fought one of the key battles of the 1956 Suez War. He led the armored division that seized control of the Sinai Peninsula in the 1967 Six-Day War and an armored division during the 1973 Yom Kippur War. Having led his division across the Suez Canal and encircled the Egyptian army, Sharon emerged from the Yom Kippur War as a national hero.

Sharon then entered politics and was minister of defense when Israel invaded Lebanon in June 1982 to drive the PLO from that country and end its attacks against Israeli territory and civilians. In September, when the fighting was almost over and the Israeli army had surrounded Beirut, Lebanese Christian militiamen entered two refugee camps near the city and murdered hundreds of Palestinian civilians. Although Israeli troops were not involved, the incident shocked the Israeli public. A special government commission found Sharon indirectly responsible because he had not anticipated what the Lebanese Christians might do and stopped them from entering the refugee camps. He was forced to resign, but he remained active in politics and held several ministerial posts in various Israeli governments in the 1980s and 1990s. In February 2001, he was elected prime minister in a landslide victory. He served as Israel's leader until incapacitated by a stroke in January 2006.

TEHRAN

Capital of Iran. Tehran has a long history of settlement but remained a minor town until chosen as Persia's capital in the late eighteenth century. In 1943 it was the site of the first World War II meeting of U.S. president Franklin Roosevelt, British prime minister Winston Churchill, and Soviet leader Joseph Stalin. After the war, the city grew rapidly and underwent modernization under Mohammad Reza Shah Pahlavi, leaving little of significance that is more than a half century old. Tehran is Iran's industrial center but also a sprawling, overcrowded metropolis with severe pollution problems and teeming slums. The population has fallen slightly in recent years as people who fled the fighting of the Iran-Iraq War have begun returning to their native towns and villages.

TEL AVIV

City in Israel. Tel Aviv was founded on sand dunes in 1909, a few miles north of the ancient port of Jaffa. Since then, enveloping Jaffa in the process, Tel Aviv, whose name means "hill of spring," has grown into Israel's center of business, culture, and commerce. It is considered one of the liveliest cities in the world. Although Tel Aviv proper is smaller than Jerusalem, it is the core of Israel's largest metropolitan region. If Jerusalem is known for its history and religious shrines, Tel Aviv is known for its thriving commercial activity, beachside hotels, and nightlife. It was in Tel Aviv on May 14, 1948, that David Ben-Gurion proclaimed the independence of the state of Israel.

TERRORISM

Terrorism is the systematic organized use of extreme violence against civilians to achieve political ends. While terrorism is an old tactic, it did not become a significant political weapon until the 1960s. This occurred in large part because modern electronic media, especially television, spread the news and the frightening reality of terrorism to hundreds of millions of people, therefore exponentially increasing the impact of any given act. Modern terrorism includes acts such as bombings, hijacking and skyjacking, and assassinations. Most terrorist acts are committed by independent organizations, but often they act as proxies of governments. As of 2001, the U.S. State Department listed seven countries that sponsored terrorist groups. Four of them—Iran, Iraq, Libya, and Syria—are Middle Eastern Arab states. The fifth, Sudan, has an Islamic fundamentalist regime. The two remaining countries, Cuba and North Korea, are Communist states.

The most frequent target of terrorism in the Middle East has been Israel. Terrorism against Israel has been carried out by a variety of Palestinian and Islamic organizations. While most of the Palestinian groups joined the PLO, they continued to operate independently. These organizations turned to terror after Arab states failed to defeat Israel on the battlefield in 1948–1949 and again in 1967. Among their more notorious actions was the murder of eleven Israeli athletes at the 1972 Olympic Games by Yasser Arafat's al-Fatah group; the murder of twenty-two schoolchildren in the Israeli town of Ma'alot by the Democratic Front for the Liberation of Palestine (DFLP) in 1974; and al-Fatah's 1978 hijacking of an Israeli bus that ended with thirty-seven Israelis dead. Sometimes terrorist actions did not target Israel itself but were designed to take hostages, including Israelis, who could be used for political purposes. Examples are the hijacking of four European and American airliners in September 1970 by the Popular Front for the Liberation of Palestine (PFLP) and the hijacking of a French airliner to Entebbe, Uganda, by Palestinian and German terrorists in July 1976. That episode ended with almost one hundred Israeli and Jewish hostages being rescued in a daring raid by the Israeli army.

In the 1980s and 1990s, Islamic fundamentalist groups opposed to an Israeli-Palestinian peace tried to derail the peace process with suicide bombings inside Israel. The most deadly attacks were carried out by two groups, Hamas and Islamic Jihad. They were responsible for a series of attacks that killed more than sixty Israelis in just two months in 1996. Between the signing of the Oslo Accords in September 1993 and September 2000, more than 250 Israelis were killed in terrorist attacks.

Middle Eastern terrorism has not been used only against Israel. Radical groups have murdered moderate Palestinian officials who favored negotiations with Israel. That was the fate in 1983 of PLO moderate Issam Sartawi, who was murdered by the Abu Nidal group, and of two moderate West Bank mayors, Aziz Shehadeh of Ramallah and Zafir al-Masri of Nablus, both assassinated by the PFLP. Nor is Middle Eastern terrorism always linked to the Arab-Israeli conflict. Syria has used terrorism against both moderate Palestinians and Jordanians for its own purposes, some of which have little or nothing to do with Israel. Libya and Iraq have followed similar courses of action.

The United States also has become a target of Islamic and Arab terrorists for several reasons. Libya's planting of a bomb that destroyed an airborne American airliner in 1988, killing 270 people, grew out of a number of U.S.-Libyan confrontations. U.S. support of Israel and the Israeli-Palestinian peace process has angered Arab and Islamic extremists. On a deeper level, Islamic fundamentalists consider American values and American influence in the Middle East as threats to the Islamic way of life. They believe they must end Western and U.S. influence in the Middle East to achieve their goal of establishing strict Islamic regimes everywhere in the region. The 1983 suicide truck-bomb attack by the Iranian-backed group Hezbollah that killed 241 U.S. Marines in Lebanon was an effort to drive Western peacekeeping forces from that country. The bombing of the World Trade Center in New York City in 1993 killed six people and injured one thousand. It was carried out by an extremist Islamic group whose goal was to overthrow the secular Egyptian government, which the United States strongly supports. In 1996 Islamic fundamentalists backed by Iran bombed the Khobar Towers, a U.S. military residence in Saudi Arabia, killing nineteen U.S. military personnel. In 1998 terrorists controlled by Saudi exile Osama bin Laden bombed two American embassies in Africa. Those bombings killed 244 people, including 12 Americans, and wounded more that 4,600. In September 2001, in the worst terrorist act in history, terrorists loyal to bin Laden destroyed the World Trade Center in New York City and damaged the Pentagon in Washington, D.C., killing over three thousand people.

AL-THANI, HAMAD BIN KHALIFA (1950–)
Emir (ruler) of Qatar. Sheikh Hamad came to power in 1995 after engineering a bloodless coup against his conservative

father. Like several other Persian Gulf rulers, he graduated from a British military academy and held military and defense positions before becoming emir. He became crown prince in 1977 and had accumulated considerable political power by the early 1990s, prior to deposing his father. Sheikh Hamad, one of the most reform-minded Arab monarchs, is best known for his support of the Al Jazeera television station, the only station in the Arab world permitted to broadcast free of government censorship or bias.

TRIPOLI

Capital of Libya. Tripoli was founded as a Phoenician colony and port more than twenty-six hundred years ago. For centuries a terminal point for several trans-Sahara caravan routes, it currently is an important Libyan transportation, commercial, and industrial center. In 1986 the United States bombed Tripoli in retaliation for Libyan-sponsored terrorism attacks in Europe in which several Americans were killed. Since 1996 the city has benefited from Muammar Qaddafi's Great Man-Made River project, which is being built to transport water from aquifers deep in the Sahara desert to the parched Libyan Mediterranean coast. People in Tripoli no longer have to drink brackish local groundwater. As one shopkeeper exulted, "What used to be salty is now as sweet as can be."

SOURCE NOTES

40 Quoted in Martin Gilbert, *Israel: A History* (New York: William Morrow, 1998), 487.

46 *New York Times*, April 1, 1999.

49 *New York Times*, November 29, 2005.

49 *New York Times*, November 28, 2005.

58–59 *New York Times*, November 3, 1999.

59 Ibid.

60 *Boston Globe*, May 8, 1999.

77 *The Illustrated Jerusalem Bible*, English translation, edited by M. Friedlander (Jerusalem, London, New York: Jerusalem Bible Publishing Co., 1958), 1525.

78–79 Quoted in Abba Eban, *My Country: The Story of Modern Israel* (New York: Random House, 1972), 48.

81 Quoted in Martin Gilbert, *The Arab-Israeli Conflict: Its History in Maps* (London: Weidenfield and Nicolson, 1974), 68.

82 Quoted in Howard M. Sachar, *A History of Israel: From the Rise of Zionism to Our Time* (New York: Knopf, 1996), 673.

87 Quoted in the preface to *The Rabin Memoirs*, 2nd ed. (Bnei Brak, Israel: Steimatsky Ltd., 1994), v-vi.

88 Quoted in Robert Slater, *Rabin of Israel: Warrior for Peace* (New York: HarperCollins, 1996), 583.

90 U.S. State Department Daily Press Briefing, Thursday, January 22, 1999.

90 *New York Times*, July 7, 1999.

93 *New York Times*, April 4, 2001.

96 *New York Times*, May 5, 2006.

103 *New York Times*, November 25, 1998.

104 *Jerusalem Post*, December 15, 2000.

105 *Washington Post*, September 16, 2001.

106 MEMRI Special Dispatch Series-No. 1083, http://www.memri.org/bin/articles.cgi?Page=archives&Area=sd&ID=SPI108306 (June 16, 2006).

114 *New York Times*, February 8, 1999.

135 Quoted in Avraham Sela, *Political Encyclopedia of the Middle East* (Jerusalem: The Jerusalem Publishing House, 1999), 710.

137 *New York Times*, May 9, 1999.

137 Ibid.

152 *New York Times*, December 23, 1998.

155 *New York Times*, May 21, 2006.

163 *New York Times*, May 26, 1999.

163 *New York Times*, July 4, 1999.

173 *Boston Globe*, January 18, 1999.

174 *New York Times*, May 3, 1999.

174–175 Ibid.

175 *New York Times*, May 4, 1999.

175 *New York Times*, April 17, 1999.

175 *New York Times*, April 30, 1999.

176 *New York Times*, May 11, 1999.

176–177 *New York Times*, June 30, 1999.

178 *Christian Science Monitor*, May 17, 2004.

194 *National Geographic* 196, no. 1 (July 1999): 14.

196 *National Geographic* 196, no. 1 (July 1999): 6.

197 *New York Times Magazine*, November 1, 1998, 53.

197 Ibid.

197 *New York Times*, July 19, 1999.

198 Ibid.

198 *New York Times*, February 4, 1999.

199 Ibid.

199 *New York Times*, July 15, 1999.

200 CNN.com. October 27, 2005.

201 U.S. Department of State, Office of the Coordinator for Counterterrorism, Country Reports on Terrorism 2005, 173[0].[0] http://www.state.gov/s/ct/rls/crt2005/

217–218 "Saudi Arabia's Curriculum of Intolerance: With Excerpts from Saudi Ministry of Education Textbooks for Islamic Studies," Center for Religious Freedom, of Freedom House, Washington, D.C., 2006, 11, 25 (June 16, 2006).

218 *New York Times*, May 24, 1999.

222 *New York Times*, January 16, 1999.

235 Fouad Ajami, "What the Muslim World Is Watching," *New York Times Magazine*, November 11, 2001, 50.

235 *New York Times*, July 4, 1999.

242 *New York Times*, September 19, 1999.

242 Ibid.

302 *New York Times*, October 3, 1998.

SELECTED BIBLIOGRAPHY

Ajami, Fouad. *The Arab Predicament: Arab Political Thought and Practice Since 1967*. New York: Cambridge University Press, 1992.

Banks, Arthur, Thomas Muller, and William Overstreet. *Political Handbook of the World, 2006*. Washington, DC: CQ Press, 2006.

The Europa World Year Book, 2005. London: Routledge, 2006.

Gilbert, Martin. *Israel: A History*. New York: William Morrow, 1998.

Hiro, Dilip. *Dictionary of the Middle East*. New York: St. Martin's Press, 1996.

Hourani, Albert. *A History of the Arab Peoples*. Cambridge, MA: Belknap Press, 1991.

Kedourie, Elie. *The Chatham House Version and Other Middle-Eastern Studies*. London: Weidenfeld and Nicolson, 1970.

Laqueur, Walter, and Barry Rubin, eds. *The Israel-Arab Reader: A Documentary History of the Middle East Conflict*. 5th ed. New York: Penguin, 1995.

Lewis, Bernard. *The Middle East: A Brief History of the Last 2,000 Years*. New York: Touchstone, 1995.

Livingstone, Neil C., and David Halevy. *Inside the PLO: Covert Units, Secret Funds, and the War Against Israel and the United States*. New York: William Morrow, 1990.

The Middle East. 8th ed. Washington, D.C.: Congressional Quarterly Inc., 1994.

Miller, Judith. *God has Ninety-Nine Names: Reporting from the Militant Middle East.* New York: Touchstone, 1996.

Montaign, Fen. "Iran: Testing the Waters of Reform." Photographs by Alexandra Avakian. *National Geographic* (July 1999): 2–33.

Quandt, William B., Fuad Jabber, and Ann Mosely Lesch. *The Politics of Palestinian Nationalism.* Berkeley: University of California Press, 1973.

Ross, Dennis. *The Missing Peace: The Inside Story of the Fight for Middle East Peace.* New York: Farrar, Straus, and Giroux, 2004.

Sachar, Howard M. *A History of Israel: From the Rise of Zionism to Our Time.* 2nd ed. New York: Knopf, 1996.

Sela, Avraham. *Political Encyclopedia of the Middle East.* Jerusalem: The Jerusalem Publishing House, 1999.

Sinai, Anne, and Allen Pollack, eds. *The Hashemite Kingdom Jordan: A Handbook.* New York: American Academic Association for Peace in the Middle East, 1977.

Sinai, Anne, and Allen Pollack, eds. *The Syrian Arab Republic.* New York: American Academic Association for Peace in the Middle East, 1976.

Slater, Robert. *Rabin of Israel: Warrior for Peace.* New York: HarperCollins, 1996.

FURTHER READING AND WEBSITES

Anderson, Dale. *Sadam Hussein.* Minneapolis: Twenty-First Century Books, 2004.

Broberg, Catherine. *Saudi Arabia in Pictures.* Minneapolis: Twenty-First Century Books, 2003.

Behnke, Alison. *Syria in Pictures.* Minneapolis: Twenty-First Century Books, 2005.

Di Piazza, Francesca. *Libya in Pictures.* Minneapolis: Twenty-First Century Books, 2006.

Gilbert, Martin. *The Arab-Israel Conflict: Its History in Maps.* Israel: Steimatsky, 1985.

Goldstein, Peg J. *Israel in Pictures.* Minneapolis: Twenty-First Century Books, 2004.

————. *Lebanon in Pictures.* Minneapolis: Twenty-First Century Books, 2005.

Headlam, George. *Yasser Arafat.* Minneapolis: Twenty-First Century Books, 2004

Katz, Samuel M. *Against All Odds: Counterterrorist Hostage Rescues.* Minneapolis, MN: Twenty-First Century Books, 2005.

———. *At Any Cost: Natitonal Liberation Terrorism*. Minneapolis, MN: Twenty-First Century Books, 2003.

———. *Global Counterstrike: International Counterterrorism*. Minneapolis, MN: Twenty-First Century Books, 2005.

———. *Jerusalem or Death: Palestinian Terrorism*. Minneapolis, MN: Twenty-First Century Books, 2003.

———. *Jihad: Islamic Fundamental Terrorism*. Minneapolis, MN: Twenty-First Century Books, 2003.

———. *Raging Within: Ideological Terrorism*. Minneapolis, MN: Twenty-First Century Books, 2003.

———. *Targeting Terror: Counterterrorist Raids*. Minneapolis, MN: Twenty-First Century Books, 2005.

———. *U.S. Counterstrike: American Counterterrorism*. Minneapolis, MN: Twenty-First Century Books, 2005.

Kort, Michael G. *Yitzhak Rabin: Israel's Soldier Statesman*. Minneapolis: Millbrook Press, 1996.

Landau, Elaine. *Osama bin Laden: A War Against the West*. Minneapolis: Twenty-First Century Books, 2002.

Laqueur, Walter, and Barry Rubin. *The Israel-Arab Reader: A Documentary History of the Middle East Conflict*. 5th ed. New York: Penguin, 1995.

Lewis, Bernard. *The Crisis of Islam: Holy War and Unholy Terror*. New York: Modern Library, 2003.

Reich, Bernard. *A Brief History of Israel*. New York: Facts on File, 2005.

Schaffer, David. *The Iran-Iraq War*. San Diego, CA: Lucent Books/Gale, 2003.

Spencer, William. *Iraq: New Nation in Conflict*. Minneapolis: Twenty-First Century Books, 2000.

Taus-Bolstad, Stacy. *Iran in Pictures*. Minneapolis: Twenty-First Century Books, 2004.

———. *Iraq in Pictures*. Minneapolis: Twenty-First Century Books, 2004.

Wowlf, Alex. *Osama bin Laden*. Minneapolis: Twenty-First Century Books, 2004.

Zuehlke, Jeffery. *Egypt in Pictures*. Minneapolis: Twenty-First Century Books, 2003.

———. *Jordan in Pictures*. Minneapolis: Twenty-First Century Books, 2005.

Websites

CIA World Factbook
    https://www.cia.gov/cia/publications/factbook/index.html
    This official CIA website provides up-to-date information on countries throughout the world.

Freedom House
    www.freedomhouse.org
    This website contains the annual Freedom House "Freedom in the World" rankings. It also contains other information, including a report on freedom of the press in countries around the world.

U.S. Department of State
    www.state.gov/g/drl/rls/irf/
    This website contains the U.S. State Department's annual "International Religious Freedom Report."

INDEX